The Phoenix Chronicles

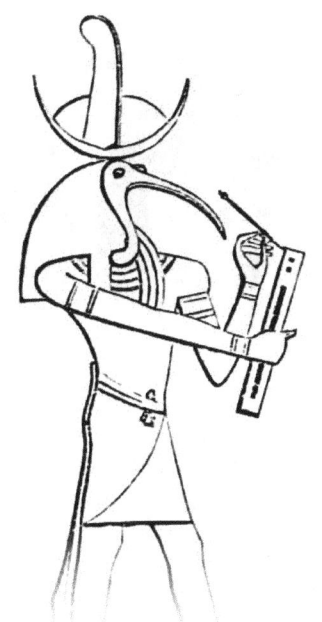

STEPHEN H. PROVOST

All material © 2012, 2014, 2018 Stephen H. Provost

Some material published under the name Stifyn Emrys.

Cover artwork: Public domain images
Cover concept and design: Stephen H. Provost
All interior images are in the public domain.

No part of this book may be reproduced, or stored in a retrieval system, or transmitted in any form or by any means, electronic, mechanical, photocopying, recording, or otherwise, without the express written permission of the publisher.

Dragon Crown Books 2018
All rights reserved.

ISBN: 978-1-7320632-6-6

Contents

Title	Page
Introduction	vi
The Book of Eden (Inception)	1
The Book of Babylon	27
The Book of Pharaohs	79
The Book of Journeys	133
The Book of Contendings	177
The Book of Tales (Parables)	213
The Book of Teachings (Proverbs)	279
The Gospel of the Phoenix	327

Praise for other works by the author

"The complex idea of mixing morality and mortality is a fresh twist on the human condition. ... **Memortality** is one of those books that will incite more questions than it answers. And for fandom, that's a good thing."

— Ricky L. Brown, Amazing Stories

"Punchy and fast paced, **Memortality** reads like a graphic novel. ... (Provost's) style makes the trippy landscapes and mind-bending plot points more believable and adds a thrilling edge to this vivid crossover fantasy."

— Foreword Reviews

"Whether a troubled family's curse or the nightmarish hell created by a new kind of A.I., the autopsy of a vampire or Santa's darker side ... Provost's sure hand guides you down gloomy avenues you do not expect."

— Mark Onspaugh, author of The Faceless One and Deadlight Jack, on **Nightmare's Eve**

"**Memortality** by Stephen Provost is a highly original, thrilling novel unlike anything else out there."

— David McAfee, bestselling author of 33 A.D., 61 A.D., and 79 A.D.

"Profusely illustrated throughout, **Highway 99** is unreservedly recommended as an essential and core addition to every community and academic library's California History collections."

— California Bookwatch

"As informed and informative as it is entertaining and absorbing, **Fresno Growing Up** is very highly recommended for personal, community, and academic library 20th Century American History collections."

— John Burroughs, Reviewer's Bookwatch

THE PHOENIX CHRONICLES

Introduction

This volume is a compilation of three previously published works — *The Osiris Testament, The Way of the Phoenix* and *The Gospel of the Phoenix* — which together make up a new vision of ancient myths across the diverse cultures whose lore and legends, when woven together, make up the tapestry of Western mythical tradition.

The Osiris Testament corresponds roughly to the Pentateuch, *The Way of the Phoenix* to the Book of Proverbs (and the parables of Jesus) and *The Gospel of the Phoenix* to the canonical gospels. Each presents familiar material, together with more obscure traditions, in a fresh presentation. Among the myths and historical accounts incorporated are those from ancient Mesopotamia, Canaan and Egypt, together with legends from Scandinavia and the Celts. Somewhat obscure traditions from the Gnostics and the Ebionites, as well as apocryphal material from early Christianity, also served as source material for this volume.

Each of the three volumes contained here is also available separately, with more illustrations and, in the case of *The Gospel of the Phoenix*, an author's commentary on the tex. A comprehensive analysis of these and other traditions can be found in my expansive companion work, *The Phoenix Principle*, available in two volumes as *Forged in Ancient Fires* and *Messiah in the Making*. Much of the research conducted for that work is reproduced her in poetic form.

The Book of

Eden

1

¹ In the time before times, when the world was young, the gods came together and fashioned for themselves a dwelling among the clouds to the north in the highlands. ² This place they named Aratta, which is called Ararat, and they adorned it with all manner of bounty from their storehouse, with gold and silver, and lapis lazuli. ³ It was the land where the sky and the earth came together, for which reason they called it the Kingdom of Heaven.

[4] They named it in the ancient tongue "Anu," which means the vault of the sky, that place where the lady of the mountain dwelt. [5] It is she whose womb brings forth new life, who joins the sky above with the earth beneath and binds them together that they might bear fruit. [6] Her caves are bedecked with jewels and crystals, and gold may be found in the depths of her dwelling. [7] The clouds are her crown, and the stars are the jewels set within it.

[8] In those days there came forth from heaven the brothers Enlil and Enki, who contended fiercely with one another. [9] Enlil was given dominion over the airy heights of Aratta, and his companion was the eagle who soars across the firmament.

[10] But Enki was given the plain below called Eden, and his sigil was the serpent that was entwined about his staff.

[11] He who has ears to hear, let him hear.

The Gardener and the Vineyard

[12] It came to pass that Enki became the father to a son, Asar. He it was who became the first to harvest grain and plants, for which reason he was called "the Gardener."

[13] His beloved was Inanna, who was crowned the queen of heaven and enthroned in Aratta's heights.

[14] At her bidding did Asar plant a garden on the plain of Eden, where the soil was rich and fertile. [15] Sheltered by the snow-covered peaks of Aratta and nourished by the waters

of heaven's chalice, it was a haven for all who came to dwell there.

16 Give heed to the words that are written here, that you may understand these secrets. For Asar is the name of Osiris, and Inanna is called also Aset, whose name is Isis.

17 A brother and sister were born alongside them, whose names are Seth and Nephthys.

18 In his garden, Osiris planted an orchard of trees rising up from the earth, which were pleasing to the eye and good for food. 19 In the midst of the garden he set a watchtower and a vineyard, also with its winepress.

20 The first of these he called "the tree of life," for by ascending one could survey the open firmament and look out upon the land unto the horizon, as if from heaven itself. 21 Inanna gave it her blessing, and in her honor did he build it. Therein would she dwell.

22 And in its heights did he set all the great lights of the firmament, like jewels for her adornment, and appointed them to keep watch over times and seasons. For this reason were they called the Watchers.

23 The vineyard he called the "tree of knowledge, good and ill," for the fruit of the vine brought both inspiration and folly to those who might partake of it.

24 And around about the vineyard were arrayed all manner of fern and vine, shrub and grassland, tree and orchard. 25 These were watered by a spring that went forth out of Eden and became a torrent of four great rivers.

26 The first is the Pishon, which winds across the sands of the desert in a nation rich in gold. In this place, resin is

found in plenty, and onyx is also there. ²⁷ The second river's name is Gihon, which traverses the land of Cush. ²⁸ The third is the Tigris, which runs before Assyria, and the fourth is the great Euphrates.

²⁹ Now men and women were in the midst of the garden, as newborn children at a mother's breast. The queen of heaven was a mother to them, and Osiris was their father. ³⁰ And they were naked, clad only in the shelter of the sky.

³¹ The men were called sons of Adam, which in Hebrew means "the earth" but in Egypt is rendered as Atum, who is honored in the city of the sun as creator of all men. ³² The women were called daughters of Eve, which means "giver of life," their name for holy Inanna.

³³ For this reason was Inanna herself called the "tree of life" and "the tower," which in Hebrew is rendered as Migdol or Magdala. For through her alone does man ascend unto the heavens.

³⁴ And the lady of the tower came to be called the Magdalene.

³⁵ He who has ears to hear, let him hear.

2

¹ Osiris taught the sons of Adam the way of reaping and sowing, and the means by which they might water the fields. ² The cultivation of the grapevine did he teach them, and the ways of wheat and barley. "For behold," he said,

"It is I who created the barley and wheat to make the gods live and, after the gods, the herd of man."

³ He therefore gave them charge of all the animals that were in that place, to care for them, and he taught them the use of speech so that they might name them. ⁴ And he gave them laws, engraved in stone from the heights of Aratta, his own commandments, ten in number, that in keeping them they might prosper. These were the laws that he gave them:

⁵ Speak not in the name of any god, for such is unfettered arrogance, but let thy words redeem themselves.

⁶ Honor thy mother, who is the earth, and nourish thy children, who are fruit upon the tree of life.

⁷ Accuse no man falsely, but cast aside deception and hypocrisy.

⁸ Slay neither man nor beast for gain or glory, and spill no blood on the altar of pride, for such is the way of the ingrate.

⁹ Bind none to thy will through debt or servitude.

¹⁰ Smite no man in vengeance, yet bear not abuse of thyself or thy neighbor.

¹¹ Steal nothing from thy neighbor, through force, guile or the hand of the king.

¹² Obey no man blindly, as the dog licks the boots of its master, yet pursue wisdom in all things.

¹³ Curse not love, lest she flee from you.

¹⁴ Walk in humility; cast out fear; ask none to bear what you would not.

The Priests

¹⁵ And Osiris appointed three classes of priests to watch over the sons of Adam, charging them to guide and nourish the people in his absence. ¹⁶ These men did he leave to care for his garden. And their classes were as follows:

¹⁷ The most worthy among them he called the Elohim, which means "the men who are as gods." To these he granted authority to mediate disputes, to maintain good order and to create such edicts as were good and just for the people. ¹⁸ These together convened a council of seventy-two elders which was called The Highest, and he who was chief among them bore the title of Most High.

¹⁹ The second class of priest he named the Cherubim or, in the ancient tongue, Kiribu. Their name meant "mighty protectors," and they were warriors charged with defending the land of Eden. ²⁰ In those days did they wield a sword of flame and fury.

²¹ Theirs would be an enduring legacy. In the time of the pharaohs in Egypt, long after the fall of Eden, their order would survive as the Kher-Heb priesthood, and their number was charged with reading out the sacred scrolls in official ceremonies. ²² As the garden's protectors, their symbol was the carob tree, which is preserved in Hebrew lore as the symbol of return. To this day, it bespeaks contentment with one's blessings, which are kept secure by the flaming sword of the Cherubim.

23 The third class of priest was the Seraphim, whose name means "burning serpents." These were the dragonlords of old, the keepers of wisdom and sacred renewal, and the people revered them for their craft and for their cunning. 24 They were masters of herbs and potions that could restore life to the infirm, making them whole again as surely as the serpent itself found new life by shedding its skin.

25 Anyone among the people, man or woman, who studied well and swore an oath to do no harm might join their ranks. And many sought to do so, for no one doubted that they were the wisest among all the people. 26 It is for this reason that one among their number was appointed the guardian of a vineyard that lay in the midst of the garden — the tree of knowledge. This one was Seth, true brother of Osiris.

27 And when he had done these things, Osiris himself departed from them, that he might travel throughout the lands and teach men in all places the way of life, the way of cultivation, of song and music.

28 And men knew nothing of war or of killing.

3

1 When Osiris had gone forth from there, he sojourned long away from Eden. 2 And in time, the Elohim grew bold and haughty, saying to themselves "Our father will never return to us" and "We are the masters of Eden now." 3 Therefore did they take power unto themselves and

reward their favorites with great wealth, neglecting those who did not meet with their approval.

⁴ Seth saw this and was troubled, for it was not his brother's way. And he resolved to go forth beyond Aratta, that he might find Osiris and inform him of these things.

⁵ Leaving another among the Seraphim to guard the tree of knowledge, he set forth boldly with strength of purpose, confident that his quest would bear fruit.

⁶ Over land and sea did he cast his gaze. He searched the slopes of the great mountains, yet he found his brother not. He went to the mouth of the two great rivers, yet discovered no sign of him there. ⁷ South to the land of Sheba did he roam, then also to the mighty Nile, but in neither place did he find Osiris.

⁸ At last, despairing, he returned to Aratta having failed in his purpose, and there was he met with the council of the Elohim.

⁹ "Where have you come from?" the Most High asked of him.

¹⁰ "From roaming throughout the earth, going here and there across the face of it," Seth answered.

¹¹ And the Most High knew of Seth's intention and was pleased that he had failed in his purpose. ¹² Therefore did he taunt him, saying, "Have you considered my servant Job? There is no one in all the earth who is his equal. He walks blameless and upright before me, fearing the Most High and shunning all unrighteousness."

¹³ Now Job was one whom the council had favored because he was loyal to their ways. ¹⁴ To reward him, they

had allotted him livestock numbering more than ten times a thousand. ¹⁵ Therefore his family prospered, and his household did flourish. Seven sons and three daughters had come from his loins, and among men he was counted the greatest in all the east. ¹⁶ But Seth knew the source of his riches, that it issued forth not from the toil of his hands but instead from council's favor. And he challenged them, scoffing. "Does this one fear you for nothing? Have you not put a hedge around his household and a shield on all he has? ¹⁷ You have guaranteed the work of his hands, that nothing may fail him, so that his flocks and his herds spread out across the entire land? But if you were to stretch forth your hand and remove from him this bounty, he will most surely curse you to your face."

¹⁸ And the pride of the Most High was wounded, for he knew that Seth spoke truly, yet he did not dare admit his own connivance. ¹⁹ He therefore removed his protection from Job, who at once became afflicted with disease and misfortune. All he had was taken from him. And just as Seth has foretold, curses were found upon his lips.

²⁰ "The Most High destroys the innocent and the guilty in like manner," he charged. "And if a scourge calls forth death in a moment, he mocks the despair of the blameless."

²¹ When these words reached the ears of the Elohim, they were embittered, for they had placed spies among Job's closest friends, men who were as kin to him. And these told the council all the things that they had heard. ²² And the Most High became wroth with Job for his curses, but more so because they had proved the truth of

Seth's accusations. ²³And his words burned into the quick of his marrow and the core of his being, until his pride was wounded and his fury kindled beyond reason.

²⁴And he spoke thusly: "Would you annul my justice? Would you condemn me to exonerate yourself?" he shouted. "Is your arm like that of the Most High, and does your voice issue forth like thunder from his mouth? ²⁵ If it be so, then clothe yourself in splendor and glory, and put on the garments of majesty and honor. Send forth the fury of your wrath, that you might bring the proud to their knees and lay the haughty low. ²⁶ Crush those who are, in your esteem, doers of evil. Turn them to dust and consign them to their graves. ²⁷ If you can do these things, then I will heed you and acknowledge that your destiny is your own to command."

²⁸ Seth heard these things and marveled at the arrogance of the Most High. Yet more than this, he marveled at his folly. ²⁹ By the word of his own mouth, the Most High had proved the case Seth had presented, that Job was no better than any other person, and that he relied altogether on the favor of the council. ³⁰ The Most High, in his conceit, had been forced to admit that he was the source of Job's prosperity and good fortune, just as Seth had argued all along. ³¹ Yet vindication came at a price for the brother of Osiris and those who, like him, cast their lots with the cause of wisdom. For when the Elohim understood that they had been made sport of, they feared the power of wisdom and of knowledge.

³² Therefore did they seal off the tree of knowledge from all the sons of Adam, placing a fence around it, so that no man could henceforth challenge them by way of greater knowledge. ³³ They forbade any others among the people to join the ranks of the Seraphim, decreeing that none among them should partake of the tree's sweet fruit. ³⁴ "Of every tree in the garden, you may eat your fill," the Most High said in a proclamation. "But in no wise shall you partake of the tree that is in the midst of it, for in the day that you eat from the tree of knowledge — in that day shall you most certainly know death."

4

¹ Seth did not answer the Elohim, neither did he rise up against them. Yet he chafed at their words, and a fire burned within him. ² Taking his own counsel, he said to himself, "How dare these men act as though they were gods! ³ Do they not walk on two legs in the garden like any others? And yet they betray the very spirit of all they were appointed to uphold! ⁴ Did my brother not travel from this place to spread knowledge among the peoples, and would such knowledge then be denied to the people of his own land?"

⁵ He questioned his brother's wisdom in departing, and in appointing the men who had betrayed him. ⁶ And the sons of Adam, in like manner, grew restless, saying, "How long shall we toil for our father who has left us?" ⁷ They awaited his return, but he tarried. And they chafed under

the decrees of the Elohim and beneath the heavy hand of the Cherubim who enforced the council's decrees.

⁸ In due course, a woman of their number came to the tree of knowledge and inquired of Seth concerning these matters, for she reasoned that in wisdom she might find the answers to their questions. ⁹ Then did he speak and say to her: "Did the Most High verily deny you any fruit from this garden he has planted?"

⁹ She said to him, "Of the fruit in this garden we may eat, yet from the tree that is in the midst of the garden he has warned us, 'You must not eat from it, or touch it, or you shall know death.'"

¹⁰ But Seth knew that this was not so, and that the Elohim had spread this lie so that members of the council alone should have access to sacred knowledge. ¹¹ "Nay!" he told her. "For the Elohim know that in the day you eat of it, your eyes shall be opened and you will become as they are, knowing good and evil." ¹² And when she stepped forward to partake of it, he did not stop her. And when she offered it to her husband, he did not prevent it. ¹³ But instead did he instruct them in many things concerning knowledge and true wisdom, and they understood what the Elohim had done to them and how those who sat upon the council had, in jealousy, withheld this knowledge for themselves.

¹⁴ Therefore did they pick the fruit of the vine and take it forth unto the winepress. And when the juice from it was fermented, then did they partake of it.

¹⁵ And behold, it came to pass just as Seth had counseled them. They drank a little for inspiration, and seeing it was good, they partook again for folly. And they grew drunk on the strength of the elixir, and they heeded not the decrees of the high council. ¹⁶ But when they came to themselves again their eyes were opened, and they felt naked beneath the heavens, for they knew that their deeds would become known to the Elohim.

¹⁷ None of these things escaped the notice of the Watchers, who gazed down from the master's watchtower. They were witnesses of these events, which are recorded in this chronicle.

¹⁸ And the sons of Adam were no more as children, having dared to challenge the dominion of the Elohim. ¹⁹ It came to pass that the Most High received word of what had happened, and went in search of them. ²⁰ But they heard the sound of him walking in the garden in the cool of the day, and they hid themselves. ²¹ He called out to them, saying, "Where are you?" because he could not find them.

²² After a time, however, they knew they could hide themselves no longer and they came forth and presented themselves to the Most High, saying, "We heard you in the garden and were afraid, knowing that our deeds would be laid bare before you. We felt as naked, fearing punishment, so we hid."

²³ The Most High said to them, "Have you partaken of the tree that is forbidden?"

²⁴ But the two of them, having seen what had befallen Job for his insolence, feared the wrath of the Most High.

[25] And they sought instead to place the blame on Seth, saying, "That serpent Seth deceived us, and we partook."

[26] And the Most High rose up in wrath against each one of them. [27] Full of anger, he directed his fury first at Seth, proclaiming, "Henceforth shall you crawl on your belly before me. Your food shall be dust all the days of your life! [28] No alliance shall you form with the sons of these commoners, for there shall be enmity between you and their offspring. They shall crush your head, and you shall strike at their heels."

[29] Then to the woman who had partaken of the fruit, he declared, "You shall never escape the pains of childbirth. Lust for your husband shall consume you, and he shall subdue you."

[30] And to the man, he said, "The ground shall be cursed on account of you. All the days of your life shall you toil without respite. [31] The ground shall bring forth naught but thistle and briar, and your wages shall be the sweat of your brow. From the ground have you been taken; to the ground you shall return!"

[31] But Seth stood up proudly against the Most High and opposed him to his face, declaring, "Henceforth, I am your adversary! [32] Wisdom shall triumph over folly, and knowledge over base ignorance. No more shall you rule the peoples! [33] In my brother's absence, his duty has become mine. It is your vanity that shall be crushed. Mark my words well, pretender, for they will surely come to pass!"

[34] And Seth gathered to himself those who would oppose the Most High. Among these were many of the

Seraphim, and some also of the Cherubim. ³⁵ But few of the common people joined him, for they trembled before the Most High, who had used the fear of death these many years to keep them in his thrall. ³⁶ When a people is long oppressed, such fear can weave itself into their very being, and so it was with the people of Eden. ³⁷ For Osiris had been so long away that many of them knew no other path but that of submission to the Elohim.

³⁸ So without them did Seth wage war against the Elohim and their minions for control of Aratta, the Kingdom of Heaven. ³⁹ Seth, the great adversary, fell like lightning from the sky upon his enemies, visiting terrible wrath upon each of them. ⁴⁰ But the Cherubim struck back with their flaming swords and fiery chariots, trampling the garden beneath them and ruining all that Osiris had planted there, so that it was fallow. ⁴¹ And the Most High laughed to himself, saying, "Behold! The curse that I laid upon the sons of Adam has come to pass! The garden is uprooted and fit only for thorns and briars!"

⁴² And the two sides fought bitterly, one against the other, yet neither could prevail. ⁴³ The wisdom of Seth and the Seraphim who fought alongside him was great. Yet the soldiers of the Elohim were twice their number. So it was that neither side could gain the advantage. ⁴⁴ Blood flowed in the rivers that washed down the slopes of Aratta. Smoke from the fires of the warring armies blotted out the very sun. ⁴⁵ Yet nothing was accomplished. No victory declared. No dispute resolved. Only terror and carnage in battle after battle.

5

¹ Osiris, so long away, was forgotten. Yet he lived still.

² And in the course of time, he sent messengers to collect some of the bounty from his people's harvest, that he might share it upon all the earth. ³ Yet in war, the land had been laid waste. There was no harvest. ⁴ And the Elohim feared that he would discover their poor stewardship of the garden he had left to them, so they waylaid each messenger sent forth to greet them. ⁵ One they beat, and another they killed, and still another they stoned.

⁶ When they failed to return to him, Osiris sent forth still more servants, only to have them dealt with in like manner.

⁷ And the Elohim took counsel among themselves, lamenting, "What if the king himself should return and punish us?"

⁸ But the Most High said to them, "Come, therefore, and let us kill him also."

⁹ And they were sore afraid, saying, "He is a god, and are we not priests sworn to his service?"

¹⁰ Then did the Most High say to them. "Have we not been given the keys to this, the Kingdom of Heaven? ¹¹ See how the people fear us, how they tremble before us. Never did they cower so in the presence of Osiris. ¹² Indeed, our power has surpassed his, and our glory has eclipsed his

fading memory. ¹³ Am I not the Most High? Do I not sit on the throne of this absent god? And so, have I not become a god in my very being? ¹⁴ Verily I say to you that it is so. I am a god, and more: I am a jealous god. These sons of Adam — they shall worship no other god before me. I have sworn it by my own name!"

¹⁵ The others murmured among themselves, but stilled their tongues, for they knew there was danger in this madness.

¹⁶ Then he said to them, "Is it not better that this one die to preserve our position?" And none dared oppose him.

¹⁷ He told them: "No man shall blame us that his life is ended. He has been so long away that few recall his benevolence. ¹⁸ And those who would find fault shall cast their gaze upon another: the one who has opposed us from the beginning. For who should inherit the throne of Aratta if not the king's own brother? ¹⁹ We shall cast the blame upon him, and none shall dare to question it!"

²⁰ The council went out from that place, united in their purpose to do as he proposed. They spoke of these things to the Cherubim and counseled them as to what they should say.

²¹ And in due course it happened just as the Most High had said it would. ²² At last the king returned to the garden he had planted, and he found it rendered desolate by the war for the Kingdom of Heaven. The fields stood empty and abandoned, and the tree of knowledge had been forsaken. ²³ And when he saw this, he searched for his brother, Seth, whom he had charged to tend the tree of

knowledge, but found him not. ²⁴ Yet when he came to the tree of life, and he saw the Cherub priest beside it, Osiris questioned him, saying, "What has happened in this place?"

²⁵ And the priest told Osiris the words that the man himself had spoken: "That serpent Seth deceived us, and we partook."

²⁶ Osiris therefore cursed his brother loudly. And he laid a curse also on the tree of knowledge, saying, "No tree can impart true knowledge, which is gained alone from a life lived fully. ²⁷ The knowledge of the vine is fleeting, but the knowledge of struggle endures. And the struggle for Eden shall be its own reward."

²⁸ So it was that henceforth would the sons of Adam struggle.

²⁹ As youths they had not known death, yet now would he be their companion. ³⁰ The hyena would stalk them and the vulture would trace their paths across the wastelands. The South Wind would sear their flesh, and the North Wind would howl its contempt for them. ³¹ No more would the branches of the garden shelter them, but the tents of the wasteland would be their home. ³² As children had they been granted the garden's succor, but their defiance marked them as those who had grown beyond childhood. Yet still they lacked maturity. ³³ Their cruelty toward the great king's servants testified against them, and their neglect of the garden condemned them. ³⁴ He knew not that they had acted in the fear of the Elohim, and would not listen to their protests when they sought to speak of it.

⁳⁵ Instead did he banish them from the garden he had planted, setting at its entrance a Cherub priest with a flaming sword to guard against their return. ³⁶ And as each man leaves the home of his father at the appointed time, so now they set forth from the garden to make their own way. ³⁷ They went out into the wastelands, enduring each day by their sweat and their sinew. And death hunted them always like a thief at midnight, as it stalks each man at his coming of age.

³⁸ Seth also went out with them, banished in like manner from the garden under a charge of conspiracy. The barren wastes and red sand deserts became his realm, and his name was changed to Satan, for he had declared, "I am your adversary!" ³⁹ This, too, became the realm of Adam's progeny, for which reason they were called sons of Seth. These were the nomads of old who were called the Hebrew or Habiru, that is, the wanderers. ⁴⁰ Forgetting the crafts Osiris had taught them, they drifted from place to place across the land, taking their fill of her and passing on to the next place as though she were a harlot.

⁴¹ But the Elohim and those who had stood beside them remained in the land of Aratta, in the heights of the great mountains, the place that would ever be known as the Kingdom of Heaven.

⁴² There did they plot out the death of a god.

6

¹ Now Seth was filled with fury at what had been done

to him, but he spoke not of vengeance, remaining ever loyal to his brother's decree.

² And the sons of men were, likewise, sorely vexed at their banishment from Eden. "Shall we ever again see the land of our fathers?" they lamented.

³ And Seth could not answer them, for they had lost faith in his brother and still feared the wrath of the Most High.

⁴ So they wandered from that country, pitching their camp at the base of the mountains. And there did they tarry for a time, where they planted a few simple crops and sought to live as best they could in the shadow of their former home. ⁵ And they bemoaned their lot but found courage in one another, and in their escape from the tyranny of the Elohim. And with this balm did they start to heal.

⁶ Such was their state when an emissary from Aratta came to them from out of the mountains one day. And they knew him to be one of the Malachim, the angels who were official messengers of the Elohim. ⁷ He came to them from the council of the seventy-two, bearing greetings with the words, "Peace! Peace!" ⁸ And he said to them, "The Most High has forgiven your trespass, and you have been summoned to return by his good pleasure. For the Most High has prepared a feast to honor Osiris, and all the people have been called to join him."

⁹ At this did the sons of Adam rejoice, for though they feared the Elohim, they longed to see their home again.

¹⁰ Seth, too, had been summoned. And though he was

loath to trust a Malach of the Elohim, even so he sought to be reconciled with his brother. [11] Therefore did he accompany the sons of Adam back to Eden, unaware of the intrigues that his enemies had prepared against him.

[12] For the Most High had devised a scheme to supplant Osiris on the throne. And with the seventy-two as his co-conspirators, he set the plot in motion. [13] The artifice unfolded in this manner: The council crafted for themselves a large ark of the finest wood, covered in gold and precious jewels, and waited until the day of the great feast they had prepared. [14] Then, when all the people had gathered to pay tribute to Osiris, the Most High presented this ark before the entire company, saying, "This is the gift of the wise Seth to this assembly, in tribute to his brother!" [15] Yet Seth knew nothing of this, and when he opened his mouth to protest, the words were lost amid the murmurs of the crowd.

[16] And the Most High spoke up once more, presenting to the guests this challenge: "Whosoever shall fit inside the box perfectly shall then claim it as his own!"

[17] Now the Elohim had so fashioned the box that none save Osiris would be able to enter it. So each of the guests stepped forward one by one, but none was able to meet the challenge. [18] Then at length did the turn pass to Osiris, and so he climbed inside and found it fit him perfectly! [19] But at that same moment, men in service to the Elohim rushed forward to seal the ark while the king reclined there. They poured molten metals over the lid to hold it fast. [20] And with great alacrity did they make their escape, shouting,

"Glory to Seth, the true king!" though they served not Seth but his enemies, who would have him faulted for the death of his brother.

[21] These men spirited the ark away from the assembly, but Queen Isis followed them in haste.

[22] And the servants of the Elohim took it many miles across the land, down from the mountains and over the plains between the waters; through the deserts and down into the heart of Egypt. [23] And there did they cast off the ark containing the mummy of the fallen king, Osiris, thinking at last they would be rid of him in this land so far from Eden.

[24] But the queen was diligent in her quest to recover his body, and after a long search came upon the ark at last. A tamarisk tree had grown up around it, preserving it from wind and rain, sun and storm. [25] When she opened it, she saw her beloved reposed as if in sleep, and in joy set forth to return him again to his homeland. [26] Yet still did the servants of the Elohim wait silent in the shadows, among the reeds beside the river. And as the queen slept, they came in stealth to open the ark. [27] And they cut the king's body into many pieces, which they scattered across all the land.

[28] When Isis discovered what had befallen her king-husband, she cried out to all the gods in lamentation. [29] She called to her sister Nephthys, who was also the wife of Seth, so that they together scoured the land from marsh to desert in search of the king's lost body. [30] And Seth himself did aid them, though he dared not show his face, for the

blame for his brother's demise had been cast now squarely upon his shoulders. Yet he helped them from the shadows and he assisted from the shelter of the rushes along the Nile. [31] To this task did they dedicate themselves for many years. And when at last they had gathered the pieces, Isis assembled them anew and wrapped them in linen cloths. [32] Breathing her healing magic upon Osiris, she restored him in a moment, and in that moment conceived a child by him in spirit. This was Horus of the Horizon.

[33] And when Horus had grown to manhood, he became the king of Egypt. His sign is the falcon and the fiery sun, for which reason he also bears the nature of the mystical bird that is called the phoenix. [34] In his honor do the kings of Egypt adorn themselves with the name of Horus, and when they pass from the realm of men they are honored as Osiris. [35] But Osiris himself ascended to the highest of heavens, whence he had come; to the heights above Aratta, so that he was found no more among them. [36] But some said he could be seen among the stars drawing back his bow there. And they called him also Anu, after the heavens themselves, for he became the lord of heaven, whence he reigned supreme over all he did survey.

[37] And Seth withdrew to the shadowy places, where he took refuge from the lies that were spread against him. [38] From time to time would he emerge to face derision, scorn and mockery from the sons of Adam who had shared his fate. [39] For the Elohim, having accomplished their purpose in destroying the king of heaven, did once more cast the sons of Adam out of Eden, saying, "Your seed is

tainted by evil from now to eternity, for you have followed the way of Seth, the father or lies and deception!"

⁴⁰ Therefore did the Elohim claim Eden for themselves, and rule there over the host of their minions.

7

¹ But those who had been exiled from the Kingdom of Heaven chose one from among them as their king. This one was a fisherman called Adam, after their tribe, and he took to wife a maid who was found in the wastelands. ² This one was Lilith, "the breath of the moon," who came to him in the night on the South Wind and who was the queen of heaven in the guise of a maiden. ³ She bore to him two heirs, who became the first great rulers among the race of men. The first of these was Cain, whose name means "king" and "conqueror," and the second was A'bel, whose name, rendered elsewhere as Ba'al, means "lord."

⁴ But there arose a dispute between Adam and Lilith, for he demanded that she submit and lie beneath him. She, however, refused him and departed to the shadows. ⁵ To this day is Lilith's scorn heard to echo across the wastes and canyons. Hers is the voice of the night owl who flies solitary, casting shadows on the moon. ⁶ Even still she submits to no man, but guards with jealous eyes her wisdom.

⁷ For this purpose is a veil drawn full across woman's countenance, that it might be hidden from the sons of men

until the bridal chamber. ⁸ This is not done for modesty, as the sons of men in their wounded pride falsely claim. But it is done after the manner Lilith, who hid herself from proud Adam rather than be made his servant. ⁹ As the veil of darkness is drawn across the moon, so it is with the veil of this mystery. And no man may remove it, but each woman has it in her choosing to wear or reject it.

¹⁰ He who has ears to hear, let him hear.

¹¹ Now Cain remembered the ways of Osiris and planted for himself fields of grain to harvest, but A'bel was a nomad like his father and a wanderer tending flocks and herds. ¹² It was in those days that men began to sacrifice to the gods, hoping to gain their favor. Cain therefore offered up a sacrifice of the fruits of his labors, but A'bel brought forth a sacrifice of from among his flocks. ¹³ For the first time then was blood spilled out upon the earth, and the gods were grieved that it was so.

¹⁴ But Cain, seeing what his brother had done, thought that the gods had approved this thing. ¹⁵ Therefore did he come upon his brother in the fields and slay him, reasoning that the blood of a man would be all the more pleasing to heaven. ¹⁶ At this, however, the gods were sore afflicted, for blood begets blood, and vengeance begets vengeance. Death begets death, and hardship begets hardship. Once the cycle is begun, men are hard-pressed to break it.

¹⁷ For this reason did the gods send Cain forth with a mark upon his flesh, that no man might do violence against him for the deed that he had done, lest he be avenged sevenfold. ¹⁸ And they banished him from the fields that he

had planted, casting him out into the land of Nod, which means "wandering." [19] So it was that he became a wanderer like the brother he had slain, and he came down out of the mountains into Shinar beside the mighty Euphrates. [20] For this reason is it said that in those days, the kingship came down out of heaven, for it descended with Cain who had been king.

[21] And Cain lay with his wife, and she gave birth to a son, who was called Enoch.

The Book of Babylon

1

¹ This is the book of Babylon, the land between the rivers, which is at the center of the Earth. It is the book of Enoch and Etana, of Ur and of Eridu. Therein lies the gate of the gods.

² Enoch came first to this place from Aratta. He was strong of mind and heart, and he set forth to build for himself a dwelling place in Shinar near the southern sea,

which was the first great city in all the land. ³ He named it Irad or Eridu, which means "a place far away," for it was far from the garden that his forebears left behind. ⁴ For this reason was he called the father of Irad, because he laid its foundation stone.

⁵ For its placement, he chose the marshlands near the mouth of the great Euphrates, where the sweet waters of the abyss rise up from beneath the earth to join the bitter waters of the stormy sea. ⁶ Enoch was lord of the sweet waters, which nourished the land and the people round about.

⁷ So it was that when kingship descended from Aratta, it came upon Eridu, and Enoch, heir to the throne of Cain, was the first to rule. The people called him Enki, which means "lord of the land," after the lord of the earth in Aratta. ⁸ He built for himself a habitation which rose above the city, and was magnificent in all its aspects. ⁹ So was it written of his dwelling place:

> Enki the Lord who decrees the fates
> Built his house of silver and lapis lazuli,
> Like sparkling light.
> The pure house he built
> He adorned lavishly with gold.

¹⁰ In Eridu he built the house of water-bank,
Its brickwork speaking words of wisdom,
Like an ox roaring,
The house of Enki gives voice to his oracles.

¹² Indeed did he rule in wisdom and in power. He walked with the gods and wrote down their ways on many tablets, which he called the ME. Some say he inscribed them in precious emerald, and others on bricks of clay. ¹³ It was he who wrote down the ways of the gods for the generations of men to remember, setting forth sixty-four decrees for them to follow. ¹⁴ Among these were the way of power and the way of wisdom, the way of peace and the way of judgment, the way of the bridechamber and the way the throne. ¹⁵ Taking reed stylus in hand, he set forth, too, the way of the shepherd and the way of the divine lady, and also the ways of many musical instruments. And also did he leave instruction concerning the rivers, should they rise over their banks and flood the earth.

¹⁶ Casting his eyes to the heavens did he study the ways of the Watchers until he learned them all according to their order, committing every detail of the sky's secrets to writing, that men might know the seasons of the year and their progressions. ¹⁷ From far and wide men came to hear his wisdom, which he shared with them freely, as a father shares bounty with his children. He taught them, as Osiris had before him:

¹⁸ "The sun rises in six portals and sets in six portals, as also does the moon. And the leaders of the stars also, six in the east and six others in the west, follow one after the other in orderly fashion. ¹⁹ First goes forth the great luminary called the sun, whose face is like the face of heaven, yet full of a fire that sends forth heat and brilliance.

[20] The wind drives the chariot on which he rises, and he descends in from the heavens toward the north that he might find a haven in the east."

[21] "The moon is a circle like the fields of heaven, and the wind drives the chariot upon which she rides. Her light does she impart in varied measure, waxing and again waning with each new month. [22] Her days are like those of the sun, and her head faces in an easterly manner when, on the thirtieth day, she is manifested."

[23] So great was Enki's wisdom that it was said of him:

When Enki rises, the fish rise,
The abyss stands in wonder,
Joy enters into the sea,

[24] Fear comes over the deep,
Terror holds the exalted river,
The Euphrates, the South Wind lifts it in waves.

[25] And the people likewise built dwellings of reed and mud-brick. From the earth they dug canals to water their cropland, and they made square boats called arks to bear them across the land. [26] And Enoch's grandfather Adam came down from Aratta, near bountiful Eden whence he had been banished, and ruled with him at his side. [27] He was the first of seven sages in the time before the flood who served as counselors to seven great kings. These men were the Annunaki, mighty men of old who came down from heaven to dwell upon the earth. [28] They came down

from Aratta and took the daughters of Shinar to wife, and made alliance with them.

²⁹ They are called by some the Nephilim and called Lugal, which means "giant" or "big man."

2

¹ Adam the fisherman fashioned for himself the vestments of a sage, which were sewn in the shape of a fish. So it appeared he had the head of a man but also of a great sea creature as his crown, along with the scales of its back upon his own. ² And he came forth by day to teach the people of Eridu the ways of heaven, whence he had come, but each night he withdrew to the ocean and plied his trade among the waves.

³ As it is written:

His word commands
Like the word of the gods
Who granted him wisdom to reveal the way of the land
To him is given wisdom
Yet not eternal life
A sage, no one rejects his word

⁴ He bakes with the bakers
Preparing food and water for Eridu by day
He sets the table with pure hands
And plies the waters in his boat

He does the fishing for Eridu

⁵ One night, he embarked in his sailing boat to bring forth fish for the good of Eridu. Without a rudder, his boat would drift. Without a steering pole would he set forth.

⁶ Now Lilith, who had spurned him, had not forgotten his mistreatment. Though he had beckoned her, she had not returned to him, but had stored up her anger for the appropriate time. ⁷ So it was that on this evening, she sent forth the South Wind to punish him, and it overturned the sailing vessel from which he was fishing. ⁸ Therefore in his wrath did Adam curse the South Wind, boasting, "I shall break your wing!" And in the moment that he said it, the South Wind's wing was broken, so that for seven days it did not blow toward the land.

⁹ It therefore came to pass that he was called to account by the gods, and he was summoned to Eden in the highlands to explain his actions.

¹⁰ But Adam was anxious for his welfare, and he knew not what awaited him in Aratta, from which place he had been cast out once before. ¹¹ Would Osiris judge him again from the highest heaven as Anu? Would he be consigned to the abyss beneath the earth?

¹² So did Enoch offer counsel, that he should flatter the sentinels at Eden's gate, saying, "They will speak in your favor."

¹³ But he warned him, "They will hold out the bread of death for you, so you must not eat. And they will offer you the water of death, so you must not drink. ¹⁴ Only adorn

yourself with the garment that they give you and anoint yourself with the oil they provide. [15] Neglect not the instructions I have given you, and keep to the words I have told you."

[16] After a time did an envoy arrive from Aratta and accompanied Adam up to the heavens. [17] When he arrived at the gates did he repeat the words of Enoch to the sentinels, who spoke out in his favor so that Osiris was appeased. [18] And he spread forth his hands and asked them, "What shall we do for this one? Fetch him the bread of life eternal and allow him to partake!"

[19] Yet Adam recalled when Osiris had cast him out from Eden, withholding life eternal from him. And he remembered his offense against the South Wind and the warning that Enoch had given. [20] Surely he could not have been so easily forgiven. Surely this was a trick, that he might taste the bread of death.

[21] So when they fetched him the bread of life, he would not eat.

[22] And when they brought him the water of life he would not drink.

[23] They brought him a garment, and he put it on himself.

[24] They fetched him oil, and he anointed himself.

[25] So was he made fit for burial, in the manner of all the great kings throughout the ages. [26] Once they pass from this world, no more do they eat. [27] Once they pass from this lifetime, no more do they drink. [28] But they are anointed with balm and adorned with white cloth for their passage to

the world to come. And they are seen no more.

²⁹ Therefore did Osiris question him, saying, "Why did you not eat? Why did you not drink? Do you not wish to be immortal? ³⁰ Take him, therefore, and send him back into the earth from which he came."

³¹ So it was that the mystery of the bread and the cup continued, and men partook in the hope of eternal life. But Adam's body was prepared for burial, and Enoch saw him no more. ³² Still, it is said that he came to Eridu a shade, no longer eating and drinking but teaching the men there all the secrets he had learned in Eden.

³³ It is written:

> He would pass the day among men
> But took no food in that season
> He gave them insight into letters and science
> And art of every kind
>
> ³⁴ He taught them to build cities
> And to found temples
> To compile laws
> And the way of shapes and patterns
>
> ³⁵ He taught them to distinguish the seeds of earth
> And showed them how to collect fruits
> And he instructed them in all things
> To ease their manner and give them reason
>
> ³⁶ Since then nothing has been added

To improve his instruction
And when the sun set, he retired to the sea once more
And passed the night in the deep

3

¹ Enoch mourned the passing of his grandfather, and sought to return likewise to the land from which he had come. ² When therefore all things that had been appointed to him were accomplished, the gods sent forth the chariot of the sun to greet him. ³ And he returned to the land of the heavens, to Eden, as Osiris had done before him. ⁴ There did he accept the bread of life which Adam had refused at his bidding. ⁵ He inscribed the wisdom of the ages from which the race of men would turn away, and so became known as Enoch the scribe, the heavenly chronicler. And the Watchers did his bidding.

⁶ Now it came to pass that other cities rose up with their kings to rival Eridu, and the kingship passed from one to the next over the course of many years. ⁷ Two kings ruled from the throne of Enki before the scepter passed to the coppersmiths to the north in Bad-Tabira, at the edge of the marshlands.

⁸ After this, the kingship passed to Larak, on the right hand of the Euphrates between Eridu and Bad-Tabira, and thence to Sippar, upstream many leagues to the north. ⁹ This was the "city of the birds," a place of trade whence goods were shipped down the great river to the cities and

fields below, a way station between the rich mountain highlands of Aratta and the river plains of Shinar.

¹⁰ And when the kingship passed from Sippar, it came at last to Shuruppak, the "place of healing" along the Euphrates. Here two kings did reign.

¹¹ The first of them, named Lamech, took to himself two wives, whose names were Adah and Zillah, and they bore him many sons. ¹² Adah gave birth to Jabal the herdsman and also Jubal, master of the flute. ¹³ Zillah bore him Tubal-Cain, a master forger of bronze and iron who dwelt in Bad-Tabira, and a daughter, Naamah.

¹⁴ But there was strife in Shuruppak, and a young man entered into the presence of Lamech to assail him, wounding him. ¹⁵ Lamech, however, slew him in his own defense. ¹⁶ After these things had come to pass, he called his wives to him, saying, "Adah and Zillah, hearken to me; wives of Lamech, attend my voice. I have slain a man for wounding me, a young man for doing me violence."
¹⁷ therefore issued a warning to any man who would seek to do him violence, that the gods would avenge him: "If Cain is avenged seven times," he declared, "then Lamech seventy times seven."

¹⁸ After this he sired another son, who would become his heir. ¹⁹ The newborn's body was white as snow and red as the blooming of a rose, and the hair of his head and his long locks were white as wool, and his eyes beautiful. When he opened them, his radiant joy lit up the whole house like the sun. ²⁰ His appearance was a source of great hope to the king, whose land had long been plagued by drought and

famine. [21] It is written:

> When the second year arrived,
> The storehouse was depleted
> [22] When the third year arrived,
> Men's faces showed starvation
>
> [23] When the fourth year arrived,
> Their proud bearing was downcast
> [24] Their well-set shoulders slouched
> They went in public hunched over
>
> [25] When the fifth year arrived,
> A daughter would see her mother coming in
> A mother would not so much as open the gates to greet her daughter
>
> [26] When the sixth year arrived,
> They served a daughter for a meal
> They served a son for nourishment

[27] It was in these days that Lamech's son was conceived. And he named the child Noah, which means "comforter," for he said, "This one will comfort us amidst the afflictions of our toil, for our hands labor in vain to till the soil that has been cursed of the gods."

[28] For the gods had grown weary of the ways of men, and the din of their boasting was deafening as they made war one with another. [29] They took the names of the gods

in vain, claiming their sanction on war and violence. And no sooner did one city lay claim to the scepter of kingship than another assailed it, besieging its walls and denying it the earth's bounty for the sake of dominion. [30] These were the ways of the lowland cities, and the gods feared that should they continue, the sons of men might presume even to attack Aratta.

4

[1] Noah ruled wisely and soothed Shuruppak with the balm of peace. [2] He prospered in his kingdom, and as his years advanced, he increased in wisdom, so that his people called him Ziusudra, the long-lived one, and Atra-Hasis, which means "exceedingly wise." [3] He took the sacred tablets of his forefather, Enoch, and consulted them in all things. And when he watched the heavens, he saw the clouds begin to gather. [4] When he cast his eyes to the earth, he saw the wells spring up and the Euphrates overflow its banks. [5] And he knew that the gods had grown wroth with the men of the lowlands, but knew not what to do.

[6] So he took refuge in his reed hut and hearkened to the words that Enoch had written on the sacred tablets in days long past, in the tablet of the flood. It was as though he spoke to Noah through the very walls of his hut. [7] And he counseled him on the things that he must do. [8] Should the gods lament the ways of man and bring destruction upon them in the form of water, these actions should he take:

⁹ Tear down your house and build an ark
Abandon your goods and seek after life
¹⁰ Forswear belongings, but preserve your soul
Aboard this vessel take the seed of all things living

¹¹ Build for her a covering
That the sun may not see inside her
Let her be covered, fore and aft
¹² The rigging must be firm
And the bitumen be strong!

¹³ So Noah did as Enoch bade him. He found the falcon and the osprey, the owl and the vulture. ¹⁴ He brought to him oxen and asses, cattle and swine, goats and sheep, the gazelle and the dromedary. ¹⁵ He built for himself an ark to house his flocks and herds, and all the animals that lived upon his lands. ¹⁶ In it also he placed the sacred tablets, so that they might be preserved amid the destruction. ¹⁷ So it came to pass that the tablets thenceforth would be housed within an ark, a vessel to protect them for his children and their children, the heirs to the wisdom of Enoch.

¹⁸ And when he had prepared everything as Enoch had commanded him, he gave a feast for all the people, and invited them to partake. But Noah could neither eat nor be still, for he feared the deluge that was to come. ¹⁹ Whilst all the others ate their fill, Noah's heart was torn and bile rose up from his inward parts.

[20] And in that moment, the face of the heavens changed, and the thunderer bellowed from on high. [21] Noah called for bitumen and sealed the ark's door shut. He cut the rope that held the vessel fast. [22] And in this very moment the winds did rage, and the bird of heaven, Anzu, tore at the sky with his talons.

[23] The flood burst forth upon them like an army attacking. Eyesight was vanquished, and the skies were black as night. [24] The deluge roared like a bull in fury, and the winds howled like a wild ass screaming. [25] The Tigris was swollen like a womb awaiting childbirth, and the Euphrates overflowed its banks from Sippar to Eridu. [26] The heavens opened up and crashed down mightily on the land, as wells sprang up from the abyss. [27] Great cities were inundated, the crops of the field were ruined, and the sea rose up to devour the marshes. [28] Such was the fury of it that it seemed the entire earth might be swallowed, for the clouds filled the heavens as far as the eye could see.

[29] Like dragonflies, the bodies of men filled up the river. Like a raft they moved the edge of the boat.

[30] And the storm was upon them many days and nights. It did not abate, nor did it falter, until finally the gods were appeased in their anger. [31] The sun shone forth once more, and clouds were driven from the face of heaven; at night the stars were seen again, and the moon shone forth in pale brilliance. [32] Only then did Noah venture forth from within the ark. [33] He sent forth a raven, which flew to and fro until the waters had receded. Then he sent forth a dove, but it returned to him, and so he waited seven days before he

sent it forth again. ³⁴ Then did it go out from him and return to him come evening with an olive branch, newly plucked, within its beak. ³⁵ By this did he know that the flood had not destroyed all things within the river valley, but that some life was preserved.

³⁶ Yet when Noah surveyed the land, he saw that the waters had claimed every field of the lowlands. ³⁷ The roads and the byways were now as canals, the pastures were as lakes, and the cities belonged to the watery abyss. ³⁸ But when he cast his eyes to the far-distant highlands, they fell upon the peaks of Aratta, which rose up proudly above the waters all around him, and he thought, "This is where the dove found haven." ³⁹ So he released it yet again and went after it, and the ark journeyed forth until it reached the base of the mountains, where the waters could not follow.

⁴⁰ Then he climbed up until he reached Eden, the great plain in the land of Aratta whence his fathers had come. ⁴¹ He climbed the mountains of the gods and built in that place an altar, for he said to himself, "The waters shall not rise to this land of heaven, therefore shall it be preserved should a flood again come upon us." ⁴² And he set the sacred tablets of his forefather Enoch on the altar there, within an ark, for which reason it is said that the ark came to rest upon the mountains of Aratta.

⁴³ And the men of Shinar remembered this, and they held it in their hearts.

⁴⁴ And the gods made a covenant with Noah never again to flood the land with such a deluge, saying:

As long as the earth endures
In seed time and in harvest
In cold and in heat
In summer and winter
Day and night shall never cease

[45] They pledged then no more to do violence to the sons of men, and the great archer of heaven so declared it: "This is the sign of the covenant we affirm with you, and with every creature for all generations." [46] And Osiris, the great archer of the heavens, set his bow upon the clouds; it was a bow of many colors for the many shades of life, from those who dwell in Shinar to the sons and daughters of Aratta, and for all things that draw breath or take root within the earth.

5

[1] Noah planted a vineyard there in Eden, for he wished to restore the tree of knowledge. Yet he understood not the way of the vine, and in his greed drank too much of its harvest. [2] When, therefore, his sons came upon him, they found him naked and began to quarrel amongst themselves, until their disputes reached the ears of the Elohim. [3] And the Most High said to his brethren, "Shall we yet again abide these fools? Nay, let us be rid of them! For they are wicked sons of Adam, bearing within themselves the very seed of iniquity!"

⁴ Therefore did the Most High speak lies to the sons of Noah and cause their hearts to be hardened against one another in enmity. ⁵ Then did they part ways from one another, removing themselves to the ends of the earth so that Ham traveled southward to Egypt and beyond, while Japheth sojourned among the Greeks and Scythians. ⁶ But Shem took for his portion the land beneath Aratta, whence his father had come, and his people were called the Shemites.

⁶ And the sons of Shem were close by the black-headed people of the river delta, who had abode in Shinar since ancient times.

⁷ Now the lowlands were destitute, and few men still dwelt there. But when the waters receded and the rivers withdrew again to their appointed courses, the fields blossomed and the land again became fertile. ⁸ Then did men multiply once more upon the earth, increasing their flocks and their herds alongside them. ⁹ So it was that the kingship descended from heaven a second time, and it came to the city of Kish, which some call Cush. ¹⁰ This was a mighty city, with walls and battlements. Such was its fame and glory that thenceforth did all the kings of Shinar take to themselves the title King of Kish.

¹¹ And their kings demanded worship like the gods, after the manner of the Elohim. They claimed Inanna herself as their consort, and appointed their sons to bear the scepter at their passing. ¹² So it was with the kings of Kish. And the greatest of these was Etana.

¹³ The star queen descended from heaven
In search of a shepherd
She sought a king across the lands

¹⁴ Inanna came down out of heaven
In search of a shepherd
She sought a king to rule them

¹⁵ And the Lord of the Air measured the dais of Etana
Whom the star queen loved steadfastly
And so he decreed

¹⁶ "She has sought for herself a shepherd
Let kingship be upon the land
May the heart of Kish be joyful
At kingship, the radiant crown, the throne of splendor."

¹⁷ For this reason kings are called shepherds to this day, and the pharaoh takes to himself the shepherd's crook as a sign of authority, and Etana was henceforth called "The Shepherd."

6

¹ Etana ruled the land for many years, yet had no heir, and for this reason was he greatly troubled. ² He wished therefore to procure for himself the plant of birthing, which only grew in the heights of heaven, in the highlands

of Aratta. ³ For this was the place of his fathers' fathers, the land of beginnings where the gods still dwelt. Surely, he reasoned, they would impart to him the plant of birthing.

⁴ And in a reverie, this dream came to Etana. ⁵ He saw himself building a tower to heaven, which he named High Water, and in the shade of it grew a poplar tree. ⁶ In its crown of this tree an eagle settled, and a serpent at its root. ⁷ The eagle said to the serpent, "Come, let us make ourselves a friendship. Let us be comrades, you and I!" ⁸ This pleased the serpent, so they made a pact between themselves to share the food of all the land. ⁹ They would go forth together toward the mountains, and there would the eagle hunt gazelle and wild oxen, whereupon he would bring this bounty to the serpent and its offspring. ¹⁰ In like manner would the serpent go forth and hunt the beasts of the field, and return with them as an offering for the eagle's nest.

¹¹ Because of this, the eagle's children flourished and grew strong. ¹² And before long, the eagle became bold and said to himself, "I do not need the serpent, but in my own strength shall prosper!" ¹³ He therefore plotted against his ally, saying, "I shall eat the sons of the serpent. The serpent I shall betray! And I shall ascend to heaven like the gods!"

¹⁴ Now the smallest of his fledglings, who was exceedingly wise, counseled him not to pursue these ends, lest he incur the wrath of the sun god. ¹⁵ But he hearkened not to this warning, neither did he heed the words of his offspring, but determined in his heart to carry out his evil purpose. ¹⁶ And when the serpent went forth did the eagle

assail his nest, and when the serpent was gone did he devour his young.

[17] When the serpent returned from the hunt, bearing his burdens, he cast them down at the foot of the poplar and looked about him. [18] Behold, his nest was gone! Behold, his children were no more! [19] The eagle had gouged the ground with his talon, and a cloud of dust rose up toward heaven.

[20] The serpent wept. And the sun god, the god of enlightenment, counseled him.

[21] Then did he plot revenge against the eagle, and he laid an ambush for his betrayer. [22] He hid himself inside the carcass of an ox, and when the eagle came forth to partake of it, he sprang upon him. [23] He clipped his wings and plucked his pinions, and cast him down from his nest into a pit from which he could not escape. [24] And the eagle screeched in protest, so that his voice reached the ears of Etana.

[25] And he thought, if he did befriend the eagle and free him from his prison, perhaps the great bird would bear him up to the heavens on its wings!

[26] So Etana took the eagle by the hand and lifted him up out of the pit, whereupon he took food like a ravening lion. And gaining strength, he said to Etana, "Let us be friends, you and I. Ask me whatsoever you may desire, and I shall grant it."

[27] Therefore did Etana make known the desires of his heart, and the eagle agreed to bear him up into the heavens, that he might procure the plant of birthing. [28] The eagle spoke thus to Etana, "By the grace of Inanna, place your

arms against my sides. Place your hands upon my wing feathers, and let us now ascend!"

²⁹ And when he had borne Etana aloft one league, he said to him, "Look, my friend, how the land is now! It is as a circle one-fifth its size, and the sea is as a paddock."

³⁰ And when he had borne him aloft a second league, he said to him, "Look, my friend, how the land is now! It has become as a garden, and the vast sea has become as a trough."

³¹ And when he had borne him aloft a third league, he said to him, "Look, my friend, how the land is now!"

³² But Etana could not see the land, nor could his eyes behold the vast sea far below. And he reconsidered going farther up to heaven, and he entreated the eagle to set him down and let him return again to his city. ³³ One league did the eagle drop him down, then plunged to catch him on his wings. ³⁴ A second league did the eagle drop him down, then plunged to catch him on his wings. ³⁵ And a third league did the eagle drop him down, then plunged to catch him on his wings, until at last he returned to the city whence he had come.

³⁵ Waking from his reverie, Etana wondered, and he sought out the meaning of this dream. ³⁶ This is its interpretation: The eagle was a ruler of the people, who in his pride betrayed an alliance with the serpent. And these two made war, one with the other, because the serpent sought to cast down the eagle from his lofty perch.

³⁷ Now would the eagle, in his zeal, seek for himself an alliance with Etana, that together they might defend the

heavens against the serpent's scions. [38] And Etana would agree to these things, on condition that he be given the plant of birthing, which is a shoot from the tree of life.

[39] Because of these things, Etana made peace with the land of Aratta and obtained the plant of birthing, whereupon his wife conceived and gave birth to an heir, Balih. In this manner was the royal line was preserved in Kish.

[40] So Aratta and Kish remained at peace, and Etana entered into his rest. And ten more kings ruled after him, until at last Eanna went out to battle against Kish and defeated her, and the kingship was carried off to Eanna. [41] And though the Elohim yet ruled in Aratta, their time of lordship there was drawing to a close, for soon would there arise a king who would challenge the very gates of heaven and prevail.

7

[1] As the world has its ages, so does also the race of man, whose epochs are marked at the gates of the stars.

[2] The first of these is the age of the lion, during which the great sphinx of Egypt arose. This was the golden age when the tides rose up from their sea beds and the desert sands washed new across the lands called Libya.

[3] The second is the age of the protector, whose shell is hardened and whose mistress is the moon. This was the age

when man dwelt in the protection of the gods, in the place between land and sea.

⁴ The third is the age of the partners, who stretch forth their hands to one another in homage to their likeness. It was in this age that the sons of the earth joined together in the first great enterprises, and they mastered the crops of the field.

⁵ The fourth is the age of the bull, the age of bronze, in which the sons of men did harness the beasts of the land, placing yokes upon their necks and mounting them in conquest. In this way did they greatly expand their dominion. And they began sacrificing animals on their altars to please the gods, for which the gods turned away from them.

⁶ The fifth is the age of the ram on the mountain cliff, when the bull was slain in violence. And men did seek to reach the heights of heaven but were cast down again in shame. ⁷ This was the age of iron, when great armies fought like rams for land and glory. And all men trembled before them as they invoked the names of their gods. Yet still the gods forsook them.

⁷ The sixth is the age of the oceanborn, when men shall seek the depths of their own souls, yet find them not amidst the rancor. And the gods shall speak, but men shall not have ears to hear.

⁸ The seventh is the age of the water bearer, when the heavens and the earth shall be reconciled, and the sons of men shall once more know the gods.

⁹ He who has ears to hear, let him hear.

¹⁰ In the age of Eanna, men exalted the bull god who raged in the heavens and raised banners to wage war like beasts that trample down the earth. ¹¹ They turned away from the sun god who gives light from on high and, bent on conquest, they knelt before the storm god who thunders from heaven. ¹² As a bellowing ox, he does violence to the land. As a mighty dragon, he casts fire upon the earth.

¹³ This was the age of mighty cities and great warriors, the hunter kings who subdued the land. ¹⁴ The greatest of these cities was Eanna, and the greatest of these kings was Enmr-Kar, whose name means Nimrod the Hunter.

¹⁵ He placed on his head the horns of the bull god, and with his armies subdued the land between the rivers. ¹⁶ He took for himself Babel and Akkad, and other cities across Shinar. And thence he went forth to Assur and built up Nineveh as his own. Yet his throne was in Eanna, the "House of Heaven" by the banks of the Euphrates.

¹⁷ There did he build the great city of Unuq, which he named for his ancestor Enoch. Those who dwelt there were the Anakim, the sons of Enoch whom some men knew as Anak. ¹⁸ And Enmr-Kar built a wall around this place so as to enclose it for a vast distance and secure it against his enemies. ¹⁹ But his crowning glory was to be in the midst of the cities, wherein he sought to build anew the tree of life that was in Eden, a great new watchtower as a tribute to the goddess queen of heaven, whose name is Isis and Inanna. ²⁰ This tower he built as a ladder and a mountain, with steps carved into the sides of it that the sons of men might ascend to the heavens.

²¹ For he said to himself, "The gods are safe in their heavens. Now what if they should forget their promise, and again unleash the waters of the abyss upon this land? ²² Therefore shall we become like the gods and build a place of refuge, that we may ascend the stairway to heaven and commune with them."

²³ This place would be nothing less than a new dwelling place for Inanna. Adorned with all the finest jewels and every precious metal, it would be a gateway for the gods between the heavens and the earth.

²⁴ Therefore did he name this place Babilim, which means "Gate of the Gods."

²⁵ Enmr-Kar boasted that no more would the sons of men pine for Aratta, for he would make a new heaven and new earth in Unuq. ²⁶ And Innana would come down from the highlands to dwell among them, forsaking her abode in the land of Eden. ²⁷ So he besought Inanna, saying:

Let Aratta fashion gold and silver skilfuflly
On my behalf, for the sake of Unuq
²⁸ Let them cut lapis lazuli without flaw from the blocks
That I may build a holy mountain in Unuq

²⁹ Let Aratta build a temple brought down from heaven
Let Aratta fashion your abode
³⁰ Let Aratta submit beneath the yoke of Unuq
On my behalf

³¹ Let the people of Aratta bring down stones from the mountain
    To build a great shrine
    Erect the great abode
    The abode of the gods

³² Make the abyss rise up for me like a shining mountain
Make Eridu gleam like the range of mountains
³³ May the abyss shine forth like silver from the lode
I shall bring the ME from Eridu

³⁴ When I am adorned with the crown of lordship
Like a purified shrine
³⁵ When I place upon my head
The crown of Unuq Kulaba
³⁶ And the people shall marvel
With the sun god as my witness
In my joy

³⁷ Yet Inanna scorned his advances, for would any temple made with human hands be wondrous enough to contain her majesty? Not she, the queen of heaven, whose canopy was the night sky and whose doorposts were the tall cedars. ³⁸ Enmr-Kar sought to woo her and, by subtlety, entrance her. Yet the subtlety of men is like a clamorous gong to the ears of a goddess. ³⁹ So she spurned him, though he did not know it, and she rebuffed it, though he would not accept it. ⁴⁰ For the declaration of a goddess is like a whisper to the ears of proud men, who wage war in

the name of the heavens and defile the names of the gods with their folly.

8

¹ When he was convinced that he had received the blessing of Inanna (though he knew not the truth, that she had scorned him), Enmr-Kar called to himself a messenger to make an embassy to Aratta and give word to the lord of that land what was required of him. ² "Let Aratta pack nuggets of gold in leather sacks," he said. ³ "Place alongside it the kumea ore. Package up also precious metals, and load the packs on the donkeys of the mountains"

⁴ He sent him also with this word of warning, should the lord of Aratta defy him, that he would make people fly forth from that city like a dove from the bough of a tree, and that it would gather dust like a city utterly ruined.

⁵ So the messenger went forth from there. He journeyed by the starry night and traveled by day with the sun of heaven. ⁶ He brought his message up into the highlands and descended with it from the highlands. ⁷ In Susa and Ancan did they salute Innana humbly, like tiny mice. In the high mountains, the multitudes groveled in the dust for her. ⁸ He traversed five mountains, six mountains, seven mountains. He lifted up his eyes and saw Aratta. ⁹ Then did he step forth into her courtyard and make known boldly the authority of his king. ¹⁰ Openly did he speak the words of his heart, transmitting his message to the lord of Aratta.

[11] Now the Elohim yet ruled within Aratta. As ever were they proud and haughty, and they would not submit.

[12] Yet in those days, a famine was on the land, and Aratta was sore afflicted. In Shinar there was plenty, while Aratta was in want. [13] So they struck a bargain, the two of them, that the lord of Aratta would bow his knee to Enmr-Kar should he send forth from his storehouse new barley and grain to ease the great hunger.

[14] When the messenger returned, he told Enmr-Kar of these things, and the great king agreed to abide by this agreement. [15] He measured out in full the barley from his granary, accounting also for the teeth of locusts. He loaded it on the pack-asses, and dispatched them at once to the highland kingdom. [16] With them he sent his messenger to demand recompense from the lord of Aratta, the prince of Eden.

[17] But again the Most High of Aratta would not submit. And the herald was sent back to Unuq empty-handed.

[18] For five years, for ten years Enmr-Kar waited. He bided his time as his chief steward fashioned for him a great scepter, and when it was completed, he sent it forth with his herald to the throne of Aratta.

[19] Then the lord of Aratta despaired, saying, "Aratta is indeed slaughtered like sheep. Its roads are indeed like the rebel lands, since Innana has given the kingship of Aratta over to the lord of Unuq. [20] Now Innana looks with favor on this man who has sent a herald, whose message is as clear as the light of the sun. [21] Where in Aratta can one go in this crisis? How long before the yoke we bear is

tolerable? ²² As for us, in the midst of our direst hunger, most extreme famine, are we to prostrate ourselves before the lord of Unuq?"

²³ Still, he was not willing to submit.

²⁴ He therefore summoned the herald and said to him: "Say to your master, 'Let my champion compete with your champion, and let the better man prevail!'"

²⁵ Upon hearing this was Enmr-Kar enraged with his brother from the mountains. ²⁶ So told his messenger, "Accept this challenge." And he gave him other words to speak in his behalf, demanding once more gold and silver for the house of Inanna he would build in his city, and rare lapis lazuli to adorn it. ²⁷ Uttering new threats, he spoke to his messenger in an oracle at such length that the herald could not repeat all that was said. For his mouth was heavy and speech forsook him.

²⁸ Therefore did Enmr-Kar inscribe his message on a tablet of clay, as had been done in former times by Enoch. ²⁹ Until that day, the way of the scribe had long been neglected, and the practice of writing was no more established. Only the ME preserved from former times remained. ³⁰ So it was that Nimrod revived the ancient art of writing then and there, dispatching the herald with his new message engraved in clear lettering for all to see.

³¹ He brought these tablets to Aratta and presented them to the king there. And the message inscribed upon them told of what Enmr-Kar had already achieved as he built his tower up to the highest heavens: ³² "This tree has grown high, uniting the heavens with the earth. Its crown

reaches up to the heaven, and its trunk is secure upon the earth. [33] So does his kingship shine forth upon the land; it is he who sends you this clay tablet."

[34] When the lord of Aratta saw it, his brow was creased in anger. And at that very moment did the storm god unleash thunder from the heavens, and the earth shook also beneath them. [35] Like the roar of a great lion, the storm raged all about them, and the mountains convulsed beneath them, rising up in thirst to accept heaven"s offering. [35] On the parched flanks of Aratta, in the midst of the mountains, wheat sprang up of its own accord. Chickpeas grew unbidden. [36] And the men of Aratta brought these things into the granary of their lord, wherefore he looked upon them and saw that the famine had ended.

[36] Emboldened, the lord of Aratta therefore declared to the messenger: "Behold! Innana has not forsaken her people! She has neither fled from Aratta nor taken up residence in Unuq. [37] She who preserved Aratta in the midst of the flood has now blessed her anew. For as the flood swept over and we stood in the face of it, now Innana, the lady of all the lands, has seen fit to sprinkle the water of life upon her children."

Yet he knew not that in the rain she wept for them; that the waters were as tears shed for the strife he had created.

9

¹ So the lord of Aratta defied Enmr-Kar once more, and he called to him a champion who came wrapped in lion skins with a turban of many colors around his head. ² This man was a sorcerer, and boasted, "I shall make Unuq dig canals! I shall make them submit to the shrine of Aratta! ³ The lands from below shall submit to the lands from above, from the sea to the cedar mountain. Let Unuq bring its goods by boat in tribute in a flotilla to the great city of Aratta!"

⁴ So the lord of Aratta gave him silver and gold, promising him fine food and sweet wine should he succeed in his purpose. ⁵ "When their men are taken captive," he vowed, "your life shall be full, and you shall enjoy every happiness; in your hand shall be wealth and prosperity."

⁵ And the sorcerer directed his steps toward Unuq.

⁶ When he arrived, he cursed the livestock, so that no milk came from the udder of cow or she-goat. The kid went hungry and the cow grew bitter toward her calf. ⁷ The churn lay empty, and the day was given to starvation. ⁸ The cow-herd dropped the staff from his hand in amazement, while the shepherd hung the crook at his side and wept bitterly. ⁹ They sat down amidst the debris of their ruin and cried out, saying, "The sorcerer of Aratta has invaded the stables; he has made the milk scarce so young calves are wanting. He has made butter scarce and diminished the milk of the she-goat. So have we been dealt a disaster!"

¹⁰ And their voices were heard across creation, and reached the ears of a witch named Sajburu.

¹¹ Hearing of their plight did she turn her face toward Unuq and make her way down the Euphrates, continuing until at last she came to the great city which the sorcerer afflicted. ¹² And she challenged him, saying, "I am the champion of Unuq. Let us have a contest, to see whose magic is from heaven, and let the loser declare on his honor that his country shall submit to the one whose magic shall triumph."

¹³ To this was he agreeable.

¹⁴ So both of them took a fish and threw it into the river. And in place of the sorcerer's fish, a giant carp arose from the waters. ¹⁵ But in place of the witch's fish, an eagle emerged and seized the carp between its talons. Then did it ascend out of the waves and away into the heavens.

¹⁵ A second time they threw a fish into the river. And the sorcerer caused a ewe and its lamb to rise up from the waters, but the witch made a wolf come forth and lay hold of them, dragging them into the desert.

¹⁶ A third time they threw a fish into the river. The sorcerer made a cow and its calf arise from the waters, but the witch called forth a lion to drag them away into the reedbeds.

¹⁷ A fourth time still they threw a fish into the river, the mighty Euphrates. The sorcerer brought forth an ibex and wild sheep, but the witch summoned to her a mountain leopard that laid hold of it.

[18] A fifth time yet the sorcerer threw a fish into the water, and a gazelle kid came up from out of its current. [19] And the witch likewise threw a fish into the river, where it was transformed into a tiger that sprang up and captured the gazelle.

[20] And the sorcerer's countenance darkened, and his mind became confused. [21] He begged that she show him mercy, but she refused, saying, "You have caused great distress in the stable and the cow shed. [22] You have removed the lunch table; barren are the tables of the morning and the evening. [23] You have cut off butter and milk from the evening meal of the great dining hall. Such wickedness is deserving of death under the law, and I shall not pardon your life."

[24] Therefore did she lay hold of him and cast him headlong into the river, whereupon his life force departed from him and Aratta was finally vanquished.

[25] Then did Enmr-Kar send forth a mighty army against Aratta, ascending the highlands through the seven mountain passes that are the seven gates of heaven. [26] There did he lay siege to the city whence his ancestors had come. His men made their encampment in the ditches and posts that surrounded the city. [27] But for a year did javelins fly down at them from atop the city walls, and slingstones like raindrops fell as if from the clouds above them to the roadway where they stood. [28] Around about they were hemmed in by briars and dragons, so that they despaired of ever taking the city.

²⁹ But Lugalbanda, the great general, instructed Enmr-Kar as to how he might vanquish Aratta.

³⁰ Cut down the lone tamarisk tree
By the banks of the water meadows!
Tear out the reeds that grow in that place!
³¹ Catch the fish that swims there and cook it!
So shall the waters be fouled, which are life to Aratta!

³² Then carry off the metalworkers
and stonemasons of the city
³³ Renew it once more and settle it
Then it shall be his!

³⁵ So Enmr-Kar did as he was bidden. He cut down the tamarisk tree which grew alone by the banks of the water meadows, and he uprooted the reeds from that place. ³⁶ He caught the fish from the river and cooked it, so his armies renewed their strength. ³⁷ From the tree's wood he made himself buckets, so that water was diverted from Aratta. ³⁸ Those within the city thirsted, but they could not drink. They hungered, but they could not eat.

³⁹ They opened their gates to Enmr-Kar, who took away the metalworkers and made slaves of the masons. ⁴⁰ The proud Elohim of Aratta were made humble. The Most High of their number was laid low and cast down from the Kingdom of Heaven, just as the mountain lord and his minions had cast down Seth and the sons of Adam. ⁴¹ And they who had served him became as wanderers upon the

earth, seeking a new home for themselves in the southern reaches of the lowlands.

⁴² From that day forward did Unuq claim dominion over Eden, and the great kingdom that had been the cradle of Adam become no more than memory. ⁴³ Ever more the vassal, it passed from one king to another, until the garden was uprooted by the feet of many armies and the wide plain was subdued beneath long caravans and new cities.

⁴⁴ But no man forgot her glory. And still, few dared defy the name of the Most High.

10

¹ Enmr-Kar built his tower to the heavens and adorned it with all manner of precious stones and metals from Aratta. ² His armies crossed the plains and mountains, subduing the lands around him, and he laid waste all who came against him. ³ With each new conquest, his pride was magnified and with each new victory his arrogance increased. ⁴ In a vision he conceived of a kingdom which would span the breadth of creation, wherein the great god of Unuq would reign from horizon to horizon and he, Enmr-Kar, would rule the entire world as his very embodiment. The Enki, lord of all the earth.

⁵ During his conflict with Aratta, he had sent his messenger forth with the following oracle:

⁶ On the day when there is no snake

On the day when there is no scorpion
On the day when there is no hyena
⁷ When there is neither lion, dog nor wolf
When there is no fear nor trembling
When man shall have no rival

⁸ At this time, may the lands of Shubur and Hamazi,
The many-tongued
And Shinar, the mountain of the ME of magnificence
And Akkad, which possesses all that is fitting
And Martu, which rests in security
May the whole universe, the well-guarded people
All address the lord of the air together in a single language

⁹ At that time shall all the ambitious lords
And all the ambitious kings
And all the ambitious princes
Submit to the wise lord Enki

¹⁰ The lord of abundance and steadfast decisions,
Known for his wisdom, the lord of Eridu
Shall change the tongues within their mouths
As many as he placed there
So the speech of mankind is truly one.

¹¹ Yet it was not to be.
¹² For the sorcerer of Aratta had placed a curse upon him. And the gods did listen, because he had acted so in

violence. [13] His offense against Aratta was not to be forgiven, for he had trampled the garden of Osiris and had vanquished the land of Eden. He had cut down the tamarisk tree, where Osiris had been preserved. [14] So the gods took vengeance upon him and turned the oracle against him. Within his empire there arose conflicts and disputes, and these multiplied with each new phase of the moon. [15] Many men sought to ascend the great tower he had built, but each prevented his neighbor from so doing.

[16] In the midst of their arguing, a single tongue became many. The people of Shinar were dispersed across the land while the tower was torn asunder by ruin and folly.

[17] No man understood his neighbor, for they had forgotten how to listen. The names of ancient cities were changed, so that they were no longer recognized. [18] Unuq became Uruk, and men also called it Erech. [19] Likewise the names gods and heroes from the first times were corrupted, with each tribe calling them by different appellations.

[20] Isis was Inanna and Diana and Astarte.

[21] A'bel became Ba'al, and also Bile, and Adam was Adapa.

[22] Osiris was a new name for the one once called Asar.

[23] Even the name of Enoch was dispersed upon the winds, so he was known as Thoth to the Egyptians, and Hermes to the Greeks. [24] In Akkad he was called Ea, and in the west he was Yah the Righteous, who lays his bow upon the heavens at the passing of each storm.

[25] And it came to pass that the men of each nation blessed one name and cursed another, as though the names

themselves were a source of power. ²⁶ "This name alone is holy!" they declared, condemning the use of any other.
²⁷ On pain of death did men oppose these sacred names. And in these names were the seeds of untold violence sown to generations of widows and beggars and orphans that would follow.

²⁸ And the men who spoke these names defiled the sanctity of the land.

²⁹ They appointed priests to guard their altars, to speak in the name of their god.

³⁰ They appointed kings to guard their treasures, to rule in the name of their god.

³¹ They appointed warriors and armies, to fight in the name of their god.

³² And the priests hid the face of their god behind a mask, saying, "No man may see the face of a god and live!"

³³ And the masks they fashioned to hide the sacred they made in their own image, saying, "Our god is jealous," when it was they who became jealous; and "Our god demands vengeance," when the demand was their own.
³⁴ They proclaimed, "Our god is angry" to justify their anger, and "Our god commands it!" to support their bloodshed.

11

¹ In the course of time, it came to pass that one named Lugalbanda rose up and took the throne of Unuq. ² There

were wars and rumors of wars across the land. Treaties were made and broken, and alliances were sundered. ³ Lies were the currency of commerce, and no man valued the life of his neighbor. ⁴ Even firstborn sons were set on the altar and butchered for the sake of their gods. ⁵ Yet still every tribe recalled the days of Noah. And though they called him by different names, the story of his time was preserved in their memory, and it remains so to this day. ⁶ They took courage in his example and sought solace in his wisdom.

⁷ As this wisdom had preserved him, so they would seek it.

⁸ As his great ark had guarded him, so they would guard themselves.

⁹ As he had set forth upon the waters, so would they too venture forth.

¹⁰ Nevermore would the waters of the floodplain overwhelm them, but would bear them aloft to a land far distant. ¹¹ They would build great vessels as their father had before them, and they would turn the power of waters to fit their purpose. ¹² Rising up, the great Euphrates would bear them forward to Dilmun and beyond. Through the place of the two waters, sweet and bitter, would they pass, out across the open sea that some call Ocean.

¹³ This was the time of going forth, when mariners claimed new lands in the name of their masters. ¹⁴ The men of Kish made their way along the coastlands of the desert, never venturing far from shore as they passed beyond the realm of Sheba to the south and on to the land which is on two sides of the water. ¹⁵ On one side they came ashore and

built a port which they named Aeden, after the garden of their fathers. [16] Here they buried the bones of their ancestors, Cain and A'bel. And they named the land across the channel Cush, after the city whence they had come.

[17] Others, though, called it the land of Punt and those who dwelt there the Punic tribe.

[18] These were the people of the Phoenix who came from the land of the rising sun, the followers of Horus from beyond the horizon. [19] For this reason they came to be called the Phoenicians. [20] Many wild animals roamed in their kingdom, from the elephant to the hippopotamus to the baboon and leopard. [21] Their land was rich also in myrrh and incense, in ebony and short-horned cattle, and they brought into their kingdom goods from other lands around about: gold and ivory and animal skins. And they prospered there.

[22] It was they who created the first true system of letters, in the tradition of Enoch, setting them down upon scrolls of papyrus and gathering them together in libraries.
[23] Indeed, the great port city of Byblos, which they founded, took its name from the inner bark of the papyrus plant.

[24] It was but one of many trading posts they established. Some took their great boats with them across the desert, finding their way at last to the Nile and making a kingdom for themselves along the banks of the great river. [25] These were the fathers of Egypt, who founded great dynasties and gave rise to a mighty empire. [26] Yet always they remembered Punt as the land of the gods, whence their

ancestors had come, and traded with her rulers to the advantage of both lands.

27 The queen of Egypt brought shiploads of goods across from Aeden to her country, loading her ships heavily with marvels from the land of Punt: all goodly fragrant woods from the gods' land, heaps of myrrh-resin with fresh myrrh trees. 28 There was pure ivory and ebony, cinnamon wood, green gold of Amu, khesyt wood, ahmut and senter incenses, and cosmetics for the eyes. 29 Also on board were monkeys and apes, dogs and the skins of the southern panther, all brought forth by the Phoenicians and their children. 30 Never had the like of this been sent to any king enthroned since the beginning.

31 In the image of the towers in Shinar, the kings of Egypt raised up the pyramids. And the Phoenicians built ships even greater than those that had borne them to Cush and Aeden, seeking out new lands to extend their wealth.

32 They built Tyre on the coast of Lebanon.

33 They built Carthage in the north of Libya.

34 And they traveled onward to the gates of the Sea at the Center of the World, where they built Tangier on the southern land Cadiz in the north. 35 Thence they ventured farther still, driven by strong winds away from the coast of the known world. 36 They challenged the dragons that guard the ends of the earth and monsters that plied the depths of the great ocean. Yet their courage failed them not, and the pressed on until they came to a land both vast and bounteous. 37 Here they found a level plain of exceeding

beauty, with mountains rising high above it, from which flowed navigable rivers that were used for irrigation.

[38] Gardens in great multitudes were traversed by streams of sweet water. Its inhabitants had built for themselves private dwellings and great halls for banquet feasts, with fields of flowers arrayed around about. [39] In the highlands were dense thickets and fruit trees of every variety, among which could be found secluded valleys and springs of fresh, clean water.

[40] All manner of beast and wild animal did dwell there, in a land where the climes were mild and forgiving.

[41] This place became a secret and a legend, undiscovered for its distance from the known lands, until the Phoenicians landed their ships there. [42] Some among them proposed to establish a colony on those shores, but the men of Carthage sought to prevent it, fearing their own city might be forsaken because of the excellence of this new land, farther even from their homeland than was Shinar from Libya.

[43] Yet however far they traveled from their homeland, the people of the Phoenix remembered always the sacred land of Aratta, and they mourned their departure from their abode in the highlands. [44] So they built for themselves new mountains in the midst of their cities, by which they could ascend to the heavens. [45] And they fashioned for themselves arks to set at their summit, wherein they placed the tablets of truth they had inherited from their father Enoch.

12

¹ Years passed, and the tablets were forgotten, guarded by priests who neither knew their wisdom nor shared it with those who sought it.

² When they had locked their wisdom away, they locked themselves away as well, taking refuge behind walls and battlements thicker and higher than any built before.

² Proud Gilgamesh took the throne of Unuq and raised the walls so high he boasted that no man could breach them. He was the son of Lugalbanda, hailed as one part man and two parts god.

³ It was in his day that the power of Kish was broken, for its lord Agga sent an army to besiege Unuq. Yet the city's wall held firm, and the assault on its ramparts failed.

⁴ So it was that Unuq reigned supreme in the land between the rivers. ⁵ But Gilgamesh's pride restrained him from true greatness, so Osiris sent a man from the mountains to test him, a man with strength and power to equal the great king's. ⁶ This one was called Enkidu, and he came out of the highlands like a terror, his body covered in hair and his mane long and flowing.

⁷ He went forth like a prowling lion, eating with the gazelles and drinking with the beasts. He struck fear into the hearts of all who saw him. ⁸ So it was that when a certain hunter came upon him at the watering hole, this man was astonished, and retreated at once to his own home. ⁹ Thence he went to Unuq, and reported to Gilgamesh the marvel that he had seen.

¹⁰ "I saw a young man come down from the mountain, strong and powerful as a sky bolt from heaven. His feet tread upon the mountains and he eats among the cattle. ¹¹ When he comes to the watering place, I dare not approach him. When I dig a pit, he fills it. When I set a trap, he destroys it. ¹² Because of him, the beasts of the field elude me, so that I can no longer make my living there."

¹³ So Gilgamesh called to him the wise woman Shamhat and sent her with the hunter, and he told the man what he must do. And they went their way.

¹⁴ At length they came to the watering hole, and they waited there for Enkidu. ¹⁵ When at length he came to that place, the hunter said to his companion, "Shamhat, shrink not from him when he approaches, but let him know the ways of a woman. Then will he forget the beasts of the open field, and will lavish his attentions upon you!"

¹⁶ And it came to pass as he had said, and Enkidu abode with the wise woman for six days and seven nights. ¹⁷ And when the time was completed, behold, no longer did the beasts of the field approach him, but were wary and kept their distance. ¹⁸ His strength had been diminished, but yet had he acquired judgment. The woman's gift to him was wisdom. ¹⁹ Gazing hard upon his face, she spoke thus to him:

"You have grown wise now, Enkidu, like unto a god. Why should you roam the open country with the beasts? ²⁰ Come and let me show you the sheepfold of Unuq, where Gilgamesh rules in perfect power like a wild bull, stronger yet than all the people."

[21] And she divided her garments between them, so he could clothe himself, and she took him to the tents of the shepherds. [22] There did the shepherds gather round and look upon him in amazement. Surely this was not the same one who had roamed about the open lands so freely? [23] Quickly did they bring him bread and strong wine, yet he knew not how to partake, for he had but suckled the milk of wild creatures. [24] Yet the woman came to him and showed him, saying, "Take of the bread, the staff of life, and drink of the wine, for it is custom."

[25] For this was the mystery of the bread and the cup, the first for life and the second for knowledge.

[26] And he did as she had bidden. He partook of the fruit that came from the vine, the nectar of knowledge for good and for ill. [27] And he broke bread, which was the food of Osiris, in the hope of eternal life. Yet eternal life would not be his.

[28] Then did the mighty Enkidu array himself in the clothing of men, so that he took on the aspect of a bridegroom. [29] And when he did so, the shepherds cheered him, and he exulted in the spirit that the wine bestowed upon him. [30] And he became a watchman for the sheepfold, hunting lions and wolves that stalked them while the shepherds took their rest. [31] He was a mighty guardian, and in strength he knew no rival.

[32] Thus did the days pass, good and many.

³³ Then at length did a weary traveler come upon them from the land of Unuq. And Enkidu welcomed the stranger into his presence.

³⁴ "What news? And wherefore have you come?" he asked him.

³⁵ And the man replied, saying, "Gilgamesh has gone into the marriage house and shuts out the people. He does strange things in Unuq, the city of great streets. ³⁶ He commands work at the roll of the drum for men and women, and he demands that he be first to share a new bride's marriage bed, before even her husband can know her. ³⁷ For he says this is his birthright, ordained by the gods themselves in the heavens. Even now does he prepare to enter into the bridal chamber!"

³⁸ Therefore did Enkidu grow pale with anger. And he clenched his fists, declaring boldly, "Now I will go to this place where Gilgamesh afflicts the people! ³⁹ Now will I challenge him to his face, and will proclaim aloud in Unuq, 'I have come to abolish the old order, for in strength no man can surpass me!'"

⁴⁰ So he strode forth with the wise woman until he came to the great city of Unuq. ⁴¹ And he made his way into the great marketplace, parting the crowds as they exclaimed of him, "This is the man who was raised with the beasts. Behold! He is a match even for the great Gilgamesh!"

⁴² And as Gilgamesh made ready to enter the bridal chamber, Enkidu stepped forth and stood before him, barring the way so he could not pass. ⁴³ Gilgamesh sought to move forward, yet he put out his foot and so prevented

it. ⁴⁴ Then did the two men fall upon one another, grappling and snorting like two great bulls. The walls shook and the doorposts trembled until they shattered, unable to bear the strength of the two great warriors.

⁴⁵ At last did Gilgamesh bend his knee and plant his foot in the earth, and he turned his body so Enkidu was thrown. ⁴⁶ Thus was the great contest between them ended, and Enkidu said to the man who had bested him, "There is no one like you in all the earth. Your strength surpasses the strength of all men." ⁴⁷ In that same moment, the two men were bonded, and from that time forward, they were constant friends.

⁴⁸ But the gods did not forget Gilgamesh's hubris, nor did they ignore the grave offense he had shown in taking other men's wives to his own bed. ⁴⁹ And they said to themselves, "Behold, here is one who might have been worthy to be called immortal. Yet now he is cursed to know not only his own greatness, yet also the certainty of his death."

13

¹ Such was the fame of Gilgamesh and Enkidu that great tales of their exploits are told to this very day. Are they not to be found in the "Book of Gilgamesh and Enkidu" and "The Bull of Heaven"?

² There is it written that the two warriors fought the bull of heaven, and that Enkidu seized it by the horns while Gilgamesh slew it with a single thrust of his sword. ³ Its

heart they offered to the sun, and its horns they took with them to adorn the walls of Gilgamesh's palace in Unuq. ⁴ But Inanna was enraged at their actions and took her case before the council of the gods. Therefore was it decided that, in exchange for the bull's life, one of the two heroes would forfeit his own.

⁵ It was decreed that Enkidu should be the one to die, and though Gilgamesh lamented long over his stricken friend, there was naught he could do to spare him from the fate that awaited him. ⁶ One day passed, and Enkidu lay still, taken by fever. A second day passed, and his sickness increased. A third day, and he grew weaker, his eyes blinded by tears from weeping. ⁷ And after twelve days, he called out to Gilgamesh, saying, "My friend, the great goddess has cursed me to die in shame. I shall not die like a warrior in battle. I feared that end, yet happy is the man who dies in combat, for I must die in shame."

⁸ And at length he breathed his last, leaving his companion to weep bitter tears at his passing. Gilgamesh touched his heart, yet it beat no more. ⁹ So he laid a veil across Enkidu, as one puts a veil across the countenance of a bride. Such was his affection for his fallen friend.

¹⁰ Then did Gilgamesh rage about like a lioness whose cubs are taken from her, and he flung his royal garments from him as if they were abominations. ¹¹ He declared, in his grief, "All the people of Unuq shall weep over you, and they shall raise a dirge of the dead. The joyful shall bend low in sorrow, and I will grow my hair long in tribute to

your greatness! ¹² Then shall I wander the desert places, adorned in nothing more than the skin of a lion!"

¹³ And so it came to pass that he departed the gates of Unuq, knowing not where he would go, yet fearful in his heart that he should suffer the same fate as his companion. ¹⁴ "How can I rest?" he asked himself. "How can I know peace? My heart is stricken with despair. What has become of my brother shall likewise befall me at the end of my days."

¹⁵ So he determined in his heart to find his ancestor Noah, of whom it was said he had never perished, for he had found favor with the gods. ¹⁶ He traveled a great distance until he came to the waters of death, across which lay the land of the rising sun. This, he had been told, was the land of Noah. ¹⁷ And on the shore was a ferryman, a servant of Noah, who stood ready to bear him across the waters.

¹⁸ When he arrived at the habitation of Noah, he asked the ancient one to share with him the secret of life eternal.

¹⁹ This, then, is what Noah told him: "There is a plant that grows under the water, thorny like a rose. It will wound your hands when you try to lay hold of it, yet if you succeed in so doing, you will hold in your hands that which restores lost youth to a man!"

²⁰ Gilgamesh therefore found the deepest channel in the open waters and tied heavy stones to each of his feet, that he might descend into the depths of the ocean. ²¹ There he found the plant of which Noah had spoken, and he plucked it from the place it was growing. ²² Its thorns

pierced his hands, but he held it fast. Then he cut the stones from the chords by which they were fastened to his feet, and the water's current took him until he was safe upon the shore.

²³ Gilgamesh, triumphant, boasted of what he had accomplished. He exulted to the ferryman, saying, "Come and see this marvelous plant, by virtue of which a man may regain his former strength! ²⁴ I shall bear it forth to Unuq of the strong walls, and once there, I shall give it to all the elders of the people to eat. ²⁵ Its name shall be 'Old Men are Young Once More,' and at the last I shall partake of it myself, that my lost youth may be restored."

²⁶ Then did they go on their way, and at length did they stop for the evening at pond of cool water. And laying the plant aside, Gilgamesh went down to the water to bathe. ²⁷ Yet deep within the pool there lay a serpent, and it sensed the sweetness of the flower. So it rose up from out of the water and snatched it away before Gilgamesh could reach the place where he had lain it. And he knew he could not recover it.

²⁸ At the end of his appointed days, therefore, Gilgamesh breathed his last. And a dirge was sung for him when Unuq laid him in the earth.

²⁹ The king has laid himself down — he will not rise again

The lord of Kullub — he will not rise again

He conquered evil — he will not come again

30 He was strong of arm — he will not rise again
He had a countenance well-pleasing —
    he will not come again
He is gone into the mountain —
    he will not come again

31 On the bed of fate he lies — he will not rise again
From the couch of many colors, he will not rise again

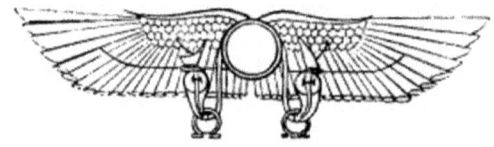

The Book of Pharaohs

1

¹ Hearken now to the Book of the Pharaohs, who ruled the land called Egypt by the Nile. These rose up to challenge Babylon, to become its equal and surpass it.
² They raised up monuments in the desert and sought their counsel among the stars. These were the people of Osiris, the servants of the sun.

³ In Babylon, the kingdom of Gilgamesh was weakened, and a new city rose to claim the mantle of greatness. This was Akkad, which Enmr-Kar had ruled in earlier times. ⁴ Yet now a king arose there even greater than he, whose empire stretched from Elam to the cedars of Lebanon.

⁵ In Kish did he rise to power, emboldened by a dream in which he saw the king there meet his death by drowning. ⁶ He said, "I am the Gardener!" after the manner of Osiris. And "Isis is my consort!" that he might claim the mantle of wisdom. But he called her Ishtar, after the manner of his people.

⁷ "My mother was high priestess, yet my father I knew not," he declared. ⁸ "My city is Azupiranu, on the banks of the great Euphrates. There did my mother conceive me; in secret did she bear me. ⁹ She set me in an ark of rushes, sealing the lid tight shut with bitumen. Then did she cast me into the river, which rose quickly. And it bore me on its waters to the home of Akki, the water drawer. ¹⁰ Then he became as a father to me, raising me up to be his gardener. And Ishtar did love me, and did grant to me the kingship."

¹¹ Sargon was from the tribe of the Shemites, and he was the first among his people to rule in the land of Shinar. ¹² His tongue was foreign to them, but his armies swept across the land like locusts, and none could stand against him. ¹³ Lugalzaggesi of Unuq had bound all of Shinar to him as a single land. Yet he fell to the Akkadian like a sandman shaking his fist in defiance at the sea god Yam.

¹⁴ Sargon tore down the battlements of Unuq and brought Lugalzaggesi in a dog collar to the gates of Enlil.

15 Then did he march forth against Ur and Lagash, and thence to the shores of the southern sea, where he cleansed his weapons of all enemy blood and proclaimed himself master of all that met his gaze.

16 He had no rival, and no man was his equal. His splendor covered all the lands, and by the eleventh year of his reign he had subdued the lands in the west to their most distant shoreline. 17 In his pride did he set up statues to his glory, and took from the far lands tribute, which he ferried on barges to his palace in Akkad. 18 And when the land of Kazallu defied him, he laid it waste so that not a single perch was left for the birds of the heavens.

19 Mari he subdued, and Ebla did submit to him. He made himself Susa's master and traded with the cities of India, Crete and Cappadocia.

20 And the Shemites prospered in the land between the rivers, and their numbers multiplied while Sargon and his scions reigned there. 21 For fifty-six years did he hold the seat of power, and after him his children, and their children after them. 22 But Naram-Sin, the grandson of Sargon, stretched forth his hand against the city of Nippur, and he defiled the temple of Enlil in that place. 23 Therefore did the gods grow wroth with his insolence and withdraw their favor from Akkad.

24 For the first time since the foundation of their cities, the great fields yielded no grain. The fisheries yielded no fish. The orchards produced neither wine nor syrup. 25 Clouds gathered but withheld their rain, and the masgurum tree grew not. 26 In that day, a shekel's worth of

oil was but half a quart, and a shekel's worth of grain was but half a quart. Such were the prices in the markets of every city. ²⁷ He who slept on the roof died on the roof. He who slept in the house had no burial. And the people scourged themselves in the anguish of their hunger.

²⁸ So did the empire of Sargon fall. And in its place rose a new line of rulers who restored the name of Shinar to its former place. ²⁹ The sons of Shem were cast down from their places of privilege, and their language was stricken from the books of the law. And those who were of royal heritage feared for their safety, that they might be set upon and slain by men who hated them. ³⁰ So it was with one named Terach, who dwelt in the precincts of Ur during those days. And he had three sons there with him, whose names were Abram, Nahor and Haran.

³¹ Abram was the eldest among him and heir to the lineage of Terach, for his name meant "exalted father." ³² He married a woman of Shemite noble lineage, for her name was Sarai, which translated means, "my princess." ³³ Haran, in like manner, was of noble heritage, for his eldest daughter he named Milcah, which means "queen." He was also the father of Lot. ³⁴ Yet he departed this earth while his father yet lived, and Milcah married his brother, Nahor, that he might care for her.

³⁵ Now it came to pass that Milcah was with child by Nahor, and she gave birth to eight sons, the youngest of whom she called Bethuel. And Bethuel begat a son named Laban and a daughter named Rebekah.

2

¹ Upon the death of Haran, a dispute arose concerning Terach's inheritance. Although Abram was the eldest, his wife was barren and had given him no child to preserve their lineage. ² Haran's son Lot therefore sought the inheritance, and this was a cause of strife between them, for Abram said, "Sarai may yet conceive." But Lot said, "She is past the age of childbirth, and the birthright shall pass to me."

³ News of their dispute was heard upon the streets of Ur, and it reached the ears of the king in Shinar. ⁴ He feared lest the clan of Terach raise an army to fight against them, whereupon he sought to quench the fire of rebellion ere it was kindled. ⁵ He therefore set forth a decree that the clan of Terach be exiled from the city of Ur and from the entire land of Shinar, so Terach took his kinsmen and fled that place for Harran, a city of Ebla to the north and to the west. ⁶ There did they settle, in Paddan Aram (which means "the highland plain"), until the death of Terach.

⁷ But there was famine upon the land, and the people of Harran were loath to share their pastures with the sons of Terach. ⁸ Then there arose a dispute within the clan of Terach, for some proposed that they should leave that place while others among them wished to tarry there. ⁹ So it was that Nahor and his family remained upon the highland plain, with his son Bethuel and his kinfolk Laban and Rebekah. But Abram and his kinsmen departed that place

and went down into Canaan, and thence into the land of Egypt, by the banks of the fertile Nile. [10] Lot and his wife accompanied them. [11] Their numbers had swollen, both in men and among their livestock, and their servants were as an army of invaders in lower Egypt. To the Egyptians, they were the Hyksos or the "foreigners," and others called them the Habiru.

[12] Now the pharaoh in that day was weak, and feared the numbers in the Hyksos caravan, so he sought an alliance with Abram as a means to secure the throne of his kingdom. [13] When he saw Sarai among their number, that she was comely and pleasing in her manner, he sought her hand as a way to seal their friendship. For Abram had said to him, "She is my sister." [14] And knowing not that they were married, the pharaoh became set on having her. [15] To this end did he invite her to the palace, and in return for her attentions did he give Abram a wealth of sheep and cattle, with donkeys and camels for his herdsmen, and servants male and female.

[16] But his household became afflicted with disease and pestilence, and he grew fearful when his ministers said to him, "Your betrothed is wed already, and Abram is her master."

[17] So he summoned Abram to him and said to him, "What is this that you have done to me? Why did you withheld from me the knowledge that she is your wife?"

[18] And Abram had no answer for him. Yea, he had kept this a secret knowingly, for he sought to enrich himself with gifts from Egypt, that he might enhance his own

might at the pharaoh's expense. [19] And this much did he indeed accomplish, for the pharaoh pleaded with him to go his way, saying of Sarai, "Take her and go!" [20] And the king instructed his servants to send Abram on his way, along with his wife and everything he had — the herds he had arrived with and the gifts he had been given from the pharaoh's own wealth.

[21] So it was that Abram's power greatly increased, and the pharaoh's hand was weakened. [22] Therefore did the pharaoh withdraw to his capital in the south, leaving to Abram and his people the marshes and lowlands near the mouth of the mighty Nile. These lands became a kingdom to him, and he prospered in all his endeavors. [23] To the Egyptians, he was Maibre Sheshy, pharaoh of the lower kingdom, and his lands extended into the desert south of Canaan. [24] He amassed great quantities of gold and of silver, and the pharaoh of old became his servant, and he ascended the throne of Egypt.

[25] In the course of time, he went forth, up out of Egypt into the Negev, and thence to a place called Bethel. But the quarreling between Abram and his nephew Lot was resumed, for Lot had grown jealous of Abram's wealth and Sarai still had borne him no issue. [26] Abram therefore called his nephew to him, saying, "Let there be no more quarrels between the two of us, or between your herders and my own. [27] Is not the whole land spread forth in front of you? Therefore, let the two of us part company on this day. If you take the path to the left-hand side, I shall continue on the right. And if you choose the right-hand path, I shall

follow the left." ²⁸ For he knew that his armies were the stronger among the two of them, and that the lowlands of the Nile had sworn allegiance to his lordship.

²⁹ Therefore Lot surveyed the land before them and, seeing the verdant plain of the Jordan to the east of them, chose this path for his men and his livestock. ³⁰ He came upon the city of Sodom and abode there, in lowlands so rich with pasture that they recalled the land of Eden. This was the Vale of Siddim, which means "valley of broad plains."

³¹ But Abram took his retinue to the west and settled there in the land of Canaan. And the Elohim dwelt there in that day, as did also descendants of the sons of Adam. ³² And the Elohim mingled among the men who were with them, and they went in among the daughters of Adam and knew them, for they saw that they were comely and delightful to the flesh.

³³ And they built themselves a city and called it Salem, and this became for them a new Eden, forged on a hilltop in the midst of Canaan. There did they reconvene the council of the Elohim, and choose one among themselves to bear the title of Most High, as in days of old. ³⁴ A priest was chosen among them as the leader of the Malachim, who would serve as messenger to the country around about there. ³⁵ The name of this one was Melchizedek.

Like Abram, he was a Shemite.

3

¹ Now when Lot had settled in Sodom, he did not seek to make himself king there, for that place was in thrall to Chederlaomer the king of Elam. ² In those days the Elamites had marched westward out of Susa, gathering to themselves the lands between the rivers in Shinar where Sargon had once held sway. ³ Two kings from this place did they count among their servants, and likewise the ruler of the Hittites to the north. ⁴ With the armies of these cities at his side, Chederlaomer had swept down to claim all the lands to the east of Canaan as his own, and none dared oppose him.

⁵ When Lot arrived in Sodom, he likewise fell under the sway of Chederlaomer, who was the enemy of Abram. ⁶ But when the five kings of Siddim learned of his presence, they said to himself, "Who is this among us now? Is it not the nephew of Egypt's pharaoh? And shall he not protect us from the wrath of the Elamites?" ⁷ They did not know that Abram and Lot had parted ways, and that the two were yet at enmity over the inheritance of Terach. They knew only that they could never oppose Chederlaomer alone. ⁸ Yet if Egypt could be persuaded to send its army to fight alongside them, then they might free themselves of the shackles that had bound them to Elam these twelve years.

⁹ Therefore did the kings of Siddim refuse to send the tribute demanded by Elam, and did defy Chederlaomer. ¹⁰ Being enraged at this, the king assembled the armies of

the Hittites and of Shinar and of Larsa, along with his own, and marched forth to meet the five kings who had dared to rise up against him. They were as follows:

[11] The king of Gomorrah, which means "submerged," for it lay low in the plain and the waters would assail it when the floods came. Therefore was it well watered.

[12] The king of Admah, which means "earthen," for it was on higher ground and surrounded by earthen ramparts.

[13] The city of Bela, also called Zoar, which means "small," for it was the smallest of the five cities.

[14] The city of Zohim, which means "place of the gazelle," for deer and other animals could be seen around about there.

[15] The city of Sodom, which means "burning," as it was lacking in shade and the rays of the sun beat down upon it so fiercely that its people could find no refuge in the heat of summer. Yet this was the greatest of the cities.

[16] Though they gathered together, the armies of the five kings who assembled could not hope to match the strength of the Elamite minions, even as these had come a great distance to do battle. [17] It therefore came to pass that the Elamites and their allies fell upon them with great fury, and the kings of Sodom and Gomorrah fled before them, their armies retreating in such confusion that many among their number fell into the tar pits that were there in the valley. [18] And Abram's armies did not come forth, as they had hoped, to join their numbers. So it happened that all their goods and food were plundered, to be taken away as the spoils of war to Elam.

²⁰ Lot was taken captive also, along with his possessions, for the Elamites knew well who he was. And they said to themselves, "Behold, we have captured the nephew of the king of Egypt! He shall bring a great ransom, and his uncle shall bow the knee to Chederlaomer!"

²¹ When news was brought to Abram of what had happened, he took counsel with his advisors as to what he should do. ²² On the one hand, he reasoned, he could allow the Elamites to go their way and rid him of his nephew. Then could he claim at last Terach's inheritance. ²³ Yet this matter had become to him as a flea on the back of a donkey. ²⁴ Was Abram not now the ruler of Lower Egypt? And was not his wealth many times that of his father's treasure? ²⁵ No, it availed him little to let the Elamites have their way, and were he to do so, he knew that his name would mocked in the camp of his enemies.
²⁶ Then might Elam beset him from the north, or the king of Upper Egypt from the south.

²⁷ The appearance of such weakness he could in no wise allow, so he set out with more than three hundred mercenaries and pursued the enemy. ²⁸ He fell upon them to the north of Damascus, dividing his men up to attack from this and that way. ²⁹ There he routed the armies of the Elamites and set them on their heels, recovering all that they had taken from the five kings and increasing his own wealth accordingly.

³⁰ Lot's wealth he did also recover, ensuring that his nephew would remain indebted to him from that day forward. In this way was the matter of Terach's inheritance

laid to rest at last between them, for Lot knew that he dared not broach the matter again in the face of his uncle's power.

³¹ Therefore did Abram pledge his inheritance to Eliezer of Damascus, a servant who had followed him faithfully into battle against the Elamites.

³² After these things, they marched back down to Canaan.

4

¹ When the Elohim heard news of Abram's success, they saw the chance to magnify themselves as in days of old. Drunk with success, Abram would be generous if they could persuade him to accept their blessing — along with the promise that they would guard his eastern flank for him in wartime. ² So they sent Melchizedek forth to meet him, bearing a feast of bread and wine as an offering of peace, for Salem's men had taken no side in the war with Elam, and they feared that the king of Egypt might hold this against them should they presume to approach him empty handed.

³ Abram therefore made a treaty with him. And he gave Melchizedek a tenth of all the spoils, that he might fortify the land against Elam. ⁴ But Melchizedek said to him, "Keep the spoils, but let me have the people." (He said this that Abram might leave a contingent behind him to help fortify the frontier against incursion.) ⁵ And Abram was

pleased with this, and received the blessing of the Most High as the seal of their friendship.

⁶ The name of Salem was greatly magnified, and the power of the Elohim was strengthened by the hand of Egpyt.

⁷ Then did the king of Sodom come forth likewise to greet Abram in that place, the Valley of Shaveh, which was called the Valley of the King. ⁸ And he, too, brought an offering to appease the pharaoh, for the disgrace of his retreat had become known across the land, and he was full of dread that Abram might deal harshly with one who had yielded up his nephew into the hands of the enemy.

⁹ But when he brought forth his offering, Abram received it not, saying, "I have sworn an oath to the Most High that I will take nothing which belongs to you. ¹⁰ Not so much as a thread or a strap from one of your sandals shall I accept. For I have sworn that you shall never say, 'Abram I have enriched.' ¹¹ Nay. All that I shall have from you is what my men have eaten and the portion that belongs to those who went out with me: let the men of Aner, Eshkol and Mamre have their share."

¹² He did this because of the Sodomite king's cowardice, by which Abram knew he could not be trusted to defend the eastern outposts against Elam. ¹³ His city's defenses had been breached too easily, yet the city of Salem had been built atop a plateau amid the mountains. Thence did it offer a position of a strength from which an army might withstand a siege or assail an enemy. ¹⁴ It was, Abram judged, a high place blessed by the gods.

¹⁵ So Abram asked Melchizedek, "Who are the gods of this place?"

¹⁶ Melchizedek said to him, "Our god is Enki, lord of the earth, who ruled Eden and saved Noah from the flood by the word of his mouth. And his son is the Most High, who sits upon the throne of the Elohim in Salem."

¹⁷ And Abram said to him, "Noah was the father of my ancestor Shem, for whom the tribe of the Shemites is named. I am Abram, son of Terach. ¹⁸ My kinsmen and I fled Shinar when the days of Sargon's line were ended, for we were of noble blood and they feared our people."

¹⁸ "Truly," said the priest of Salem, "it is Enki who has guided you to this place and delivered wealth into your hands more bountiful than that of all Shinar. The entire world now trembles before you, and the king of Elam cowers like a dog in the face of your army. ¹⁹ This oracle do I give unto you now, as in a vision, for in a vision it comes to us both here as we stand together. ²⁰ Ea says, 'Fear not, Abram, son of Terach, for I am your shield and your greatest reward!' "

²¹ Upon hearing this, Abram was sore afflicted, and he grieved at having pledged his inheritance to Eliezer of Damascus, but he had vowed also that Lot should never lay hold of it. ²² He grieved over these things before Melchizedek, saying, "Enki has given me no children, therefore shall a servant of a household be my heir."

²³ But Melchizedek shook his head and said to him, "This man shall no more be your heir than shall your ass or heifer. Nay, a son of your own loins shall succeed you."

²⁴ He then took Abram outside, and they surveyed the heavens. "See the sky! And count the stars! Can you count them indeed, or is it beyond your power? ²⁵ By the witness of the Watchers who sit with Enki in the heavens, as the stars are beyond numbering, so shall your offspring be! ²⁶ For did not Enki bring you up out of Ur and make of you a mighty ruler? In this same way shall he bear your sons up, and make of them a wondrous nation!"

²⁷ Then Abram believed him.

²⁸ And Melchizedek told him, "Enki would have you find a heifer and a goat and a ram, each of which have passed three summers, and find also a dove and a young pigeon. Then bring them to me!"

²⁹ These things did Abram do. And he severed the bodies of each in twain, except for the birds, and arranged the segments opposite each other. ³⁰ When, therefore, the sun had set, two servants came forth from Salem with a blazing torch and a smoking firepot to pass between the portions of each sacrifice. ³¹ And Melchizedek, the priest of my Salem, declared to Abram: "To your descendants shall Enki grant the lands from the river of Egypt to the great Euphrates — the lands of the Kenites and the Kenizzites, the Kadmonites and the Hittites, the Perizzites, Rephaites, Amorites, Girgasites and Jebusites, and all those who dwell in the land of Canaan."

³² But behold, these lands already stood in thrall to Abram, for this was the true meaning of pact the priest had set before them: that one half of all the earth should belong to Egypt, and the other half should be for Salem; that all

men's possessions should belong to the pharaoh, yet their lives should be pledged to Enki. [33] Henceforth should kings and priests do battle, and brother should rise against brother. [34] For one son of Abram, by his housemaid, would become the father of a people, and that another son, by Sarai, should give birth to a different nation. [35] There should ever be division between them. Isaac would ever crush the head of his brother Ishmael, yet Ishmael would strike in vengeance at his heel. [36] This was the legacy of Eden, and the wages of the enmity between Lot and Abraham. [37] The seeds of violence would they sow within their children, and their children's children after them, teaching them the way of rancor throughout a thousand generations.

[38] But it came to pass that Enki looked down upon these things and lamented what was being wrought in his name, saying, "The Elohim have taken my name in vain, and spoken without leave in my behalf. [39] They have forgotten the command of Osiris, who warned them to 'speak not in the name of any god, for such is unfettered arrogance, but let thy words redeem themselves.' [40] Therefore do I decree that no man's lips shall utter my name from this day forward. For no mere mortal should presume to speak for me!"

[41] Because of this, the lips of the Elohim were sealed shut against the name of Enki. They dared not speak, nor commit it to tablet or scroll, for they feared the great god's judgment. [42] Instead did they speak of him as Yah, a name like unto his ancient name of Ea. [43] And whenever anyone

asked them by whose authority they had uttered a blessing, they would say, "I am who I am, and he is who he is." ⁴⁴ And so the saying passed from generation to generation, until its meaning was lost to the children of Salem. And they said to themselves, " 'I am' is the name of the great god whom we worship."

⁴⁵ So it was that the word for "I am" in their own tongue was taken to be the name of a god. And so was Enki's purpose confounded. ⁴⁶ Yet all these things were observed by the Watchers and inscribed in the book of the heavens, just as they had been from the beginning, to be revealed in the course of time.

⁴⁷ And these words are that revelation.

He who has ears to hear, let him hear.

5

¹ Now the gods had grown weary of the ways of men, for the sons of Adam had turned their backs on wisdom to chase after their own vanity and folly. ² So the gods withdrew from the land of Canaan and left the Shemites to worship the god they had set up upon their altars. ³ The Elohim did magnify his name and say, "The seat of heaven has been carried down to Salem."

⁴ But the gods of old watched over the lands of Upper Egypt and of Babylon, of Greece and Persia, even unto the mighty Indus. ⁵ Their eyes were diverted to the Phoenicians and the Minoans, and to all the other peoples who had not forsaken them. The sons of Ham and the people of Japheth

did revere them. ⁶ Many in their number withdrew westward, to the isles beyond the Sea at the Center of the World, and further still into the mists where few dared venture. ⁷ But they left Abram and the Shemites to worship the god he called "I am" in that place which was called Salem, where he had built a fortress atop the plateau as a bulwark for his armies. ⁸ He called this fortress Zion, which means "castle," and there he housed the army that would guard Egypt's eastern flank.

⁹ Abram ruled over the land for ten years. But the god who was born on Zion gave him no heir, and his patience waned. ¹⁰ So it came to pass that Sarai, fearing he might put her aside for another, told him, "Sleep then with my slave girl, that she might conceive and we may build a family from her womb." ¹¹ And Abram did as she bade him. He took Hagar to wife, as was the custom of the pharaohs (for it was their wont to take for themselves a harem full of wives). ¹² He brought her to his bed, wherefore she did conceive the son for which he had longed.

¹³ But Sarai was ill pleased with these events, for Hagar was a daughter of Egypt and of the southern pharaoh. ¹⁴ She had not thought that Abram would accept her offer, and when he did, she had hoped that Hagar would not conceive. ¹⁵ But now that these things had come to pass, there could be no doubt that the people would laud this servant girl as their queen — this vassal who would deliver an heir to their beloved pharaoh.

¹⁶ Sarai therefore said to Abram: "May the god you serve judge between the two of us. I have delivered my slave girl

into your arms, and now she is raised up against me!"

¹⁷ There was venom in her voice, and a fury born from the fires of hatred. Because of this did Hagar flee from her sight, fearing for her safety and for the life of her son. ¹⁸ She made her way down through the desert and back toward her homeland, Egypt, for she said to herself: "There shall they accept me, and my son shall be recognized as the true king once Abram has breathed his last." ¹⁹ Yet Abram knew of her intent and sent forth one of the Malachim to find her, and the messenger came upon her beside a spring in the Wilderness of Shur, near Egypt. ²⁰ Then did he question her, saying, "Where is it you are going?"

²¹ Hagar said to him, "I am fleeing from the wrath of Sarai."

²² But the Malach said to him, "Nay, but return whence you came, and the child who is in your womb shall become the father of a race too great to count."

²³ Hearing this, Hagar knew that Abram would guard her, and that her unborn child was likewise under his protection. ²⁴ She said to herself, "surely a god has heard me," and resolved in that moment that if her child should be a son, she would name him Ishmael, which means "the god hears." ²⁵ Therefore it came to pass that she returned once again to Abram, and there gave birth to the child he had fathered upon her. And behold, it was the son whom she had longed for. ²⁶ She therefore said to herself, "My destiny is secure, for I am the mother of his only heir, and my son shall rule the earth from river to river!"

²⁷ And so it would have been. Yet there came a day

when Sarai, too, was found to be with child, though her childbearing years were thought to have been long past her. ²⁸ Her child, too, was a son, and she named him Isaac, which means "he laughs." This name was meant as a foreshadowing: that Isaac would laugh at the misfortunes of his half-brother and rejoice to see the son of Hagar serve him.

²⁹ This, truly, was Sarai's purpose and intent. And as soon as the child had been weaned, she went to Abram and laid claim to Isaac's birthright. Hatred returned to her voice, and her countenance was darkened by fury. ³⁰ "As favorite wife of my husband the pharaoh, I demand that my son be named heir to the throne!" she told Abram. "This is my will, dear husband: Be rid of that slave woman and her cursed son at once! Never shall my son Isaac share your fortune with that bastard, Ishmael!"

³¹ On hearing her, Abram was grieved and sore afraid, for he knew not what she might do to young Ishmael. ³² Yet he was determined that no harm should come to the boy, so he summoned Hagar to him and entreated her to depart from there. ³³ He gave her food and water, that they might be nourished, and he ordered his men to spirit her away into the desert. And though Sarai knew it not, his men watched over them.

³⁴ When the water from her skins was wanting, he sent one among the Malachim out to console them and to bring them sustenance. ³⁵ When they cried out in distress, a messenger from Abram gave them solace in his encampment, saying, "Fear not, but lift the boy up by his

hand, and he shall become a mighty nation!"

³⁶ And when she was let into one of the tents, she looked up and beheld the man before her, and she saw it was her husband. ³⁷ Still she feared him because of Sarai, and she lowered her eyes again before him, thinking that he should strike her.

³⁸ She therefore spoke to him this entreaty: "The gods are with you in all you do. Therefore swear to me that you shall not deal falsely with me or my child, or with his descendants after him. The nation of my father, mighty Egypt, showed you kindness when you were a foreigner."

³⁹ He said, "I swear it." And he took her to a spring of water welling up there in the desert, for which reason this spring is called to this day Beersheba, which means "the well of the oath."

³⁹ This was the oath he swore to her face. He swore it not to another king, as some have told it, but to the woman who gave birth to his first-born child, the one named Ishmael.

6

¹ In the course of time, Abram was troubled because he had cast Ishmael out, and grieved because he loved the boy's mother. ² "What is this thing I have done?" he cried out to the hills. "Have I not cast out my own flesh? Have I not shunned my own true heir?" ³ And though he had acted for Ishmael's protection, the shame of it consumed him, so that it was more than he could bear.

⁴ Now a fever came upon him, and his remorse became delirium, so that he thought to atone for this thing he had done by spilling blood — the blood of Isaac. ⁵ In his head, the voice of a phantom cried out to him. At first he betook it to be the voice of Ishmael, which was shaming him. But then, as his fever was magnified, he came to hear in it the voice of Yah. ⁶ It said to him, "Take your son, your only son by Sarai, to the place that I will show you. Bind him hand and foot, as you would an animal. ⁷ Then offer him up as a sacrifice to my glory, that you may atone now for your sinfulness and the earth may know that I am God!"

⁸ So Abram cast aside his bedclothes and made haste to call his son Isaac to him, saying, "Come, and we shall make sacrifice!" ⁹ But he told not Isaac the intent of his madness, for some portion of him recalled the commandment of Osiris: "Slay neither man nor beast for gain or glory, and spill no blood on the altar of pride, for such is the way of the ingrate." ¹⁰ And he was ashamed. In his subterfuge he therefore broke another of these commandments: "Accuse no man falsely, but cast aside deception and hypocrisy."
¹¹ He justified the one for the sake of the other, because of his guilt over Ishmael, and because he thought Yah had so decreed.

¹² So he took Isaac to the top of a great mountain and bound him there to a rock, against his will. And he raised up the knife as if to cleave his flesh. ¹³ Yet in that moment, he hesitated. His fever lifted and the voices he had heard abated. ¹⁴ And he said to himself, "What madness is this that has consumed me? I have cast out one son at my elder

wife's bidding. Will I now compound this folly by spilling the blood of his brother? Nay!"

15 In that moment his eyes fell upon a ram caught in a thicket. "What great fortune!" he exclaimed, and stepped forward toward the place where it was tangled. 16 But he pitied not the poor trapped creature, though Osiris had forbidden such a sacrifice — whether it be of animals or of men. 17 Though his fever had broken, neither his shame nor his fury had diminished. 18 And he sought to save face for himself; his pride consumed him as he slashed at the flesh of the ram and laid its carcass on the altar he had meant for his second-born son.

19 And the gods spoke among themselves and said, "Behold, the man has become as A'bel, shedding the blood of animals in the cause of pride and fury. 20 And he has become like Cain, for he would have shed the blood of his own kinsman just as soon. 21 Abram regards life not as a gift, but as a thing which he might take at his good pleasure. 22 Therefore shall we consign him to the fate which he has chosen. No more shall he be called Abram, which means 'exalted father,' for no more shall he be exalted. 23 Instead shall he be cast down among the nations. And he shall be called Abraham, which means 'the father of a multitude,' for though he would have shed the blood of his kinsmen, yet they shall multiply across the desert.

24 "And they shall raise their hand one against the other, against the Canaanites and the sons of Ishmael. Without mercy shall they slay them, invoking the name of a god to vindicate their madness. 25 Their enemies shall in like

manner rise up against them, offering no quarter, for blood begets blood and fury begets fury. [26] An eye shall be given for an eye, and a tooth shall be demanded for a tooth. Such will be the way of things, since they have forsaken the way of wisdom. [27] Therefore shall wisdom forsake them in like manner, and the gods shall turn their backs on these people in disdain."

[28] At the appointed time, Abraham's son Isaac married his kinswoman Rebekah, the daughter of Bethuel. [29] And his elder son Ishmael took to himself two wives, casting aside the first because she failed to honor his father, but keeping the other close to him because she did what was right in the sight of Abraham.

[30] And in the course of time did Sarai breathe her last, whereupon Abraham drew Hagar back to himself. [31] It therefore came to pass that she bore him more sons, six in number, but each of them he sent away from him. For they chastened him, saying, "You do not honor the gods, and have turned your back on wisdom!" [32] But he stood against them, saying, "These gods of which you speak are only idols. Get behind me if you will not honor me!" And with this did he send them away into the east. [33] It is said that he built a city to contain them, with walls so high that the sun could not be seen there.

[34] But the son of one of them, Epher, he appointed the general of his armies. [35] Epher led these armies against the men of Libya and subdued them, and he spilled their blood without mercy and the blood of their children without quarter. [36] Thus did it come to pass as the gods had

reckoned, that blood would be shed by the kinsmen of Abraham. And this was but the beginning of their bloodletting.

³⁷ Abraham by no means saw the end of it, for in the course of days, he breathed his last.

7

¹ Never had there been a time like this in all of Egypt. The great empire that had built the pyramids lay subdued by an invader. ² The shepherd kings, they called them, for Abraham and his people had arrived as shepherds in the Nile Valley, cast aside the once-great pharaohs and made themselves lords of the delta. ³ The grandson of Abraham was Yacob-Har, which is "Jacob, the Horus." He reigned during his lifetime in the land of the pharaohs.

⁴ And in Babylon there rose up a king named Ammurapi, who served the sun god Shamash. From this god he claimed to have received the tablets of the law, by which he governed his empire.

⁵ And on an island in the Sea at the Center of the World, a king ascended the throne of Minos.

⁶ Seasons passed and the spokes of heaven's wheel shifted in the sky. The stargazers marked the signs and wonders in the velvet skies overhead, and they took note of the changes in the seasons. ⁷ The Thebans from the highlands of Egypt, the ancient land of the pharaohs, chafed mightily beneath the Shemites from the north, for they were yet vassals to the sons of Abraham, who

demanded of them taxes and tribute. [8] And the Shemites built for themselves a great capital in the lowlands, and they called its name Avaris.

[9] Now the greatest of these pharaohs was Apophis, who reigned forty years over the land and was among the last of Hyksos "the shepherd kings." [10] He was also called Auserre in the tongue of Egypt — that is, in his own tongue, Israel — for it is from him that the nation of Israel was born. [11] In his day, he amassed great wealth, trading with the kings of Minos to the north in the midst of the sea. [12] Such were his riches that the name of his capital was transferred to the tongue of the Romans, who called their word for greed "avarus." [13] And he worshipped only Seth, constructing a temple at Avaris that he consecrated in the great god's name. [14] Is it not written concerning him, "He chose for his patron the god called Seth. And he worshipped no other god in all the land, save for Seth alone"?

[15] And the Elohim in Canaan despaired at this, for Apophis worshipped not the god of their choosing. [16] Therefore did they say, "He has made himself our adversary!" [17] It is for this reason that the name Seth was perverted upon their lips to the name of Satan, which has that very meaning. And he was known also as the adversary of the Horus kings in the south, which is to say the city of Thebes.

[18] Indeed, the Elohim were not the only men who opposed Apophis. [19] The Thebans and their leader, Kamose by name, complained bitterly of the tribute paid to the shepherd king.

THE PHOENIX CHRONICLES

20 "I should know how my strength is served, when one chieftain rules in Avaris and another in Ethiopia," he declared. 21 "Here I sit between an Asiatic and a Nubian, each in possession of a slice of Egypt! No man can find rest from the desolation that is wrought in the name of Seth."

22 His counselors, however, entreated him against any rash action, for they knew the strength of Apophis and the vengeance he would take upon them should they rise up to oppose Avaris.

23 "Behold," they said, "all are loyal to the Asiatics as far south as Cusae. We are tranquil in our portion of Egypt. 24 Elephantine is strong to the south, and the heart of the nation is with us north to Cusae. 25 Men till for us the finest of their lands. Our cattle pasture in among the papyrus reeds. 26 Corn is sent for our swine, and our cattle are not taken from us."

27 But Kamose would not be swayed. In his anger did he raise an army to assail Apophis and his minions, saying, "No man can settle down when despoiled by the taxes of these men from Asia! 28 Therefore shall I contend with him, that I may rip open his belly! May I deliver Egypt and smite the Asiatics!"

29 Yet it was not to be. The armies of Kamose were driven back, and Avaris remained secure. Indeed, Kamose himself was slain.

30 And the land did prosper. For seven years, the cattle of Egypt grew fat as they grazed in the fields of the delta. 31 Grain sprouted up, more plentiful than the rushes in the

Sea of Reeds. The mighty Nile rushed forth each year at the inundation, overtopping its banks and blessing the soil with life abundant. [32] The sons of Egypt blessed Osiris for this bounty; and Apophis gave thanks to Seth, the keeper of storms, for visiting the earth with such abundance.

[33] It was at this time that Apophis appointed for himself a vizier, whom he placed over all the land. This one, like the pharaoh, was a Sethite from the seed of Abraham.
[34] For he said to himself, "It is good that a kinsman should look after my abundance."

[35] This man's name was Yusuf, meaning "he that increases," and the scribes would call him Joseph.

[36] And this is how Yusuf came to be exalted in pharaoh's court.

[37] It came to pass that Apophis sought out Yusuf for his counsel, for he was known for his wisdom and discernment. Therefore did Auserre summon his kinsman to himself.

[38] And Yusuf came into the presence of Apophis, and he said to the king of Eygpt, "Behold, you have been granted many years of great prosperity. But times of bounty are ever followed by times of want. [39] Shall this time of plenty extend beyond the seventh year? If not, then what shall become of you? [40] Behold, seven years of abundance may give way to seven years of drought and famine. Then how shall you feed the people? [41] Therefore, let the pharaoh appoint a wise man to guard the land, and let him appoint also stewards of the grain in its abundance. [42] Charge these men to collect for the pharaoh one-fifth of all the harvest

during these years of bounty, that this might be preserved for the lean years ahead. [43] In this way the land shall not be laid waste by a famine, and the people of Egypt shall have plenty while others are in want."

[44] Apophis hearkened to Yusuf's counsel, and it was pleasing to his ears. [45] Therefore did he appoint Yusuf to oversee the land of Egypt and its bounty. [46] He placed a signet ring on his finger and arrayed him in fine garb, with a gold chain around his neck and a chariot driver at his command. [47] And Apophis betrothed him to the daughter of Potiphera, a priest of On, which the Greeks call Heliopolis. (Now Potiphera means "dedicated to Ra," the sun god, and On was the city of the sun). [48] It was then that Yusuf's name was called Osarseph, which means "he who magnifies Osiris."

[49] And Yusuf went out from the court of the pharaoh and into all the land of Egypt, collecting grain from the farmers and householders, and building great storehouses wherein it might be housed. [50] The grain he gathered was like the sand of the sea; so plentiful was it that the record-keepers could not account for it all. [51] And in addition to this, he had his servants carve out a canal from the mighty Nile to the Fayyum Oasis to the west of it. There was water captured, that it might provide a reserve when the rains were wanting.

[52] And behold, in the course of seven years, it came to pass as Yusuf had predicted. [53] The rains fell not in the highlands, and the waters of the Nile drew back. The inundation came not, and the land grew cracked and

barren. ⁵⁴ Heads of grain fell from withered stalks, and the lifeless soil spurned them. ⁵⁵ Cattle grew lean, for there was nothing to graze on, and men grew restless, saying, "What shall become of us?"

⁵⁶ It was then that Yusuf opened the storehouses. It was then that he threw wide the doors to the granaries. And he said to the people, "Come forth! Partake! And enjoy the fruits of the bounty you once sacrificed!"

8

¹ In those days the famine was severe throughout the earth, even beyond the land of Egypt. And all the world came to the storehouses of Yusuf to buy grain. ² In this way was the house of the pharaoh enriched. And in this way was Yusuf's name magnified in all the earth. ³ And the people called him Zaphenath-Paneah, which means, "the one who nourishes the world with life."

⁴ But the pharaoh grew disconsolate, for he was ever aware that the Thebans sought his throne. ⁵ He therefore summoned to himself a seer, and he said to him, "You are able to see the gods, as though you yourself were one of them. ⁶ Am I not king of Egypt? Yet my visions are no match for yours. ⁷ Teach me, therefore, how it is that you see so clearly the realms of heaven, that I may walk with the gods as you do." For he sought a sign from heaven, that he might guard himself against the Thebans.

⁸ The seer therefore said to him, "You must purify Avaris of the Thebans, for they are as lepers among us. If

they conspire against you, and rise up from within, how shall you guard yourself against them? ⁹ Nay, let them be gone from this place and send them out into the quarries beyond the river. There they shall work to preserve your throne, and may not overthrow it. ¹⁰ In these quarries they can mine stones to build a wall around Avaris. Such a bulwark can guard against their brethren should they rise against you from the south."

¹¹ And the pharaoh hearkened to the seer's words. So he appointed Yusuf to the task of raising new walls around the city, should the king of the south rise up against him. ¹² For though Kamose, lord of Thebes, had fallen, a new king had risen to take his place. This was the brother of Kamose, whose name was Ahmose (but in the Greek tongue, Moses). ¹³ It he now set his mind to lead an army against Avaris and to drive out the Shemites from that place, for which reason he might be known as "the liberator" of his people.

¹⁴ When news of this reached Avaris, Yusuf hurried to complete the walls, redoubling the burden on the Thebans in the quarries. ¹⁵ And he sent word to the Elohim in Salem, saying, "Make haste to bring your armies hither, for our enemies the Thebans stand ready to assail us." ¹⁶ And the Elohim heard him, and sent their emissaries to meet with him, for though they honored Yah, whom they called Yahweh, and the men of Avaris followed Seth, still they were of one blood. ¹⁷ The leaders of the Shemites from Canaan came down and appeared before Yusuf.

¹⁸ Now the famine was yet upon their land, and the

shepherds from Canaan knew of the storehouses that Yusuf had built. [19] When, therefore, they appeared to him, they told him of their want, saying, "We have come down to you from Canaan to purchase food."

[20] But Yusuf accused them, saying, "You are spies! You have come down to see where our land is unprotected!"

[21] He said this to test them, for he knew that Ahmose was eager to prevail against Avaris, and that he would certainly send spies before him.

[22] And the shepherds answered and said to him, "We are brothers who lead the people of Canaan. Only one of our brethren has not joined with us, but remains in the land of our fathers."

[23] But Yusuf heeded this not, for he was wary. He therefore demanded that they should summon to him the one who had stayed behind, that Yusuf might know he was no Theban. [24] And he said to them, "I judge that you are spies. Therefore shall you be tested in this manner. As the pharaoh lives, you shall not depart from this place until this 'brother' of yours comes forward. [25] Send one of your number to retrieve him; if you do not, your words shall be revealed as falsehood."

[26] He then put them all in custody for three days. And when these had passed, he gave them their freedom; only one was to remain as a guarantee that they should return to him with their countryman. [27] It therefore came to pass that, in due course, they returned to him with their 'brother,' and Yusuf believed their words. [28] Then did they pledge to him thousands of fighting men, that they might

gain in exchange for this both provision and sanctuary within the land of Avaris.

To this they all agreed.

²⁹ In those days also, Apophis sought to fortify himself further against the Thebans by striking an alliance with Ethiopia to the south. By so doing, he reasoned, the Theban king would be caught in a vise between Apophis' forces to the north and the Ethiopians to the south.

³⁰ He therefore invited Queen Tany of Sheba, who ruled all Ethiopia and the south, to his palace in Avaris. This invitation she accepted, bringing with her gold and precious gemstones and spices from the land of Punt, which she bore with her in a great caravan up from the source of the Nile.

³¹ She brought with her also difficult questions, seeking to measure whether an alliance with Apophis was truly in her interest and that of her kingdom. For she reasoned that the Thebans stood directly across her northern border and might begin a campaign against her should she cast her lot with the northerners. ³² Would Apophis be able to protect her in such an instance? This question was in her mind, though not directly on her lips.

³³ In answer, Apophis showed her the great palace he had built and the temple with its precincts and all the splendor of Avaris. ³⁴ He made an offering for her in the temple he had built and set forth a great banquet in his honor, so that she saw no recourse but to form an alliance with him, saying, "I did not believed the words that were spoken of this place and its wonders until my own eyes

beheld them. ³⁵ Now it is plain that the half was not told to me, for your wisdom and prosperity exceeds all the praise that formerly reached my ears."

³⁶ Thereupon they made an agreement of alliance, and the queen returned to her own land.

³⁷ When Ahmose, however, heard of these things, and that the king of Avaris was mustering an army to defend against him, he went down to Ethiopia with his own men and gained an audience with the queen. ³⁸ On his journey southward, there are those who say his forces were confronted by an army of serpents, and that he expelled these from the Ethiopian capital with the help of a great flock of ibises. ³⁹ In truth, however, the serpents were soldiers in the service of Apophis (whose own name is also that of a great sky serpent), and they were defeated by men who fought under the sign of the ibis, which is sacred to the great god Thoth.

⁴⁰ This god was said to have created Amen, the mighty god to whom Ahmose had sworn allegiance and whose name was the last word on the lips of every prayer in Thebes. ⁴¹ In the names of these gods, Ahmose expelled the forces of Apophis and occupied the Ethiopian capital, which was Sheba. ⁴² In the wake of his victory, Ahmose persuaded the men of that place to forswear the queen's pact with Avaris and renew their former alliance with Thebes. ⁴³ This pact he sealed by marrying the queen herself.

⁴⁴ Then did he call upon them to offer them provision and to guard his borders as he marched against Avaris, to

which they also consented.

⁴⁵ Once he had secured his southern border, Ahmose gathered his fighting men to him, many thousand in number. And they marched northward into the land of the pharaoh.

⁴⁶ From Thebes, they made their way down the Nile to Abydos, to Hermopolis and past the Fayyum to the sacred city of Heliopolis. Then they entered Heliopolis and laid hold of it, and brought it to heel. ⁴⁷ Then did they advance upon the fortress of Sile and assail it with a single purpose. For this fortress guarded the border between Egypt and the land of Canaan. ⁴⁸ By capturing it, he sought to cut off the Shemites of Avaris from their brethren to the north and east.

⁴⁹ In the course of time, the fortress fell. From that time forward, no more aid reached Yusuf from the shepherds of Canaan.

9

¹ Then did Ahmose send his emissary to the pharaoh there with this message: "Behold, you have held my people in your power for too long! ² Release my countrymen from the quarries beyond the river. Submit before the power of my armies. ³ Surrender, and I shall be lenient. But if you refuse, the Nile shall run red with blood. Therefore I demand this of you: Let my people go!"

⁴ But the pharaoh's heart was hard against him, and he refused the demands of Ahmose.

⁵ Instead did Apophis call forth to himself his son, Danaus, instructing him to assemble a fleet of great ships that they might fight the Thebans on the water. ⁶ For the king of Avaris had allied himself with the people of the Phoenix, in symbol of which the seafarers flew two banners: one of the eagle, or the phoenix, which was their own, and the other bearing the serpent of Apophis. ⁷ These seafarers had ports in Minos on the isle of Crete, whence they set sail around the central sea.

⁸ Now Ahmose sent a second message to Apophis, proposing a treaty between them, and that his own son marry the daughter of Danaus. ⁹ But to this Apophis did not agree, for he knew that it was Ahmose's son who would be heir to the kingdom should he accept it.

¹⁰ Therefore did Ahmose besiege Avaris, and he spilled the blood of its defenders into the river, as he had pledged. ¹¹ His men slaughtered the livestock of the shepherds and left it as testament to their assault. ¹² Yet still Avaris would not yield to the invaders. Still Ahmose could not capture it, so he withdrew.

¹³ Then again did he send his emissary to the pharaoh, and again he demanded of him: "Let my people go!"

But again, the pharaoh refused him.

¹⁴ It was then that the belly of the earth grew restless. In the north, in the nation of Minos, it rumbled from the depths of the underworld. ¹⁵ It churned in the forge of Hephaestus. And the Minoans trembled greatly at the sound of it, until it rose up out of its earthen vaults and broke forth on the surface of the land. ¹⁶ The mountain on

the isle of Thera became as if alive, spewing smoke and breathing fire. [17] Appearing as a dragon bent on vengeance, its wrath overtook men in chariots as though standing still and crushed them like ants under bootheel.

[18] The skies drew dark and thick with smoke, and this smoke spread far and wide from Knossos, the capital of Minos, to Avaris and beyond to the ends of the earth. [19] The land of Egypt was plagued with infestations. [20] Frogs rose up and covered the land, but it would not bear them. [21] Gnats and flies were loosed upon the land, drawn by the carcasses of the Shemite herds and the bodies of the frogs that were now dying.

[22] Then the army of Thebans laid siege once again to proud Avaris, and a second time were the Thebans repulsed.

[23] Yet again did Ahmose demand of them, "Let my people go!"

And again did they refuse him.

[24] So Ahmose sent his men forward to slaughter what remained of the shepherds' livestock. Neither goat nor lamb nor calf was spared. [25] Smoke from the fiery mountain overtook the entire land, so that the people were afflicted by boils upon their skin. [26] Ash descended upon them like hail from the sky, which was darkened as if a curtain had been drawn across the sun. [27] Locusts also rose up in mighty clouds as thick as a sandstorm from the red desert, so that no man could see his hand before him or the face of the man beside him.

[28] And the people of Avaris were sore afraid, for they

thought themselves cursed of heaven. ²⁹ Were these plagues not the work of the Egyptian sorcerers, who commanded serpents without being bitten and preserved the lives of the sleeping? ³⁰ Could such men not have brought these plagues down upon the people?

³¹ But the pharaoh would not yield to their fears, saying, "Behold, my heart is set against them. Have my people not resisted the Thebans in the past? Have they not repelled them? Shall it not be the same again?"

³² It therefore came to pass that Ahmose attacked a third time, but a third time was he repulsed by proud Avaris.

³³ Then did he seek out a meeting with the pharaoh, that they might speak face to face without pretense. And the Shemite did accept this, for he thought that Ahomse intended to surrender. ³⁴ But when the Theban arrived there, he bent not the knee before Avaris. ³⁵ Nay, he dared look the pharaoh directly in his eye and said to him, "You have defied the will of Egypt and the gods in heaven for too long, false king. ³⁶ Therefore, I say to you these last words: At midnight tonight, if you have not surrendered, I shall slay all your firstborn sons — from your own to the sons of your servants to the lambs and the calves that remain in your fields. ³⁷ This I swear in the name of the gods in heaven. Then and only then shall I depart this wretched place."

³⁸ At these words, the king was silent. He had repulsed this army of Thebans three times; now, he vowed, he would do so a fourth. ³⁹ He therefore turned his back to

Ahmose and departed, saying to his officers, "These men are fools, and stubborn. We shall teach them not to trifle with the sons of fortune!"

⁴⁰ That night did Ahmose send assassins into the streets of Avaris. In stealth did they pass through the city, messengers of death to the people who dwelt there. ⁴¹ The sons of Egyptians therein were spared, but the sons of the Shemites were slaughtered without mercy. ⁴² Yusuf was among the slain, and Ahmose did gather his bones as a testimony to the gods, and did carry them with him as he fought the enemy. ⁴³ Amid the chaos did the Theban army move forward, butchering all those who stood in their way. ⁴⁴ The defenders, stricken by grief as their sons lay fallen, stood helpless before the weapons of Ahmose, who stood at the head of his army crying, "Let my people go!"

⁴⁵ Then the pharaoh abandoned Avaris, and he fell back to Tanis with the remnants of his army. ⁴⁶ Thence did they flee to the home of their kin, the land of Canaan, and many of the common people went with them, but they were pursued across the desert by the fury of Ahmose. ⁴⁷ They passed through the Reed Sea to escape him and sought refuge in the desert places of Sinai. ⁴⁸ And it is said that the storms of Seth watched over them, passing before them in a pillar of cloud by day and a pillar of light blazing down from the heavens in the night.

⁴⁹ But the ships of the Phoenix could not follow them there in the marshes, and could offer no support for the fleeing armies. Therefore they sailed forth to find refuge, both from the Theban pharaoh and from the wrath spewed

forth by the dragon beneath the mountain Thera.

⁵⁰ Danaus himself, however, fled north to the city of Argos, which likewise became known for its ships, while others still rode the winds westward, founding new colonies along the sea's south coast. ⁵¹ These were the cities of Utica and Tangier, of Sabratha and Tipaza, and many others.

⁵² Others in the fleet of the Phoenix sailed to the eastward shores of the central sea, where they founded the kingdom of Dan. But they did remain in their ships, as it is written in the book called Judges.

⁵³ The name Dan in a certain tongue means "judge," and Canaan, the name of the land where they settled, means "merchant" — for they were sea merchants. ⁵⁴ Their cities there were and Tripoli and Baaelbek, Beru and Arqa and Ashkelon, Acre and Sidon and nearby Dan Jaan. The last of these means "Dan of the Woodlands."

⁵⁴ Some say it was thence that an expedition set forth westward, passing over the central sea to its farthest reaches and beyond before coming ashore at last on an island greener still than their homeland. ⁵⁵ And this, some say, is why they were called the Whelps of the Wood that Does Not Whither, as it is written also, "Dan is a lion's whelp." ⁵⁶ They called themselves the Danites or the Danaan, and the goddess Dana was their mother.

10

¹ Some of the Shemites who fled by land surrendered to Ahmose, while others continued onward toward the land of Canaan.

² To those who joined with Ahmose he gave new laws — the laws of the Thebans — but he gave them no provision as they passed through the desert, as he sought to test their will. ³ They therefore grumbled against him, saying to themselves, "It would have been better had we died in Egypt. In that place, we had all the food we wanted. ⁴ We had pots of meat that nourished us as we sat around about them. But see? Our new master has brought us into this desert that we might starve to death!"

⁵ So Ahmose gave them bread to eat in the mornings, and told them in the evenings, "You may hunt for your own food!" ⁶ There was quail in that place, so they brought it back to themselves for sustenance. ⁷ He told them not to store up the bread among them, but some of them paid no heed to him. For had not Yusuf taught them well to preserve their grain in the storehouse? ⁸ Yet they had no proper place to preserve it, and it became putrid and infested with maggots, so they could not eat it. ⁹ And Ahmose was wroth with them for wasting their provision.

¹⁰ But the people grew restless and thought to themselves, "We are now far from Egypt. Come, therefore, let us choose leaders from among us to challenge this false pharaoh, that we might prevail against him and return again

to Avaris!" ¹¹ To lead them they chose a certain Korah, son of Kohath, and at his side were two others name Abiram and Dathan. ¹² These took counsel together, preparing to rise up against Ahmose, but he became aware of it and called Dathan and Abiram to him to give account.

¹³ Yet they answered and said to him, "We shall heed not your summons. You have brought us here from a land flowing in milk and honey, and now you seek to kill us in the wilderness! ¹⁴ Would you treat us as slaves? Nay, we shall not come!"

¹⁵ Then Korah gathered his followers to him that they might rise up against Ahmose. ¹⁶ They were two hundred and fifty in number. Yet were they no match for the army of Ahmose, which set upon them with such fury that it seemed the very earth had opened up to consume them. ¹⁷ After this did Ahmose root out every rebel, and those he knew had grumbled against them. ¹⁸ He slaughtered them without mercy, as a plague sweeps down to slay man, woman and child. Fourteen thousand of them fell in the wake of the rebellion, before Ahmose was content.

11

¹ In those days did Ahmose pursue the Shemites as far as the banks of a certain river. ² Next to the Nile, it was but a stream. Beside the mighty Euphrates, it was only a trickle. But Ahmose did not cross it in pursuit of those who had fled him. ³ These, the Shemites, found succor with the

Elohim in the city of Salem, which is also called Jerusalem. [4] But Ahmose and his forces continued northward, where he subdued the armies of the Syrians as far as Byblos.

[5] Over the land of Canaan he appointed one of his own generals, Hoshea, whom the scribes have named as Joshua and whom the Greeks know as Jesus. [6] He was called the son of Nun, the Egyptian god of the ancient waters from which all things sprang forth. This is because he hailed from Hermopolis in Egypt, the sacred city of this god.

[7] The men made a pledge to Ahmose that they would follow Hoshea as they had followed their pharaoh. And they said to Hoshea, "Whoever rebels against your word and heeds it not, howsoever you may command them, shall be put to death!" [8] So they invaded the land and laid waste many cities. For Hoshea had given them this charge: "When you come upon a city of Canaan, lay siege to it and show no mercy. [9] Slaughter every living thing therein, the fighting men, their women and their children. Spare not their herds and flocks, but take only the gold and silver, that in so doing we might enrich the king's treasury."

[10] He gave this order because he had seen the rebellion of Korah, and he wished to have no part of the Shemites' rebellions. [11] And the men of Thebes did as they were bidden. They slaughtered every fighting man, their women and their children. They spared not the flocks of the Shemites, nor their herds. But they took only the gold and silver, and thus did they enrich the pharaoh's treasury. [12] In this manner was Canaan laid to waste, and so were the Shemites were utterly crushed.

¹³ But Salem withstood Hoshea's armed men, and did not yield before them.

¹⁴ It was there, in Salem, that many of those from Avaris had sought refuge. And the Elohim who were on the council there received them. ¹⁵ The city itself belonged to the Jebusites, a tribe of Shemites who had built a mountain fortress which they called Zion. ¹⁶ These people were known as "the threshers." Some say this was because they harvested grain from the fields, after the manner of Cain; they would crush and winnow it on the threshing floor. ¹⁷ Others say it is because they were fierce warriors who were able to beat down their enemies after the manner of threshers.

¹⁸ And the refugees came before the Elohim and said to them, "How shall we stand against the Egyptians? They have driven us from our homes, killed our firstborn sons and butchered all who stood against them."

¹⁹ And the Elohim said to them, "Which gods do you serve?"

²⁰ They said, "We honor Seth, the god of our king and our city."

²¹ Now the Elohim remembered their fathers in Eden, and the recalled how Seth had opposed them in Aratta. ²² These who stood before now them were kinsmen. Yet the men from Avaris had been deceived, or so did the Elohim reason. ²³ For was not Seth as crafty as a serpent? Had he not deceived them from the beginning?

²⁴ Therefore did the Elohim say to them, "Where is your king? And what has become of your city."

²⁵ And they answered, saying, "Our king is departed from us, we know not whence, and our city is in ruins."

²⁶ Then the Elohim said, "Behold, has not your god abandoned you?"

²⁷ But they said, "Truly, he did go before us in the desert, riding the clouds by day and casting down fire in a pillar by night."

²⁸ "Nay," said the councilors. "This was not Seth, but the god Yahweh, whom we worship. He is lord of the storms and the highest heights. He has sanctified this mountain where you stand, for which reason you are safe here." ²⁹ And they knew not what to say to this.

³⁰ "Behold, he has brought you out of Egypt that you might join with us, your kinsmen. And this shall be your homeland, a land of milk and honey. ³¹ Curse not the name of Ahmose, for it was by Yahweh's hand that he delivered you from the evil one — from your false god Seth, who forsook you, as ever he is wont to do. ³² This Seth is but a trickster, and has been so since the beginning. He tempted your fathers in the garden and caused them to rise up against Yahweh. ³³ A curse is upon him and all who hail him. From this curse has Ahmose liberated you, for which reason he is your savior as well."

³⁴ The men from Avaris looked hard at one another. "Then are you his servants as well?"

³⁵ But the Elohim answered, "We serve only Yahweh. His hand moves in ways that surpass reckoning. We honor his ways, which are beyond our understanding. Be thankful, therefore, that Ahmose has delivered you."

12

[1] Then did the scribes of the Elohim, in the years ahead, set forth a new history of the fight out of Egypt. Therein was Ahmose transformed from invader to deliverer. [2] His name they gave as Moshe, which the Greeks render as Moses. And his Theban heritage was stricken from memory, that he might become a Hebrew in the minds of the people.

[3] To accomplish their purpose, they drew upon the tale of Sargon, wherein his mother bore him in secret and cast him as an infant into a river, secure in an ark of rushes and bitumen. [4] So it was now, too, with Moses. The scribes of the Elohim set forth a tale wherein he was born in secret by a Hebrew woman. [5] And just as the mother of Sargon had done to him, the mother of Moses did to her infant in like manner. She placed him in a basket sealed with pitch and set him adrift upon the river.

[6] And behold, it came to pass that he was drawn out of the waters by the daughter of the pharaoh. [7] Just as Sargon had been raised by a man called Akki the Water Drawer, so Moses in the same way was drawn out of the water. [8] And some say it was for this reason that the Elohim called him "Moses," for they recalled that it was similar to the Hebrew word for "drawing out." [9] In this manner did they complete their deception. [10] In their tale was Ahmose made a Hebrew, having been transformed through the tale of Sargon into an adopted son of the Theban pharaoh.

¹¹ Then did the Elohim make laws for themselves and place them upon his lips. ¹² They remembered the manner in which Hammurabi, the king of Babylon, ascended a great mountain to receive the words of the law from the great god Shamash. ¹³ They recalled that this law had been inscribed upon a tablet of stone and displayed for all to see, and they wove a tale in the likeness of this history to fit their story of Moses. ¹⁴ In it did he ascend the mountains of Sinai and receive the code from Yahweh. In it did he deliver it to the people, saying, "All that Yahweh has commanded, these things shall we do."

¹⁵ In this way did the Elohim place the words of their law into the mouth of their god, and of Moses, that they might themselves hold sway over the people. ¹⁶ They demanded that the people should worship no other god save Yahweh, and that they should make no graven image for themselves, lest Yahweh's wrath be kindled against them.

¹⁷ "For behold," they warned the people, "Yahweh your god is a jealous god, and his wrath is a consuming fire. ¹⁸ Hearken therefore to the warning he utters: Each man who defies him shall receive recompense for his folly; and not the man alone, but his children and his children's children. ¹⁹ So shall they be cursed, even to the third and fourth generation because they have defied the will of Yahweh."

²⁰ These were the decrees of the Elohim: That every man among the people should relinquish the firstborn of their flocks and their household to Yahweh's service; that

they should never appear in his presence empty-handed; and that they must dedicate the first fruits of their soil to his storehouse. 21 That the man who defies his parents, be they just or unjust, should be stoned. That a virgin not pledged to another must marry the man who takes her by force. 22 That a woman who defends her husband by striking his rival's loins should have her hand cut off, and that she be shown no pity.

23 These laws did they craft to their own ends, that the ancient ways of Osiris might be lost. That the true laws might be obscured. 24 These were the laws of Enoch, which had been hidden from the eyes of men by the Elohim; which had been stored within an ark from days of old. 25 There were those who remembered these things and said, "What has been done with the ark of our covenant? Where have the writings of the ancients been hidden?"

26 So the Elohim crafted for themselves a new ark, which they adorned with gold. And the ark they built was fashioned after the manner of the ark in which they had slain Osiris.

27 Thus did they command their workmen: "Build for us therefore an ark of acacia wood, and let these be its dimensions: It is to be in length two cubits, and in breadth one cubit and one-half, which shall also be its height. 28 Adorn it and line it in the purest gold, and fashion gold molding around about it.

29 "Cast four rings of gold, one for each of the ark's four feet. Fashion also poles of acacia wood, and cover them likewise in gold. 30 These shall be inserted into the four

rings, that you may bear the ark from place to place. And they are not to be removed. They shall, henceforth, remain within the golden rings. 31 Now fashion also for the ark a seat of atonement to be placed atop it, and create from gold the image of two figures, placing the first at one end of the ark and the second at its opposite side. Their wings shall extend toward the heavens, that they might overshadow the ark's covering."

32 And the two winged figures were fashioned in likeness of the twin goddesses, Isis and Nephthys. For they reasoned, "Behold, this shall be a sign to all our enemies. When we march out against them, the ark shall go before us. 33 They shall witness the power of the pharaohs in its craftsmanship. And they shall cower and run in fear from us, thinking the armies of Egypt are upon them."

34 In this way did they violate their own law against graven images. Yet they cared not.

35 And when the people asked them yet again, "What has been done with the ark of our covenant?" the Most High of the Elohim said, "Behold! It is here before you. 36 And within it lies the ark of Yahweh's covenant with his people, which he entrusted to Moses: the same covenant that was handed down in Eden and lost by the folly of Seth and his minions. 37 Now it has been found and restored to us, that we might know and dwell in the presence of the one true god."

38 And the people looked, and marveled.

39 But one among them stepped forward and said to the Most High, "We would see the tablets with our own eyes,

that we may know they are secure."

⁴⁰ And the Most High answered and said to him, "Do you dare challenge Yahweh your god? Know you not that the ark is his very throne? Would you therefore command him to step down that you might test him? ⁴¹ No! For you are but mortal flesh, unfit to bind the straps of his sandals! Never shall you gaze upon the sacred stones of Moses. ⁴² If you so much as stretch out your hand to steady the ark when the oxen stumble, you shall perish on the spot. ⁴³ Woe to you, unworthy wretch! These tablets were forged by the finger of Yahweh, whose face no man may gaze upon and whose mind no man may know."

⁴⁴ The one who had stepped forward was silent. And the ones who had unspoken doubts stepped backward. ⁴⁵ No more did they dare to challenge the Most High, and the ark remained sealed before them.

⁴⁵ What lay within, no man knew. And when it came about one day that the ark was lost to them, no man fathomed what had become of it. ⁴⁶ Such is the way of deception. It survives only so long as a deceiver preserves it, until it vanishes from the sight of men like a wisp of smoke in the mists of morning.

13

¹ The Elohim laid their yoke upon the people and did warn them. Words of fury they spoke to them, words of terror and foreboding.

² Through their laws did the Elohim amass great power, drawing into their treasuries vast wealth by the word of their decree. ³ The people chafed beneath their edicts, but dared not challenge them, for these laws were the words of their god, and those who dared question them would remain not long among the living.

⁴ For the Elohim spoke thus to the Shemites of Canaan: "The prophet or dreamer who speaks against Yahweh shall be slain. You must purge the evil from among you."

⁵ And again: "The one who displays contempt for a priest or judge who is the minister of Yahweh shall be slain. You must purge the evil from among you."

⁶ These were the wages of their iniquity. These would be the penalties for rebellion. ⁷ The Elohim heaped threat upon threat, and indignity upon indignity, as they brought oppression to the people. ⁸ No freedom would they grant the men in thrall to them. No quarter did they give those who defied them.

⁹ "If any man should defy the word of Yahweh, he shall be cursed among all men. He shall be cursed in the city and cursed, likewise, in the country. His basket shall be cursed, and his kneading trough shall be cursed. ¹⁰ Hear this now, you women! The fruit of your womb shall be cursed. ¹¹ And hear this now, you men! The crops of the field, and the calves of your herds and the lambs of your flocks shall bear the curse of Yahweh. ¹² When you enter in shall you be cursed, and when you go out shall you be cursed.

¹³ "Confusion shall assail you from every side, that all you attempt shall end in ruin. ¹⁴ Disease shall come upon

you, and pestilence, until you are wiped from the face of the land you seek to possess. ¹⁵ There shall come upon you plague and fever, scorching heat and withering drought. ¹⁶ Blight shall overtake you and mold shall be found within your storehouse. ¹⁷ The sky shall be as bronze, and the earth shall be as iron. Rain will be turned to dust and powder, which shall fall from the skies until you are no more.

¹⁸ "Your enemies shall rout you. You shall attack from one direction and flee from seven. ¹⁹ The carrion birds shall pick at your carcasses, and no one shall disperse them. ²⁰ Your skin shall be covered in boils and sores, and your body filled with tumors; no relief shall you obtain from them. ²¹ And madness shall come upon you, blindness of the mind and of the eye, so that you grope in vain through the darkness. Yet the path shall elude you. ²² Robbers shall take what is yours, and no one shall deliver you.

²³ "Your wives shall be raped. Your homes shall stand empty. Your vineyards shall wither and be given to over to worms, and your oxen shall be slaughtered before your eyes. ²⁴ Your ass, your sheep and even your children shall be taken from you. Locusts shall afflict you, and the foreigner shall rule over you, that you may be a cause for ridicule among the nations. ²⁵ These things shall surely come upon you, lest you obey the commands of your god, Yahweh."

²⁶ When the people heard these things, they were deeply afraid. And they dared not question. They dared not disobey. ²⁷ It came to pass, therefore, that the Elohim

gathered to themselves such power that they grew haughty, even beyond what they had been before. ²⁸ And they said to themselves, "Come, let us impose our will upon all the land." And they sent the spies out into the land around about Salem that they might subdue it, and these brought back with them a favorable report.

²⁹ Therefore did they assemble an army, saying, "When you march out against a city to assail it, offer them peace if they submit to you. ³⁰ Then shall they be as slaves to you. The work of their hands shall be done in your service, at your bidding, without complaint. ³¹ Yet if they will not be your slaves, but engage you in battle, lay siege then to that place. And when it is delivered into your hand, put every man therein to the sword. ³² Then take the women, the children and the livestock as plunder for yourselves.

³³ "Yet in the cities of the nations that Yahweh shall give to you, leave nothing alive there. ³⁴ Spare them not a single breath, but annihilate the cities of the Hitties, the Amorites, the Canaanites, the Perizzites, the Hivites and the Jebusites. Utterly destroy them, lest they spread the filth of their gods and entice you to break the commandments of Yahweh."

³⁵ The point of the sword went forth before them, and bloodshed followed in their wake.

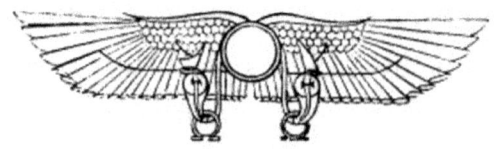

The Book of Journeys

1

¹ The Pharaoh Ahmose was fruitful and prosperous, becoming the father of many children, and inaugurating a new and golden age in the land of Egypt. ² Ahmose reigned for ten and ten and five years again. He it was who outlawed the ritual of sacrifice to the gods, which the shepherd king Abram had sought to perform amid his fever and which other nations also undertook to practice in their madness.

² The line of Ahmose abode on the throne of Egypt for ten generations and beyond, honoring the gods Amen and Thoth with their regnal names. ³ From the seed of Ahmose sprang the first woman to sit upon the throne of the Two Lands, and Thutmose, the third of his name, who ruled more than two score and a dozen years. ⁴ As Ahmose had been "The Liberator," this Thutmose became known to his people as "The Warrior," leading the armies of Egypt into Canaan and Syria, across the Euphrates and south into Nubia.

⁵ His greatest victory was at Megiddo, in the famed battle of Armageddon. It was here that he defeated an army of Canaanites and Syrians led by the king of Kadesh and supported by the Mittani. ⁶ It was here that archers first drew bows of sinew, wood and horn crafted together.

⁷ When the armies of the pharaoh came upon them, the fighting men of Canaan took counsel and became convinced that Thutmose would lead his men along the roads on either side of the mountains of Megiddo. This was a longer route, but more certain. ⁹ The third way was directly through the mountains, by way of a narrow pass called Aruna where an army would be hemmed in on either side and forced to move ahead single-file.

¹⁰ Yet this was the way that Thutmose decided upon. Though his counselors sought to sway him, he was determined to take the most treacherous path. ¹¹ "I swear by the love Ra has shown me and by the favor that Amen has shown me that I shall proceed upon this road of Aruna. ¹² Shall my enemies, whom Ra detests, think of me,

'Behold, he has begun to fear us, for he takes another path'? For this will they surely think."

¹³ The Canaanites indeed believed that he would take the easier course and, in preparation, had stationed their armies on either side of the mountains. ¹⁴ But in the end, they were undone. The Egyptians burst forth upon them at the plain of Megiddo like water gushing from a narrow channel, forcing them to take refuge in the city and laying siege to it until the men inside gave themselves over to Thutmose.

¹⁵ As it is written, Thutmose "prevailed over them at the head of his army. At the sight of him coming forth, they fled in fear, rushing headlong toward Megiddo. ¹⁶ They left their horses and chariots of silver and gold, that they might be lifted up over the walls of the town by their garments. ¹⁷ Then were their chariots captured with great ease, as their ranks lay stretched out on their backs on the field of battle, as fish lie in the cords of a fisherman's net."

¹⁸ Thutmose captured not only Megiddo, but the lands around about it as well. The city of Kadesh fell to him, and the Mittani fled before him. Even the Elohim at Salem could not resist him. ¹⁹ So complete was his victory that it was, from that day forward, spoken of in whispers of dismay and vexation by the Elohim and those who served them. ²⁰ In the time that followed, Thutmose stretched forth his hand to subdue all of Canaan and Syria, eastward to the great Euphrates and beyond. ²¹ Those taken at the point of the sword or bound to subjugation remembered this battle as the end of a great era. ²² Their stories were

passed along for generations uncounted, until Megiddo came to be spoken as the name of an age's end.

[23] For the line of Ahmose, it marked not an end but a point of turning. From that time forward, no pharaoh of Egypt would rule as great an expanse as the empire Tuthmose surveyed. [24] As is the way of things, kings go forth to conquer and return to ruin. The Two Lands prospered for a time yet, but there came a day that their splendor was not what it had been, and a new pharaoh came to the throne who was intent upon restoring it.

[25] This one, like his father and two others before him, was named Amenhotep, which translated means "Amen is content." [26] But the pharaoh was not content, for he looked to the sky and beheld there a single god, not the many gods and goddesses of his fathers. [27] This god shone down upon him, its radiance reflected in his own, and as he basked in the glory of this light, he became resolved within his heart to swear fealty to the one god who was its source.

[28] The young pharaoh dispatched the high priest of Amen to serve as overseer on a quarrying expedition, whereupon he himself seized control of the temples in the capital. [29] It was not long before he had proscribed any worship of Amen. Even the very names of Amen and his consort Mut were removed from the temple precincts, which were both defaced and defiled. [30] No festival was to be held in honor of any other god save the one god of radiance, called the Aten, and no images of theses gods were to be displayed.

[31] Then, in a moment of inspiration and conceit, the

pharaoh discarded the name of his birth and took to himself a new title to honor the name of the Aten. [32] Henceforth would he be called Akhenaten, the living spirit of the Aten, manifested on the earth as light incarnate and the founder of a great new capital called the Aten's Horizon.

[33] He chose for the site of this new city a desert place. In this place there had been neither temple nor marketplace nor simple abode. [34] "Behold," said Akhenaten, "it is I, the pharaoh, who has found it, when it belonged to neither god nor goddess; when it was ruled by neither king nor queen; when it belonged not to any people. [35] My father, Hor-Aten, declared in my hearing, 'It is to be my own abode, the Horizon of the Aten eternally.'"

[35] On the banks of the Nile toward the sunrise it rose up from the desert, with a palace for the pharaoh in the north, temples to the Aten at its heart and estates for the great families at its southern edge.

[36] But the pharaoh placed upon the backs of his people a burden too great for them to bear. [37] They cowered in fear lest they be discovered honoring any other god save the Aten, and they hid the images of their own gods, careful that they should not be seen.

[38] Such is the way of things when one god rules by force of arms. It is the way of veiled truth and hidden honor; the way of fearful smiles, of two faces and two tongues.
[39] When a general, priest or king places his own god on a stone pedestal, it is the people who become as stones, afraid to speak apart from what is accepted or act beyond

the measure of their masters.

2

¹ As Akhenaten turned his eyes inward to his new capital, he neglected the outward. A great plague swept down across the nation, so that thousands perished, and the power of his sun god could do nothing in the face of it. ² The people cried out, yet their cries were not answered. They suffered, yet their suffering was not assuaged.

³ Neither did the pharaoh answer the cries of his people from out of Canaan, the land which his fathers had subdued and made to serve them. ⁴ As the Hittite king grew in strength and boldness, he sought out an alliance with the Mittani, whose realm encompassed the headwaters of the great Tigris and Euphrates, sending to their king a statue of gold. ⁵ Yet this gold was but a gloss that covered a figure carved from wood.

⁶ At this the Mittani king was offended, and the alliance with Egypt was strained. ⁷ In due course, the growing might of the Hittites was brought to bear against the Mittani, who could not stand alone against them. ⁸ Abandoned by Egypt, they were overrun, and the Hittite armies swept southward toward Canaan along the shore of the Sea at the Center of the World.

⁹ Syria fell to the them, yet Akhenaten (whom the Greeks call Achencres) lifted not a hand to stay them. ¹⁰ The Hittites urged the men of Canaan to rise up against

the pharaoh whose fathers had subdued them, so that the men Akhenaten had favored with high office in that land cried out to him for succor. [11] The servant of Egypt who ruled in Jerusalem wrote in desperation to the capital, seeking help against the Hebrews who had risen against him. [12] These men, at the bidding of the Elohim, sought to throw of the yoke of the pharaoh and renew their own sovereignty in Canaan.

[13] Yet amidst the pleas of his own chosen governors, the pharaoh stood by, sending no help.

[14] Abdi-Heba, who had sworn allegiance to the pharaoh, was disconsolate. [15] "Why do you favor the Hebrews and oppose the rulers?" he asked. "We are bereft of troops in our garrison. [16] Oh, that the pharaoh should guard his lands! All the pharaoh's lands have entered into rebellion. [17] If only I might enter the presence of my king and look at him squarely with both eyes, yet alas, the enmity against me is strong and I am prevented. [18] May the pharaoh send troops for his garrison, that I may enter into his presence and fix my gaze upon him. [19] Then, as my lord lives, I would say to him, "Lost are the lands of the pharaoh. Do you not hear me? All your rulers are lost; the pharaoh, my lord, has not a single ruler left.

[20] "May the pharaoh set his gaze upon his archers, and may he send troops of bowmen, for the Hebrews sack the pharaoh's lands. [21] If archers are sent, his lands may be preserved, but if they do not come, all these lands shall be forfeit."

[22] Yet the pharaoh heeded him not, and did not reply.

Neither did he send archers, and so it was that the lands of Canaan and Syria were wrested from him.

^{23} The Hittites, in their coming, took many men of Egypt who were in Canaan as their prisoners. ^{24} Yet their victory became a curse at the moment they grasped it, for the Egyptians were infected by the plague that had come upon them, and this they carried northward into the land of Hatti. ^{25} There it felled a great many, even Suppiluliuma, their monarch, as well as his heir.

^{26} Nor was the pharaoh himself safe in his new capital. The golden rays of the Aten could not shield his family from the ravages of this vile affliction, nor could the remoteness of his new capital. ^{27} In the course of but a short time, his mother, three of his daughters and one of his wives were taken from him.

^{28} In those days, it happened that the sea winds bore a prince across the seas to the land of Egypt. Some say he came from Greece and others from the high steppes beyond the inland sea. ^{29} And betaking himself to the capital, he was brought before the pharaoh himself.

^{30} Now, it is said that this young man had fled his home country because his father, who was king of that land, had given him no title. ^{31} Therefore provoked to anger, he rose up and undertook a rebellion with the help of many cohorts. ^{32} Yet his uprising was not successful, and his father Nenius expelled him from the land owing to his acts of treason.

^{33} When, therefore, he sought refuge in Egypt, there were those who eyed him warily, thinking he had come as a pirate to raid that nation's treasures. ³⁴ For in those days were more and more men taking to the seas, plying the green waters of the central sea as if they were a font of ill-gotten wealth. ³⁵ Therefore did the Greek prince come to be called Gaythelos, or in the western tongue, Goídel Glas, which means "green raider."

³⁶ But when he was brought before the pharaoh, the daughter of the pharaoh was also there at court. ³⁷ This was the custom of Akhenaten, to rule with his family by his side, and his daughter was all the more precious to him now that her sisters had departed this life. ³⁸ The plague that had stricken them had not yet taken her, and the pharaoh had begun to despair of finding a way to shield her from its grip.

³⁹ When, therefore, his daughter and the Greek prince expressed a fondness for each other, it presented not a threat but an opportunity. ⁴⁰ Many were the whispers and suspicions in the capital concerning this newcomer: that he sought to plunder this rich new city or even that he sought the hand of the pharaoh's daughter as a means of supplanting Akhenaten. ⁴¹ It was unthinkable that such a one should be allowed to marry into the royal line and remain in Egypt, where he might plot to overthrow the pharaoh as he had schemed against his own father.

⁴² Yet, if he should one day return home to his own country and claim its throne, such an alliance would prove valuable. ⁴³ More than this, if he were to take the princess away from the wretched plague that was all about them, she would be preserved, along with the pharaoh's lineage.

⁴⁴ Akhenaten therefore agreed that they should wed, on the condition that Gaythelos should leave the country straightaway with his new bride and take her away to a safe distance, beyond the reach of the plague.

⁴⁵ To this did he consent, and shortly after they were wed did they make their departure, along with a retinue of ships well stocked with supplies and wares to trade as they ventured forth to their new home, wherever the waves might take them.

⁴⁶ But their departure did not safeguard the kingdom of Akhenaten, which was soon to be no more. ⁴⁷ In the passing of a few years, the pharaoh himself was dead, and the generations that followed made certain that his great god suffered the same fate. ⁴⁸ In a few short years, all record of Akhenaten and his ways were removed from the walls of the temples. ⁴⁹ The priesthood of Amen was restored to its former glory, and the images of the Aten were removed. ⁵⁰ His glorious capital sank back into the dusts of the desert, abandoned, and its pillars removed to build more temples to the glory of Amen and the old gods. ⁵¹ Akhenaten himself was all but forgotten, his name no longer uttered on the lips of the people and his countenance removed from the works of chiseled stone.

3

¹ In those days, the Elohim once again grew strong in Salem. Egypt had drawn back from out of Canaan, and the

Hittites were distant masters, having turned their eyes westward toward Anatolia and Greece.

² In place of the great empires there arose a wealth of city-states, tribes and petty kingdoms, and these were scattered across the land between the coastal plane and the river Jordan. ³ There were the Moabites and the Edomites in the south and east; the Philistines of Ashdod, Askelon and Gaza along the southern coast; and the Amalekites to the south of them.

⁴ Others among these principalities traced their lineage to the great shepherd pharaohs Maibre, called Abraham, and Yacob-har, named among them as Jacob. ⁵ Among these were the tribes of Judah and Benjamin, of Reuben, Gad, Asher, Naphtali, Simeon, Issachar and Zebulun.

⁶ One tribe boasted that it was descended from Yusuf, the great vizier of Apophis. But these did not follow Seth as their fathers had, for fear of the Elohim, and in strife was their tribe divided between two factions, called Ephraim and Mannasseh. ⁷ There was also a tribe of itinerant priests called Levi, who aligned themselves closely with the Elohim.

⁸ But the greatest among the tribes was Dan. The men of this tribe hearkened not to the priesthood in Jerusalem, which sought to yoke them, demanding, "Why does Dan linger by his ships?"

⁹ The people of Dan did not bend the knee to Jerusalem, nor did they crawl on their bellies before those who would ensnare them. ¹⁰ Their numbers were great in the land of Canaan, surpassed only by the sons of

Jerusalem and its territories. And their enmity was long set one against the other. [11] The men of Jerusalem assailed them on their southern coast, so that some among them moved northward and settled in the land called Laish, near the ports of Tyre and Sidon where their kinsmen dwelt.

[12] Tyre was found within the regions of Asher, the land of the goddess Asherah, she who treads upon the sea. [13] In Jerusalem were her sacred pillars torn down by the priests of the Elohim, but in the north were her shrines and altars guarded. [14] Some say that their name is the name of old for Osiris, that is Asar, and that the pillars they erected were an homage to his ways.

[15] During their migrations did the nobles of their race take this title for themselves, calling themselves Aesir, which means "lords."

[16] But because of the contempt that was borne them by the servants of Yawheh, they called the scion of Asher the son of a servant whore, and in so doing reviled the god who had turned from their wickedness. In like manner did they slander the Danites.

[17] The Elohim and their prophets would rail against them, saying, "I am against you, O Tyre, and I will cause many nations to come against you, as the sea sends forth its waves. [18] They shall lay to waste the walls of Tyre and cast her towers down, then shall I scrape away her rubble and leave only a bare rock. [19] To the sea shall she be consigned, and there shall she spread her fishnets, but on the shores shall her cities fall to the sword."

[20] And again: "Shall not the coastline tremble at the

sound of your downfall, at the groaning of the wounded and the slaughter that comes upon you? ²¹ I will make you a place of desolation, like a city where no one dwells. Then shall I call up depths of the ocean to wash over you and its unbounded waters to cover you. ²² Then shall I cause you to dwell in the nether regions of the earth, as in the ancient ruins, with the ones cast into the pit. Neither shall you return to reclaim your place of glory. ²³ But I will make your end a horror and you will be no more. You shall be sought, but never again found."

²⁴ Nevertheless did the Danites thrive and prosper, setting forth on expeditions over land and sea. The former joined with some among the Asherites in embarking on a journey northward. ²⁵ They passed by the land of Eden in Aratta, nearby Lake Van. Those who dwelt there were an ancient race, the Vanir, in a place they would remember as Vanaheimr, which means "the home of the Vanir."

²⁶ Moving on from that place, they traveled north at a further distance to the steppes beyond Axsaina, the Dark Sea, which is known to the Greeks as Pontus. ²⁷ In this place they were called the Scythians, known as great riders of the horse who spread their herds far and wide across the plains.

²⁸ Thence did some travel northward and west along the river called Danube, to which they gave their name. ²⁹ They did likewise navigate the waters of the Don and the Donets, the Dnieper and the Dniester, leaving their mark upon those places as well. ³⁰ It was beyond the Don, to the east in Asia, that they built their great capital of Asgard,

that is "enclosure of the Aesir."

[31] To secure themselves, they charged their smiths with creating three great treasures. (They called their ironworkers dwarves because they were always stooped over as their hammers rang against the hot iron.) [32] The first of these treasures was a great boar with golden bristles, to symbolize courage and ferocity in battle. [33] The second was a golden armband, and the third was a hammer they named Mjolnir, which means "crusher." [34] This last, it is said, always returned to the one who wielded it, for that one was the mightiest in battle.

[35] Then, to defend their city, they pressed into service a certain man of great skill and stature, whose companion in the task was a great stallion. [36] As a reward for his work, he was promised the hand of a true goddess as a sign that he should be one of them if he were to complete the task by springtime. [37] The workhorse and its kind helped the craftsman and his servants move all the stones into their proper places, and it appeared that he would indeed achieve his goal. [38] But the Aesir were loath to welcome him into their company, so they set loose a mare before the craftsman's stallion, which then chased its quarry far into the fields. [39] Thus delayed, the man could not finish his task in the appointed number of days, and the Aesir slew him in recompense for his failure.

[40] Forgiveness was not the way of the Aesir, nor was mercy in their aspect. [41] Though their own name meant "lords" or "high ones" and was close akin to the name Asar — that is, Osiris — they had abandoned his ways and

made war on one another, as had the Elohim and their followers. ⁴² Their way was to sacrifice the lives of men to their gods, hanging them from a tree and piercing them through with their spears.

⁴³ Their master was named Odin, who had come from the city of Troy when it fell, and his armies made war upon the Vanir, whose own forces came northward and laid siege to the capital. ⁴³ The hooves of the Aesir horses pounded like thunder upon the steppes. ⁴⁴ Odin himself rode the stoutest of Scythian steeds, Sleipnir, whose speed was such that men drew him with eight legs instead of four. ⁴⁵ And when the battle came, he cast his spear into the throngs of the Vanir, yet even still they could not overcome their foes. ⁴⁶ The Vanir rushed forward, trampling the plains on their own steeds, and broke the wall of the Aesir stronghold. ⁴⁷ Yet neither side could prevail, and the two peoples made a truce so that they were thenceforth were one nation.

⁴⁸ In honor of their peace, they created a potion known as mead, the strength of which was such that it could keep men from battle or compel them to it, depending on how much of it was drunk.

⁴⁹ At length, some say that many years after this, a group of them ventured as far as shores of the Baltic Sea, to the place that was to become the realm of Denmark. ⁵⁰ They remembered the stories of Asgard and Odin, and these they told to their children and their children's children, until the kings and heroes of old became as gods to them.

4

¹ Not all the Danites went north toward the lands of frost and snow. Others among them left their homeland in ships, sailing across the Sea at the Center of the World and beyond, even from the time of Ahmose.

² In those days did some of their number go forth. Among their captains was a certain Nuada, who sailed past the edge of the central sea and ventured beyond the gates to the boundless ocean.

³ This Nuada had ruled over his company for seven years, and at length he brought them to the farthest reaches of the known lands, sailing through the dark mists that conceal the sunrise to make their landing on the northern shores of an emerald isle.

⁴ When they saw this, they were keen to make landing, and they did so at a place called Tracht Mugha in Ulster.

⁵ They brought with them to this place four objects that were as talismans. ⁶ The first of these was the Stone of Fal, which attested to the kingship. The second was the Spear of Lug, which carried the battle. The third was the Sword which was called the Answerer, wielded by Nuada himself. And the forth was the Cauldron of Dagda, from which all men could eat their fill.

⁷ Nuada's people were call themselves the Tuatha De Danaan, which some say refers to the Tribe of Dan and

others interpret as People of the Goddess Dana. [8] Such was their affection for this fine new land, that they burned their ships, so there might be no retreat, for they believed they had come upon the land of their ancestors. [9] And indeed, it is said among some that the old gods had fled to the western horizon, as had been told in the tales of Egypt, having grown weary of the ways of men.

[10] Upon their arrival on the shores of the isle that would one day be called Errin, the Tuatha made their way inland a distance to a place called the Red Hills of Rian. [11] There they made their first encampment, and shortly encountered the inhabitants of that place, who were called the Firbolg. [12] These were the "men of bags," who were short of stature and dark of aspect, and who are said to have been the first to play the bagpipes.

[13] The king of that people was one Eochaid Mac Erc, and he sent out from his company a champion named Sreng, armed with two thick spears and a strong shield that was the color of the earth.

[14] And the Tuatha, seeing him come forth, said to themselves, "Behold, a man approaches without any cohort. Surely he means to gather information. Therefore let us send one of our own men to speak with him."

[15] Therefore one named Bres, son of Elatha, went forth from their encampment and strode out toward the one who approached them. [16] Each of them looked the other up and down, taking account of the one who stood before him. For a time, neither man spoke, until at last they deigned to greet one another.

¹⁷ Then Bres entreated Sreng, "Remove your shield from your body and countenance, that I may behold you and give my fellows an account of your aspect."

¹⁸ And Sreng did so, showing forth his weapons. The points of his javelins were broad, their shafts thick and sturdy. ¹⁹ And Bres said, "Woe to the one that should be smitten by them in battle. Woe to him at whom they are flung, against whom they shall be cast, for they are instruments of great torment."

¹⁹ Bres then likewise handed one of his own sharp spears to the other, saying, "Take this as a sample of the weapons the Tuatha wield." ²⁰ And as they drew near to one another, Bres said also, "Give this message to your countrymen: that they must give my people half of your island, or march forth to meet us in battle."

²¹ Sreng then answered and said to him, "Truly would I rather part with half our lands than face your weapons in battle." So they made a pact of friendship and went their way.

²² But when Sreng returned to his people, and he gave them his account of the meeting with Bres, they grew fearful. For he said to them, "Hard it would be to fight them, for their spears are sharp, their shields are strong and their warriors worthy and masterful." ²³ Then he told them of the agreement he had made to share the land with the Tuatha, at which they were chagrined, saying, "This we shall not grant, for if we agree, they shall take the whole of the land unto themselves!"

²⁴ The Tuatha then took counsel among themselves and

retreated toward the shores of the sea, saying to themselves, "Let us not stay here, but find a stronghold in the west; there we shall face whoever might come against us." [25] So they went thence over marsh and plain until they reached a place called Black Hill, where they prepared for whatever might come.

[26] They gathered to themselves seven battalions, who strode out onto the wide field called Magh Nia, which stands near a place between two lakes. And coming to meet them at the opposite side were eleven battalions of the Firbolg.

[27] Their lines stretched forth across the plain, one facing the other, and the Tuatha sent out three among their poets as envoys to King Eochaid, who received them in his tent with gifts at their coming. [28] Yet when they repeated their demand that half the land be ceded to the Tuatha, Eochaid replied, "We shall not grant this request from now to the end of time!"

[29] Both sides therefore agreed to stand down for a short space of time, that they might prepare their weapons for the battle that was to come. [30] In making ready for this day, the Tuatha raised up a fort called the Fort of Onsets, whence they went forth into battle. And the Firbolg entrenched a great fort as their stronghold called the Fort of the Pack, for the packs of dogs that would feast on the bodies of the dead when the battle was over. [31] Each side also made a well of healing filled with herbs where they might tend to the wounds of the fallen.

[32] When they first met on the field of combat, the

Firbolg charged fiercely and drove back their enemy, so that they were victorious. [33] Yet they did not pursue the Tuatha, but returned instead to their own encampment in high spirits at the end of the day.

[34] Even so, the battle was not finished. The champion Dagda fought valiantly for the Tuatha, even slaying the Firbolg warrior Cirb, who before that had sent three hundred men to their deaths. [35] For their part, the Firbolg sent forth Sreng into the melee, and it is said that he slew one hundred and fifty of the Tuatha before reaching Nuada, their king and engaging him in combat. [36] So heavy were the blows of Sreng that, though Nuada turned them aside nine times with his shield, each time was he assailed anew. [37] Then at last Sreng dealt him such a mighty blow that he sliced off the rim of his shield and severed Nuada's right arm at the shoulder.

[38] But before Sreng could deliver a killing blow, two warriors of the Tuatha, Dagda and Aengaba of the North, stood forth between him and the king. [39] Thereupon did Sreng withdraw. And it is said that a hand of silver was fashioned to replace the one Nuada had lost, though he surrendered the kingship on account of his wound.

[40] The Tuatha then made a charge to avenge their king's injury, and they drove deep into the Firbolg company until Bres came face-to-face with the King Eochaid. [41] The king slew him, but Dagda and three other champions of the Tuatha pressed forward to him. [42] That day did many men of the Firbolg die protecting their sovereign.

[43] Then did the Firbolg advance once more against the

THE PHOENIX CHRONICLES

Tuatha, but their king was weary and stayed behind, charging Sreng and his own son thus: "Continue the fight while I go in search of a drink, for I can no longer endure this consuming thirst." [44] He therefore withdrew to quench his thirst at the strand called Eothail, nigh unto the seashore. He took with him a hundred men as his guard, but the three sons of Nemed followed him from the Tuatha contingent with a hundred and fifty men. [45] There they surprised Eochaid and his guardsmen, engaging them until all fell and the king along with them.

[46] On the field of battle, Eochaid's son fell also, though he in like manner slew the son of Nuada in combat. [47] Such was the fierceness of the blows dealt by one side against the other that, after a day and a night of conflict, each was too weary to lift a hand against the other. So it came about that each side went its own way.

[48] And after each side took counsel among its leaders and champions, they came together and made peace. [49] These were the terms: that the Firbolg would retain the land of Connacht, where the battle had been waged and round about it, and that the Tuatha should withdraw to the island's farther regions, all of which would be theirs to rule by treaty.

[50] Thence did the Tuatha reign upon the island for nigh unto two hundred years, and their kings were six in number until, at the last, the realm was divided among three chieftains whose signs were the hazel tree, the ploughshare and the blazing sun.

[51] But because the land was won by force of arms and

price of blood, it was destined to be lost in the same manner. [52] For the sword that rends human flesh also cleaves asunder peace from justice, shattering one and distorting the other.

5

[1] It was during their reign that Gaythelos and the daughter of Akhenaten set sail out of Egypt in search of a land not touched by the plague. [2] Wind and wave carried them west across the waters until they found a certain watercourse in the land of Numidia, along the north shores of Africa. [3] Making their way upriver in this place, they disembarked there for a time, but could find no rest for themselves there.

[4] Then they betook themselves again to their ships and, as Nuada had done before him, they sailed through the gates to the boundless ocean, remaining near the coastline and following it northward until they found a favorable landing place where they might end their journey.

[5] At this place they removed themselves from their ships and made camp, whereupon they were assailed by the native peoples of that place. [6] Yet Gaythelos and his men prevailed against them and built for themselves a settlement upon a hill close by the ocean. [7] There they built a tower encompassed by a deep ditch, naming the settlement Brigantia, which means "high place," for the hill and the tower that rose above it.

8 But the people of the land round about Brigantia did continually harry it, until Gaythelos grew weary of warding them off, for each time he did so, men's lives were lost in the defense of their settlement. 9 He feared that, in time, the people whose land they had invaded would subdue them and subject them to an ignoble life of servitude.

10 He therefore called upon some of the seamen who had come with him to provision themselves in boats and set out to explore the boundless ocean, beyond any lands that they had known, in the hope of finding a place rich and bountiful that was not yet occupied by any other inhabitant.

11 Such a place did they indeed discover, then returned to Gaythelos with tidings of its bounty. 12 Now some say that Gaythelos himself espied the land from the top of Brigantia's high tower, yet surely they know now whereof they speak, for the land they found lay far beyond the horizon from that place and was hidden behind the mists that blanket its shores. 13 Indeed, it was the same land to which the Tuatha had come those many years earlier, and this first expedition returned with news of it.

14 Gaythelos, though, had taken ill and was close to death when the expedition returned. He therefore called his sons to him and said to them, "Whatever may befall me, go forth and make this island your habitation. 15 For in the place where we now dwell, land is difficult to acquire unless it be purchased at far too steep a price, which I fear shall be enslavement and the death of us all. 16 Far better would it be to die bravely in battle than to succumb a little each day

beneath the yoke of subjugation."

[17] Therefore he exhorted them, "Go without delay to the island that is prepared for you, in which place you shall live a life that is noble and free. [18] This is the one gem most sought after by every gentle heart: that is, to endure the sway of no foreign ruler, but to submit freely to the lineage of one's own nation."

[19] Then one of his sons, Ith by name, did go forth on an expedition to the island, taking ninety men with him but leaving his brother behind. [20] They made their landing in the north of the island, near the same spot where the Tuatha had come ashore upon their migration to that place. Indeed, the sons of the Tuatha came out to meet them on a strand called the Fetid Shore.

[21] Ith inquired of them, "What is the name of this place?"

[22] "Inis Elga," said they, which means "Noble Island."

[23] They then took him to a meeting with their kings, who were three in number: Mac Cuill, Mac Cécht and Mac Gréine. [24] Ith came before them and praised their land in their presence, saying, "Good is the land wherein you dwell. [25] Bountiful are its fruits, its honey, its grain and its fish. Temperate is its climate, neither too hot nor too cold. Truly, here you have all that you might need."

[26] But the kings of the Tuatha gleaned from his words that he wished to take possession of the land for himself. Had they not also come and, by force of arms, wrested the island from the Firbolg? [27] They therefore slew one man among Ith's company and bade him to be gone from Inis

Elga. [28] Yet when he returned to his ship where he had left them at the Fetid Shore, they fell upon Ith and killed him as well.

[29] After this, some of the men who had come with him retrieved his body and fled the island. Then did they return whence they had come, bringing tidings of what had befallen them and how the inhabitants of Inis Elga had slain their captain. [30] It was for this reason that the Brigantians took to their ships and set out for the island anew, vowing to avenge their prince who had been slain.

[31] These went out from the coast of Iberia in thirty-six ships, led by one remembered as Milesius, which means "Soldier of Spain." [32] He took with him eight sons and nine brothers, each them determined that they should fulfill Gaythelos' dying wish and build a new settlement on the island they had discovered. [33] They took with them also the wife of Gaythelos, the princess of Egypt whom he had wed, whose name in her own tongue was Merytaten, but whom they now called Scota.

[34] With them also went their judge and bard, Amergin Glúingel. And it is said that when he set foot on the shores of the new land, he spoke thusly:

[35] I am wind on sea.
I am ocean wave.
I am roar of sea.
I am bull of seven fights.

[36] I am vulture on cliff.

I am dewdrop.
I am fairest of flowers.
I am boar steadfast.

[37] I am salmon in pool.
I am lake on plain.
I am a mountain in a man.
I am a word of skill.

[38] I am the point of a weapon sent forth in combat.
I am god who fashions fire for a head.

[39] Who makes the jagged mountain smooth?
Who is he who proclaims the ages of the moon?
And who, the place where the sun falls in setting?

[40] Then, three days from their arrival did they break camp and do battle with the Tuatha. [41] It was then that Scota, the daughter of the pharaoh, fell in battle. But the Milesians were not to be denied, and they fought fiercely until they had subdued the Tuatha, who from that time forward were seen no more in all the land.

[42] Their abode became the cairns and burial mounds to which they were consigned by the Milesian invaders, and their names became echoes from a distant past. [43] The Tribe of Dan was no more in the land of Inis Elga, their memories obscured beyond the mists of time, relegated to the land of legend.

[44] Thenceforth, for many years, the island's name was

changed to Scota, in honor of the fallen queen of Egypt who never sat upon the throne of that land but who, in her death, became the queen of a new country. [45] And in the time ahead, many of her people crossed the narrow straight to another island, which land also took her name as its own, whereas in that day the people took to calling Inis Elga, Errin.

6

[1] Not all the Danites perished on that western isle. Many remained in their ships. Indeed, they grew mighty and their ships subdued the world. [2] Their captains traded with Tarshish in Iberia, which belonged to Hiram, king of Tyre, whose own city gave this distant port its name. [3] They traded in gold and silver, in bronze, in tin and copper, and thus did they magnify both their name and their fortune.

[4] They rose up from the waters as a great storm, which was born in the Sea at the Center of the World, and moved across the waters in strength and boldness. [5] The Warriors of the Great Green Sea, they called them, and the people of the Phoenix they were. [6] Such was their strength in arms that no land could stand before them. The empire of the Hittites, which had withstood the armies of Egypt's pharaohs, was laid waste at their landing.

[7] They were many in number, and no man knew their homeland, for they were from everywhere and nowhere. As ghosts they sailed the central sea, raiding the coastal

lowlands and watching all nations submit before them. [8] In confidence did they advance on Ugarit, along the seacoast in the land of Syria. And the king of that nation cried out in terror at their arrival. He pleaded for help from those who were his allies. To the king of Cyprus he sent this letter:

[9] "Behold! The enemy's ships have come. My cities are burned, and the country is beset by evils. [10] Do you not know, my father, that my foot soldiers and chariots are in the land of the Hittites, and all my ships are abroad in Lydia? [11] Thus my land is abandoned to itself. Let it be known, my father, that seven ships from the enemy have inflicted great hardship upon us."

[12] Yet he found no help from that quarter.

[13] And he sent forth also a missive to the king of Carchemish, whose land was to the north by the mighty Euphrates. Yet from Carchemish also, no more than sage advice was sent in answer:

[14] "As for what you have written me, 'Ships of the enemy have been seen at sea!,' you must remain steadfast," came the answer. [15] "Where are your troops and chariots stationed? Are they not close by you? Or if not, then behind the enemy that assails you? [16] Therefore surround your towns with ramparts. There you must await the enemy with your chariots and foot soldiers at the ready. Stand fast with great resolve!"

[17] Yet the kingdom of Ugarit could not stand fast. The enemy poured in upon them like seawater through an open floodgate. And in a moment, the nation was no more.

[18] The peoples of the sea came from everywhere, as if

from nowhere. They swept like spirits across the waves from Italy in the land of the Etruscans. [19] From Achaea, the land of the Greeks. From Sardinia and Sicily. And from the northern coast of Canaan, from the five cities of the Philistines. [20] It was there, in the land of Philistia, that they encountered the armies of the Elohim, and it was there that the land was rent asunder in bloody warfare between the servants of Yahweh and the masters of the sea, the people of Dan.

[21] First, however, the seafarers set their sights on the grandest prize of all, on Egypt, the empire of the pharaohs. [22] In the days of the Pharaoh Merenptah, they brought their ships to ground on the coast of the Nile Delta. There did they combine their men and weapons with those from the tribes of Libya, finding common cause with them against the empire of Egypt. [23] Together, they formed a fighting force of sixteen thousand men, marching inland to Memphis and also Heliopolis.

[24] Yet Merenptah repulsed them, killing six thousand of their number and routing the remainder of their forces.

[25] Even still they took courage. And in the eighth year of Merenptah's successor, Rameses, they made haste to renew their assault on Egypt. [26] Yet Rameses, the third pharaoh to bear that name, strengthened his forces in the south of Canaan and fortified the many mouths of the Nile. [27] The archers of Rameses struck down the seafarers before they could reach the shores of Egypt. [28] They lay in ambush in the mouths of the mighty Nile, in the marshes of the Delta. [29] They sent forth their arrows like a plague of stinging

locusts, and their ships emerged from hiding amid the reeds and rushes of the lowland. ³⁰ Then did the pharaoh's navy ensnare the ships of their enemies, the seafarers, using the barbs of their grappling hooks. And after this they pulled the vessels of woe aground in the marshland of the Delta.

³¹ There did the foot soldiers of Egypt assail them, until the invaders were turned back and utterly vanquished.

³² "As for those who came forth to my borders, their seed has vanished. Their hearts and souls are crushed for all eternity. ³³ Those who went forth upon the sea sailed into the heart of a flame fully kindled. ³⁴ At the mouths of our great river did we meet them. And a stronghold of lances surrounded them upon the shore."

³⁵ Thus did Rameses boast of his victory, yet the seafarers were not defeated. ³⁶ To the southern coast of Canaan they withdrew, finding refuge in their five coastal cities: Ashkelon and Ekron, Ashdod and Gaza, and Gath, the home of the Gittites.

³⁷ The coast of Asia was their domain as well. There they dwelt in a city beside Mount Ida, a city known as Troy.

7

¹ The city of Troy grew from the mists of time and memory, seated upon the eastern coast of Asia. The ancients say it was founded by one Ilus, son of Tros, who named it for his father. Yet others still called it Ilium, after him.

² Its place near the mouth of a narrow strait gave it mastery of the passageway between the Sea at the Center of the World and, to the north and east, the Dark Sea. ³ In like manner, it stood as sentinel along the land road from Asia into Europe. ⁴ As guardian of these two great passageways, over land and on the waves, the people of Troy amassed a great fortune exacting tolls from ships and caravans.

⁵ For their own part, the Trojans built an ample fleet in which they sailed forth with their allies, the same seafarers who assailed Egypt and the Hittites. ⁶ And the nations round about chafed beneath the yoke of the Trojans, saying to themselves, "It is madness that we allow this to continue! See how they rob us as we pass beside the isthmus! And they use the tolls they impose upon our travelers to build yet more ships for their navy!"

⁷ Such was the wealth of the Trojans that King Priam, who led them, sired fifty sons and a dozen daughters by his wife and many concubines.

⁸ And the tale is told that his son Paris was invited to serve as judge in the pavilion of Olympus. There, in the city of the gods, it fell upon him to choose who was the fairest. ⁹ The one so favored would receive in token of her triumph a single golden apple, inscribed with the words "For the most beautiful." ¹⁰ Yet which among them would it be? Would the honor fall to Athena, the guardian of Athens? Or to Hera, the consort of mighty Zeus? Or to Aphrodite, the foam-born maiden? ¹¹ Whichever choice he made, Paris would surely incur the wrath of two great goddesses, while earning gratitude from only one.

¹² His mind, it is said, was made up by an overture from Aphrodite, who promised that he should win the heart of the world's most beautiful woman should he decide the matter in her favor. ¹³ That woman, however, belonged to another man, Menelaus, king of Sparta.

¹⁴ So it was that Paris set sail for Sparta under the guise of diplomacy to make off with Helen, as Aphrodite had promised. It is written that he succeeded, and that the Spartans, in league with their allies from Achaea, made haste to retrieve her.

¹⁵ Yet is not Helen the name by which the Achaeans call their own people? Are they not Hellenes, and is their land not Hellas? ¹⁶ Indeed, it was no woman that the Trojans had stolen, but the wealth of Achaea itself. ¹⁷ By deception and diplomacy, through their sea tolls and taxes, they had made off with the wealth of Achaea; they had plundered her without bloodshed.

¹⁸ As it is the wont of men to blame the gods for their ambitions, to attribute to the heavens their own folly, so it was in this case.

¹⁹ It therefore came to pass that the Achaeans, weary of the Trojan tariffs, gathered an armada to recover the whole of their losses. ²⁰ And they set sail across the Aegean to face the Trojans in a war that lasted one year, two years, five years, ten years, until both sides despaired that it should ever be concluded.

As it is written,

²¹ The sun of a new day struck the ploughlands,

THE PHOENIX CHRONICLES

Rising up from the quiet water
And the deep stream of the ocean
To climb the sky.

[22] Then did the Trojans assemble together.
But they could scarce recognize each one fallen,
So with the water washed away the blood upon them,
And wept warm tears as they bore them to the wagons.

[23] But great Priam, their king, forbade them mourn aloud.
So in silence did they pile their bodies on the pyre,
Their hearts vexed with sorrow,
And did burn them on the fire,
Then returned to sacred Ilium

[24] In like manner did the Achaeans, sorely grieved,
Pile the slain among their number on the pyre,
Their hearts vexed with sorrow,
And did burn them on the fire,
Then returned to their hollow vessels

[25] The Greeks went forth and, in their fighting, desecrated temples of the Trojans around about the city, among them the sanctuary of Athena. Yet still, they could not prevail. [26] At last, the Achaeans feigned withdrawal, pulling their ships back from the coastline and leaving in their wake a single gift: a horse whose hide and mane were wood, and whose legs were borne by wheels. [27] Planks of

fur they wove across its ribs. Three days it took them to build it, and its size was like unto a mountain. ²⁸ And when it was completed the Greeks said, "Hearken to our words, you Trojans. Athena has tasked us to build her this great beast as a gift for you, to atone for our desecration of her temple in your city."

²⁹ But Laocoon, a priest of Troy, counseled them strenuously, saying, "Do you truly think the enemy departed? That he has sailed away upon the foamy seas? Do you truly judge that any Greek gift be free of treachery? Is this the reputation of their leader, Odysseus? ³⁰ Nay, either the Achaeans are in hiding, concealed by the wood of this breathless beast, or they have conceived it as a mechanism to use against our walls. Or to spy upon our homes. Or to fall upon us from above. ³¹ Perhaps then also, it conceals some other deceit. Trust not this horse, my fellow Trojans. Whatever it may be, I fear the Greeks, even bearing gifts."

³² And he let fly his spear with a mighty hand, so that it pierced the side of the creature with great force. It struck there, quivering, so that the cavity within rang hollow. And there was heard in that place a mighty groan.

³³ Yet the Trojans heeded not his warnings, and they took the horse into the city. In its belly were hidden thirty soldiers, and in its mouth two Achaean spies. ³⁴ So it came to pass, after nightfall, that the ships of Greece sailed back toward the city. ³⁵ And as the Trojans slept inside their homes, the Achaeans crept forth from the belly of the beast, and they opened the gates for their countrymen, who

flooded the city with their numbers. ³⁶ Thus was the siege of Troy ended at last, and the Trojans defeated in a rout by means of subterfuge.

³⁷ But the Trojans were not all slain in the battle. Aeneas, a cousin to the king, escaped, it is said, to the country of Latium, whence come the tribe of the Latins who are mighty to this day. ³⁸ Two of his descendants, some say, founded the city of Rome. And one among his grandsons is claimed as the founder of a line of kings in Britain.

8

¹ Aphrodite was the patron goddess of all the seafaring peoples. ² As the foam-born did she guide them to safety on the waves. From her perch in the starry heavens did she light a beacon for them to follow, the brightest in the evening sky. ³ In the form of a dove had she guided Noah to safe landing. The softness of her wings bespoke of love and inspiration, and oft did she descend upon the tongues of bards and sages.

⁴ The Greeks did name her Aphrodite, but the seafarers knew her as Astarte. She was favored of the Trojans and, in like manner, of the Philistines, who dwelt upon the southern coast of Canaan. ⁵ From their cities did they launch their many ships of trade and plunder. Yet also were their foot soldiers and chariots at the ready. ⁶ And the armies of the Elohim did challenge them, but they did answer, and it came to pass that the Danites of Philistia

lorded it over the Elohim and their followers, such that they chafed at beneath their yoke.

⁷ In that place, in those days, many strong men had arisen. The men did call them giants, for great was their brutality and vast was their ambition. ⁸ Yet their reach extended beyond their grasp, and their vanity exceeded the truth of things. ⁹ Kings they were not, but petty princes and pretenders, tyrants and usurpers. Each ruled a plot of land that was little more than a collection of fields and threshing floors, brought together by their conquests of nearby farms and pasture.

¹⁰ They boasted, "I am the king of Moab!" Or of Ammon. Or of Edom. Or of Judah. And they conscripted men to battle, waging war on one another in the manner of great empires.

¹¹ Yet no empires were these. To Egypt, they were but gnats to be swatted; to Babylon, they were but vassals to be yoked. ¹² So did Merneptah, who turned the seafarers back from Egypt, proclaim of them: "Canaan is captive to all woe. Ashekelon is conquered, Gezer seized, Yanoam banished from all existence. Israel is laid waste, barren of seed."

¹³ Ashkelon was a city of the Philistines. And another of these cities was Timnah.

¹⁴ To Timnah came the champion of the Danites, whose name was Samson. His land of birth was a short distance away, at the edge of the land called Judah. No king was he, but a man of war who sought to secure for himself a place of power. ¹⁵ For this purpose did he seek alliance with the

chief man of Timnah through marriage to his daughter.

¹⁶ He said to his father and mother, "I would have her, for she pleases me." And they sought to dissuade him, yet he would not accept their answer. ¹⁷ At length, therefore, he set out from his home town toward Timnah, which was but an hour's walk distant. ¹⁸ And when he had come to the vineyards that belonged to that place, it is said that he came upon a fierce young lion, which set upon him. ¹⁹ He therefore rose up and slew the whelp, rending its flesh in two with his own bare hands.

²⁰ Yet surely this did not occur. For is it not written, "Dan is a lion's whelp?" And likewise also, the same is said of Judah. ²¹ So it was that Samson, who was born at the border between these two tribes, would rend both of them in two for the sake of his ambition. And it happened in the following manner.

²² When Samson arrived at the Timnah, the chief man of the village agreed to his proposal to forge an alliance, and a feast was prepared according to the custom. ²³ Then the father of the man appointed to Samson thirty companions, for he said to himself, "If this man plots against me, these shall hear of it and slay him."

²⁴ But Samson knew this, and so did challenge them: "Come and answer me this riddle. If you declare to me the answer in seven days, I shall bestow upon you thirty linen garments and thirty sets of clothes. But if you fail in this charge, you must provide me the same."

²⁵ Then the thirty asked him to speak his riddle. And he said, "From the eater came forth meat, and from the strong

came sweetness."

²⁶ But they could not answer him after three days. After four days, they had no reply. After five days, they were speechless. After six days, their tongues were silent. ²⁷ And on the seventh day, they went forth to their kinswoman, whom Samson had taken as his wife, and besought her, saying, "Entice your husband, that he may explain to you this riddle. Then speak the answer to us, that we may preserve your household."

²⁸ The woman therefore went to Samson, entreating and accusing him: "Your hatred burns against me! Your love is false! For you have asked my people this riddle, yet kept from me its answer."

²⁹ He sought at first to forestall her, for he had not told even his own parents the answer. Yet she persisted, so that at the last he relented and told her. ³⁰ Then at once did she go to her people and say to them, "This is the answer to the riddle: What is sweeter than honey? And what is stronger than a lion?"

³¹ So when the time came, before the sun set on the seventh day, the men of the town approached Samson and gave him the answer his wife had told them. ³² And Samson was wroth with fury, for his own deception was turned against him. ³³ He therefore cursed and said to them, "Had you not plowed with my heifer, you would ne'er have solved my riddle!"

³⁴ And in his anger, he went forth to Ashkelon and there struck down thirty men of the Philistines in that city. He stripped them of their garments and cast them in a heap at

the feet of those who had solved the riddle. ³⁵ So did he shed innocent blood in vengeance for his wife's deception. ³⁶ Then he went forth from that place to the home of his kinsmen, but his wife had been removed from his presence and given to one of the thirty from the feast. Her father would not allow him to go in to her, saying, "She is given to another. Take her younger sister instead."

³⁷ Samson, however, was greatly offended, for he who had taken the eldest sister now had first claim upon her father's estate. And Samson said to himself, "If I cannot advance my purpose by guile, I shall turn Timnah an Ashkelon against one another!"

³⁸ Then, going out, he caught three hundred foxes and tied torches to their tails, whereupon he released them into the fields. ³⁹ These ran in terror through the stalks of grain, lighting it afire so that all the land was ablaze. ⁴⁰ And the beasts themselves were set afire, and were consumed along with the grain. Their cries did rise to the heavens, born upon their deathly anguish. ⁴¹ Some say the gods did hear them, and remembered the evil done by Samson, and turned from him. But others scorn him not only for this, but also for his murder of the Philistines.

⁴² Even so, when the burned fields were discovered, the blame was placed on the man of Timnah, who had withheld his daughter from Samson. ⁴³ So his countrymen from among the Philistines set upon both the woman and her father, and burned them to death, in the same way that their fields had been burned. ⁴⁴ In this way did Samson accomplish his purpose, setting Philistine against Philistine

because of his anger.

9

¹ Yet still Samson's ire was not assuaged, and he said to himself, "Even now I am denied that which is due to me, so I shall surely slay the ones responsible with my own two hands!"

² And madness took him, as is wont to happen in the hearts of men who are bent on vengeance. ³ He saw no farther than the point of his sword and no deeper than the depth of his fury. And he went forth to slaughter them, saying, "I will not stop until I have my vengeance!"

⁴ When, therefore, he had spilled the blood of many a man, he retreated to a high cave in the hill country of Judah, the rock of an eyrie, which is called Etam, where he hid himself. ⁵ For though the madness was upon him, he knew that vengeance begets vengeance, and in due course the kinsmen of those he had assaulted would go forth seeking retribution.

⁶ So indeed they did. They went forth against the land of Judah, the land of the Elohim, because this is where Samson had hid himself. ⁷ They spread their forces out, pitching their camp near Lehi to the south of Jerusalem.

⁸ Then the Judahites came out to meet the Philistines and questioned them, saying, "Wherefore have you come forth to fight us?"

⁹ "We have come for Samson, to take him captive," they

said. "We would do to him as he has done to us."

¹⁰ So the Judahites rode out to the cave at Etam and laid hold of Samson, binding him hand and foot, for he was not of their tribe and they wished no part of him.

¹¹ They took him from that place to meet the Philistines. But as they approached the encampment at Lehi, Samson loosed the bonds that held him, so they dropped like flax that had burned in a fire. ¹² And the tale is told that he picked up the jawbone of an ass that lay in the field there, and that with this weapon he slew a thousand men.

¹³ After these things, the men of Judah feared Samson, wherefore he held sway over them and did as he pleased. But the Philistines of Timnah and Ashkelon were ever at his heels. Yet still did he spend many days among them, for he was, like them, a Danite.

¹⁴ One day, he went in to a harlot in Gaza, and his enemies lay in wait for him, surrounding that place, yet he escaped them. ¹⁵ And he found there a woman of that country named Delilah, and he desired her. The woman's home was in the Valley of Sorek. (This is the valley where Timnah was found, the home of Samson's wife in his youth.)

¹⁶ Now Samson took Delilah to himself, but his enemies besought her, saying, "Discover the source of Samson's might, that we may subdue him."

¹⁷ So she shaved his head as he was sleeping, that he might become a mockery. And the men of Gaza came in to him as he lay with her and bound him with fetters of brass. ¹⁸ They put out his eyes and confined him. And they

presented him to their god Dagon, the lord of fishermen and ploughmen, saying, "Here is the bane of the Philistines, brought low by our great nation."

[19] Yet the gods saw these things and remarked among themselves, "How long shall this continue? Vengeance begets vengeance, and strife begets strife. And always it continues, lest at length we put a stop to it."

[20] It therefore came to pass that the men of Gaza gathered for their feast day, and they tied Samson between two pillars. And they made sport of him. [21] But there came a mighty rumbling from beneath the earth, so that the pillars shook and trembled. [22] Some then said, "It is Samson! He moves the pillars!" Yet others said, "The gods are wroth with us, and the earth shall swallow us alive!"

[23] The walls did crack, and the pillars did buckle, and the stones that had been laid one on top of the other were loosened. [24] Then did the walls come down in a torrent of dust and rubble, like a wave from the sea crashing hard against the shoreline. [25] They fell upon blind Samson. They fell upon the men of Gaza. They fell upon all who assembled in that place. [26] And so were their iniquities revisited on all of them.

[27] Yet the folly of man was not so easily ended, nor his thirst for conflict so swiftly quenched. [28] Therefore did the death of mad Samson bring no end to the cycle of violence, and the Judahites made war anew upon the Danites of Philistia, and the Danites upon the Judahites. And the gods turned away in revulsion.

[29] And the wheel of time moved forward. The ages

passed on from days of bronze, and weapons of iron fired in forges of blackest intent were made ready for great battles. [30] They drew the blood of men and rent the hearts of women. Children died without mercy. The land was laid waste.

[31] And the gods wept.

STEPHEN H. PROVOST

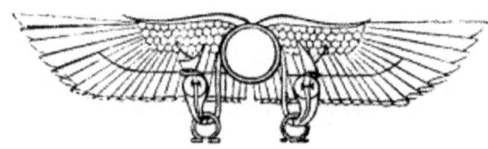

THE PHOENIX CHRONICLES

The Book of

Contendings

1

¹ These are the chronicles of the land of Judah and Israel during the time of their first princes, the record of their reigns and the violence done in the name of the gods.

² This is how the city of Zion rose to the heights of pride and vanity on the shoulders of the vanquished, how the Elohim spread strife across the land of Canaan and

how the scions of Avaris contended with the people of the Phoenix.

³ In those days, the children of Shem found no rest for themselves. Their time on earth was short, and ever were they afflicted. ⁴ On one side, the priests of the Elohim oppressed them. On the other, the nations round about assailed them. ⁵ They would rise up against the Elohim in the cause of freedom. Yet then would the nations of Ammon and Moab and Edom come against them. Then would the Philistines besiege them.

⁶ Then, having no man as a bulwark against those who would subdue them, they would cry out. They would appeal to the Elohim once more, saying, "Save us!"

⁷ So it was that the people came to seek, in their affliction, a deliverer. ⁸ Looking not to themselves for salvation, they sought instead a champion. Seeking not to guard their own freedom, they placed this charge in the hands of another. ⁹ Then would the Elohim appoint a judge to lead them, a priest and prophet whose hand was heavy. ¹⁰ In strength would he subdue the enemy, and in strength would he restrain his own people, until such time as they should rebel once more.

¹¹ In those days, the judges dwelt in Shiloh, and they passed judgment upon the people. ¹² Such a one was Eli, whose name means "ascended one of El," for he bore the ancient title of Most High. ¹³ Beside him served his two sons, Hophni and Phinehas. But their edicts were unjust, and they reeked with the stench of corruption. ¹⁴ They would take to their loins the women who served at the tent

of meeting. They would demand sacrifices for their polluted altars, and partake of the best meat themselves. ¹⁵ Plunging the fleshhook into the cauldron, they would take up for themselves the choicest portions. And if any dared resist, they would say, "We shall have it, then, by force." This was the way of the House of Eli.

¹⁶ Now in the course of time, Eli grew old and weary, and his sight had begun to fail. He therefore appointed for himself a servant, who might minister to him in all things. ¹⁷ He chose a tester of winds and a reader of portents, who might report to Eli all that transpired throughout the land. For this reason, Eli called him Samuel, which means "the ears of Eli."

¹⁸ But when Eli had grown yet more feeble, Samuel took counsel with himself, saying, "The one I serve will soon be dead, and the people abide not the ways of his sons. They shall surely rise up against Hophni and Phinehas. And then will I not be slain as well? ¹⁹ Therefore shall I arise and take the mantle of Eli to myself. In this way shall I become Most High, and gain renown the savior of the people."

²⁰ So did he contrive within his heart. He lay in wait, until he was alone with Eli and no one was there to defend the old man. Then did he enter his chamber and say to him: "I have heard the word of Yahweh."

²¹ And Eli said, "Speak. Withhold it not from me."

²² Then did Samuel say to him, "Behold! I shall accomplish something that will cause the ears of all who hear to tingle! I shall visit upon Eli what he has visited on his people. ²³ I shall judge his house for all eternity because

he knew of its corruption, yet did nothing to restrain it. He knew of his sons' perversions, yet did nothing to deny them. [24] Therefore I swear now before all the nation: My wrath upon the House of Eli shall never be assuaged. [25] No atonement shall be made for his corruption, neither by sacrifice nor by offerings on the altar. For this altar has been polluted by the wicked, and the land has been laid waste for their injustice!"

[26] Eli's eyes then flashed with anger, though they were milky white from blindness. And he cursed Samuel and spat from his dry and aged lips, "If this is the word of Yahweh, let him do what is right in his own eyes!"

[27] And he called his sons to him and warned them of all that Samuel intended. But Samuel caused the words that he himself had spoken to be heard throughout the land, and many among the people believed them, for they scorned the House of Eli.

[28] Hophni and Phinehas therefore said to themselves, "Come now! We shall raise an army against the Philistines and assail them. When therefore we prevail and make them our servants, we shall subdue the land once more. [29] Then shall the people hail us anew as their anointed ones. And then shall Samuel perish!"

[30] So it came to pass that the sons of Eli the judge rode out against the Philistines. And they brought with them the ark of the covenant. [31] This was the ark fashioned by the Elohim as a symbol of their power and dominion. And some among the Philistines were vexed at the sight of it, saying, "A god has come into the midst of them. For this

reason, we shall surely fail. ³² Are these not the gods of the Egyptians, who defeated us in Ashkelon? Is this not the ark of slain Osiris? Behold, the wings of the two goddesses who guard it!"

³³ Upon seeing it, some among them counseled withdrawal. ³⁴ But others prevailed upon them saying, "Have courage, lest these people make us their subjects, even as they themselves have been subject to us! Take courage, therefore, and fight!"

³⁵ And the Philistines went forth from that place and defeated their enemies, showing them no quarter. ³⁶ Each man from the camp of the Elohim fled in terror, abandoning their tents and forsaking their companions. ³⁷ Thousands of soldiers died that day. And the Philistines slew the sons of Eli, and they captured the ark from the encampment.

³⁸ At this did the Shemites gasp in wonder. They stood as mute children in the face of a mighty storm. They watched with eyes open, yet disbelieving. ³⁹ And when Eli himself was brought news of it, it is said that he fell backward from the place where he was sitting so that his neck was broken. ⁴⁰ Yet others say that he was murdered; some say by a Philistine, and others by the will of Samuel, at the hand of his own people who now scorned him.

⁴¹ Some among them despised the ark itself. For they said, "This is not the true ark that was crafted by the ancients! Were it so, this would not have befallen us!"

⁴² And others said, "Behold, now all is lost to us!"

⁴³ The Philistines took the ark to Ashdod, and they

showed it to the people. ⁴⁴ They paraded it through their cities as a sign of their triumph. In Gath and in Ekron they displayed it as a testament to their greatness. ⁴⁵ Yet the people were afraid, thinking the pharaoh would come to reclaim it, or that the gods might be wroth with them for taking it. ⁴⁶ (For upon seeing it, many thought it the true ark of Osiris, the one to whom their own master Dagon had bowed before the armies of Merneptah). ⁴⁷ And some said, "This ark is as a plague to us!"

⁴⁸ So they removed it from their presence and returned it to the precincts near Jerusalem. ⁴⁹ And they went back again to their own people, saying, "See? No harm or plague has come upon us! The ark is but an empty vessel, as the boasts of Eli were empty threats! ⁵⁰ Is there a plague among us? Nay, but the gold we have taken from the armies of our enemies shall be crafted in the likeness of tumors, and it shall take the form of rats. Thus shall we mock our enemies and their false god!"

⁵¹ Samuel therefore received the ark back from them with a delegation from Shiloh and Jerusalem, and in that day took credit for its return. ⁵² He told then people, "See how Dagon, the god of the Philistines, has bowed at the feet of Yahweh? For the ark became a plague upon them, and they have restored it to our people!"

⁵³ But some of the men who were with him had heard the Philistines boasting. And when the Philistines had departed, they opened the ark and looked inside it, so that the truth of the matter became known to them. ⁵⁴ For this reason did the Samuel order each of them put to death,

seventy in all, that they might be silenced and the nation might not be told of their deception. ⁵⁵ And after this, they removed the ark from their presence and sent it away to Kiriath-Jearim, which is the city of the woods, to the east of Jerusalem. There it remained for twenty years.

⁵⁶ And the people demanded a new champion, an anointed one they called "messiah." (Now messiah, in their tongue, means anointed one.) ⁵⁷ And they bestowed this honor on Samuel, who had sought it with his scheming. Then did he rise up to lead their armies against the Philistines.

2

¹ But the House of Samuel followed the ways of the House of Eli, becoming fat and wealthy from the labors of the people. ² The sons of Samuel, whom he anointed, accepted bribes and issued false decrees. They piled abuse upon abuse. They heaped injustice on injustice. ³ So now the people grew restless and weary of their lot, and they cried out, saying, "Behold! The Philistines are far from us, yet the House of Samuel is near at hand, inflicting woes more grievous than the blows of any army!"

³ Therefore they demanded of Samuel, "Give us a king, after the manner of other nations, that he may lead us."

⁴ But Samuel wished to preserve the station he had gained for himself, and so protested. ⁵ He said to the people: "This is what a king will do should he reign over

you. He will make your sons serve you with his chariots and horses, and they shall run before your horses. ⁶ Some he will assign as commanders of thousands and fifties. Others he will cause to plow his ground and reap his harvests. Others still will make weapons for his wars, or will help equip his chariots.

⁷ "Your daughters he shall take to be his confectionaries, cooks and bakers. ⁸ He will take your vineyards from you, and your fields and olive gardens, and he will give them to his favorites — his officers and servants. ⁹ He shall afflict your men and maidservants with labor, and he shall use your asses for his own purpose. ¹⁰ A tenth of your sheep he shall take from you. And you shall be his servants."

¹¹ Yet the people heeded not this warning. Did not the House of Samuel call their sons to service? Had not many of these words found fruition already by the old priest's actions?

¹² It therefore came to pass that Samuel feared the people might rise against him, as they had done in the days of Eli. ¹³ So he took counsel with himself and said, "I shall choose for this nation a king beholden to my word, who relies upon my counsel and dares not act without my sanction."

¹⁴ And he anointed for the people a man from the tribe of Benjamin, the smallest and the weakest among all the clans of Canaan. ¹⁵ This man was called by the name of Saul. He was great in stature and fair to behold, yet in truth he was as feeble as a foal made lame from its mother's womb. ¹⁶ At the coming of Samuel to his village, even he

himself protested, saying, "Am I not a Benjamite? Is my clan not the least, without significance? Wherefore should I be chosen to lead the people?"

17 But Samuel hearkened not to these words, and proceeded according to his purpose. So did he present Saul to the people, to all the sons of Israel, saying, "Behold the king who shall rule over you!"

18 And Saul did everything that Samuel instructed him, for he had not the means to challenge him. 19 Straightaway, after his anointing, he led the armies of Israel against the Ammonites, who had laid siege to Jabesh in Gilead. 20 And the king of Ammon refused their entreaties, saying, "I will withdraw this siege on a single condition: that you remove the right eye of every man among you, and in doing so bring disgrace upon all of Israel!"

21 When he heard this, Saul burned hot with anger. And he took two oxen and hacked them to pieces at the point of his own sword. 22 Then did he send messengers to all of Israel. With them, he sent the meat of the oxen, covered in flies and stained bright red from the flow of its blood. 23 And he gave them this message to proclaim: "Such shall be the fate of any man who opposes Saul and Samuel!" 24 So did he seek to procure by threat the loyalty of men, which he could not win through honor.

25 Then did he assemble an army and make haste to Jabesh in Gilead. And he feigned to the king of Ammon that he would surrender. But he did not.

26 He divided his men into three divisions, and he had them lie in wait until the sunset. 27 Then did he assail the

camp of Ammon as the night fell, and he slaughtered them from eventide to the heat of the following day. Those not slain were put to flight, until no two men were left standing together. ²⁸ Then did the men of Israel hail him, saying, "Truly Saul is a worthy king, and mighty!" And they gave him their allegiance that very day, along with the men of Jabesh whom he had rescued.

²⁹ But Samuel they credited not with the victory. And Saul alone won their praises.

3

¹ Now Samuel began to regret that he had anointed Saul as king, for he had grown mighty in his own right and beloved of his subjects. Yet Israel despised the name of Samuel for the sake his corruption and because he lorded it over the people.

² Samuel therefore assembled the people and said to them, "I have done as you asked of me and anointed a king to rule you. I am old, and the hairs on my head are gray as ashes. My sons are here among you, and I have led you from my youth until this very day. ³ So bring your charge against me. Whose ox have I taken, and whom have I defrauded? Whose donkey have I stolen, and whom have I oppressed? From whose hand have I accepted bribes, that I might shut my eyes to justice? ⁴ If I have done any of these things, I shall provide recompense. I swear it."

⁵ But the people said nothing, for they feared Saul and

his armies. Had not Samuel anointed him? And had not Saul himself carved up the ox flesh, saying, "Such shall be the fate of any man who opposes Saul and Samuel"?

⁶ In fear, yet not in truth, they answered, "You have defrauded no man among us, neither have you oppressed us. Nor have you stolen anything from the hand of any person."

⁷ Samuel therefore said to them, "Yahweh is therefore my witness against you!"

⁸ And he turned to Saul, who stood beside him, and said, "Here is the king you have chosen, the one you asked for! See? ⁹ Yahweh has given you a king to rule you. Do you think for this reason you can curse the name of Yahweh? That you can turn aside from his precepts and forsake the commands of the Most High? ¹⁰ But no! If you fear Yahweh and keep his commands, if you and the king who rules over you does not stray from him, then it will be well with you. ¹¹ But if you should rebel against Yahweh, his hand will be against you, even as it was also against your forebears!

¹² "Now raise your eyes and behold what Yahweh shall do in your sight this day. Is the wheat harvest not upon you? ¹³ Therefore, I shall call upon Yahweh to bring forth rain and thunder from the heavens. Perhaps then it shall be plain the depth of this foul deed you have done in asking for a king to rule over you!

¹⁴ "As for me, far be it from me that I might defy Yahweh and neglect to pray for you! ¹⁵ I shall instruct you in what is good and proper. Yet if you persist in doing evil,

you shall perish — and your king along with you!"

¹⁶ When Saul heard these things, he began to consider them. He pondered their import and questioned their truth. ¹⁷ And it grew clear in his mind that Samuel's intent was to betray him; that he had been chosen for the priest's own purpose, to be discarded at the proper time. ¹⁸ When Samuel had suppressed the enmity that had risen against him, he would use some pretext to cast aside his lackey and assume the mantle of leadership anew. ¹⁹ This he would pass to his sons in the proper time; in this manner would the seed of corruption be sewn anew in Israel. As their king, he could not abide this.

²⁰ Saul therefore rose up against Philistines and the other nations round about them. He smote the Philistine garrison at Geba, and he amassed an army of men to send forth against the enemy, for he sought to win the loyalty of the people through a show of force.

²¹ Samuel therefore said to him, "Go ahead of me to Gilgal. I will surely come down to you and sacrifice burnt offerings and offerings of fellowship. ²² But you must tarry seven days there and do nothing until I arrive there to instruct you!"

²³ He said this knowing that the Philistines would arrive before the appointed time, and that Saul dared not command the army without the needed offerings. ²⁴ When, therefore, Samuel failed to arrive as promised, Saul's men would be put to flight and his name would be uttered only in contempt.

²⁵ When Saul therefore did as he was bidden, this is

what occurred at Gilgal. ²⁶ The Philistines assembled there chariots beyond number with their charioteers. They gathered fighting men to that place, more numerous than the sands of the seashore. ²⁷ These went up and pitched camp at Michmash, and the men of Israel saw it. Then did they hide themselves in caves and thickets, among the rocks, in pits and cisterns. ²⁸ Some even began to leave the field, fleeing beyond the Jordan to Gad and Gilead.

²⁹ Yet still Saul waited. And when the seven days had passed, the rest of men began to scatter, saying, "This man is not fit to lead us! His army deserts him before his eyes, yet he waits for that cur Samuel's sanction!"

³⁰ And Saul knew he had been abandoned.

³¹ He therefore commanded his generals, "Bring the burnt offering to me, and the fellowship offerings with it!" And the men rallied to him, seeing now his strength of purpose.

³² But when Samuel arrived, he cursed him, saying, "What is this thing you have done? Sacrifice is a priestly duty, entrusted to the Most High. Do you dare challenge the one who made you king, when such is my right alone?"

³³ Saul therefore answered and said to him, "The men began to scatter, and you were not steadfast in your word to me. The Philistine army was poised to slaughter us at Gilgal, and I had not made the proper sacrifice.

³⁴ "What trick is this you have fashioned to ensnare me? If I made no sacrifice, the blood would have been upon your hands for your deception. Yet now you dare upbraid me for failing to keep my end of the bargain? You, who did

not keep your part with me? ³⁵ Nay! You are no more than a scheming charlatan, intent upon yoking the people to your treachery! ³⁶ You anointed a king to serve you, then thought to discard me and sacrifice the men of Israel on your polluted altar. ³⁷ May it never be! I stand now to oppose you. And my armies shall prove the right of it!"

³⁸ Then Saul therefore took six hundred men and departed from that place, together with his son Jonathan, and led his forces east toward the Philistine encampment. ³⁹ And in his fury, he swore an oath, saying, "Cursed be anyone who eats food before evening comes, ere I have avenged myself against my enemies!"

⁴⁰ But his son Jonathan had separated himself from the main company and went now in stealth with his armor bearer to the far side of the enemy camp. Then he said to his armor bearer, "Let us go up to their outpost."

⁴¹ Therefore his armor bearer answered, saying, "Do everything that is in your mind to do. I am with you, heart and soul."

⁴² So they went forward, passing between two sheer cliffs that formed a pass behind the encampment, and Jonathan said to his armor-bearer, "Come, let us cross over toward the enemy that they may catch sight of us. ⁴³ If they set forth against us, we will stand back and not engage them. But if they bid us go forth to them, we shall climb up and fall upon them." ⁴⁴ (He said this because he knew that if they should not come forth willingly, it would be because they were fearful and unprepared.)

⁴⁵ This then is what happened: When the Philistines

caught sight of Jonathan and his armor-bearer, they called out to them, saying, "Behold! The Hebrews are crawling out of the holes in which they have hidden themselves. Come up to us, therefore, and we shall teach you a lesson."

⁴⁶ At this, Jonathan and his armor bearer climbed up high into the cliffs that guarded the pass. And when the Philistines thought they had retreated in fear, they pursued them. ⁴⁷ It was then that Jonathan and his armor bearer fell upon them in ambush, and such was their shock that they ran in chaos, while Jonathan slew them from the front and his armor bearer from the rear.

⁴⁸ Now when the main body of Saul's army saw the tumult arise from the enemy camp, the king called them together and they marched forth into battle. And the Philistines fell back, but the sons of Israel pursued them.

⁴⁹ When, therefore, the men of Saul's main army entered the woodlands, Jonathan rejoined them. ⁵⁰ The soldiers were in distress from hunger, for they had not eaten because of Saul's curse. For this reason, when they saw a patch of honey on the earth, not one of them stretched forth his hand. ⁵¹ But Jonathan did not shrink from it, and reached out the end of his staff, which he dipped in the honeycomb and raised to his mouth.

⁵² Then the others who were with him drew back in fear and chastened him because of his father's curse. ⁵³ But Jonathan said, "My father has caused trouble for the nation. See how my eyes brightened once I partook of this honey? ⁵⁴ How much better would it have been if all the men had eaten this day from the plunder we gained from our

enemies? Would not our victory have been even greater?"

⁵⁵ But when Saul found out about this, he called all the men together and asked Jonathan before the entire assembly, "What is it you have done," whereupon Jonathan told him.

⁵⁶ Saul then declared, "May Yahweh deal with me in the most severe manner if you do not die, Jonathan!"

⁵⁷ The people, however, rose up and said, "Should Jonathan be put to death even as he has brought deliverance to Israel? May it never be! Not a hair on his head shall fall to the ground!" ⁵⁸ And they placed themselves between Saul and Jonathan, that no harm would come to the prince.

⁵⁹ Then did Saul go forth against Moab and against Edom and against Ammon, against the kings of Zobah and all the nations round about. ⁶⁰ But there arose a schism between the king and Jonathan because the king had ordered his own son's death and the people had prevented it.

⁶¹ Then did Saul begin to fear that Jonathan should rise against him, and that the people should support him.

4

¹ Samuel saw these things and lamented all the more that he had anointed Saul over Israel. ² He therefore sought a new way to discredit him. If he would, by force of arms, establish his name as Israel's savior, perhaps then he could

THE PHOENIX CHRONICLES

be undone at the sight of weakness.

³ When, therefore, Samuel learned that he planned to go forth against the Amelekites, the Most High sought him out and, before the assembled company, delivered him this charge: "Go now forward and smite Amalek, and utterly destroy them from the face of the earth. ⁴ Spare them not, nor any of their possessions. Slay man and woman and suckling infant. Bring forth the lifeblood of ox and sheep, ass and camel."

⁵ Now Saul could not oppose this, so he went forth at the head of his army and set out toward the city of Amalek. But to the Kenites who dwelt among them, who had been allies of old to Israel, he sent word that they should depart from there, lest they be caught up in the slaughter.

⁶ Therefore did they remove themselves and flee. And the forces of Saul descended like a great storm upon Amalek. As locusts from the desert did the appear, as if from nowhere. As hail raining down from heaven, they fell with force on the city of Amalek.

⁷ The beggar on the city street, they slew him, and his cup fell to the ground with a clang as his body grew cold and lifeless.

⁸ The child playing in the road, they slew her. Her voice rose in a wail, as she fell to the ground, then cried no more.

⁹ The woman at the well, they slew her. Never seeing their approach, she died there in a single moment. Her water pail half full still. Her body empty of life.

¹⁰ The man in the field, they slew him. With the blade of his own harvester they cut him down, like a fruit tree not

yet ripened. ¹¹ With his last breath, he cursed bitterly the name of their foreign god. And for his insolence, they separated his head from his fallen body. And they said, "For the glory of our lord!"

¹¹ Ox and the ass, they slew them. Still bound to the oxcart did the oxen fall, writhing. Still tethered to the stable did the asses fall, braying.

¹² Sheep they slew, blood spattering their woolen coats.

¹³ Cattle they slew, their udders full of new white milk.

¹⁴ Women they slew in the arms of their lovers, and children they slew at the breast of their mothers.

¹⁵ The air was thick with the dying breaths of man and beast, and the streets ran red with the blood of the city's people. ¹⁴ With the edge of the sword did Saul and his minions smite all of Amalek. ¹⁵ He spared only Agag, the king of that place, from death, along with the best of the sheep and the oxen, the lambs and the fatlings. ¹⁶ Those that were healthy he preserved. The weak and the ill, he destroyed from the face of the land.

¹⁷ All these things because of Samuel's pride and murderous intentions.

¹⁸ Yet still, it was not enough to assuage the Most High. No. For the sake of what was left alive, Samuel now cursed Saul before his assembled company.

¹⁹ "Why does the bleating of sheep fill my ears? And how is it that I hear the lowing of oxen this day? ²⁰ Did not I tell you the command of Yahweh truly, to utterly destroy the wicked Amalekites? Did I not say, 'Wage war against them until you have wiped them from the face of the

Earth'? ²¹ Why have you turned aside from the command of your god? Why did you do evil in his sight by taking the plunder for yourself?"

²² Samuel then left him and, in that day, began to plot how he might overthrow him. From that moment forward, the two never again laid eyes on one another.

5

¹ Then Samuel went forth into Judah, to the town of Bethlehem, and to the House of Jesse. ² No more would he count on tiny Benjamin as his ally. Instead would he enlist strength to back his purpose.

³ Judah was the mightiest tribe in the region, and many of its proudest men held no great love of the Benjamites. ⁴ Some had felt the sting of envy when Samuel chose Saul as king from the tribe to the north of them. And even now, Jesse grew suspicious when he saw the aging priest approach his lands. ⁵ "Are you come in peace?" he asked him.

⁶ So Samuel went forth to prepare a sacrifice before him, bearing witness of his intent.

⁷ After this, the two men took counsel together. And Samuel conferred with Jesse, that they might stand against Saul's armies. ⁸ He stated his design that one of Jesse's own sons should become king of all the land, and to this proposal the old man did hearken. To it also did he gladly assent.

⁹ But Samuel in his old age was shrewd and cunning, as

ever he had been. So when Jesse summoned his seven eldest sons before them, each appeared in order; yet not one of them found favor in the eyes of Samuel. [10] He therefore said, "Is this, then, all?" For he knew that Jesse had not summoned his youngest son, and he also had it in his mind that this youngest should be the one chosen.

[11] For who save the youngest is easier to bend? Like a reed in a soft wind, he follows the voice of his teacher. [12] And who save the youngest will serve his elders more truly? Like a pup eager for a new bone, he will do his master's bidding.

[13] So it was that Jesse brought forth the youngest before him, and Samuel anointed him straightaway.

[14] And his name was David.

[15] But though the holdings of Judah were extensive and its people many, still its armies were no match for the men of Saul. [16] So it was decided that David should swear allegiance to Saul and enter into his service until an opportune moment should arise to supplant him. [17] For, as has been told, the days of Saul were bitter days of war against Philistia, and whenever Saul heard of stout-hearted men who were strong in battle, then did he take them into his own service.

[18] It was therefore arranged that one of Saul's liegemen (who in fact had pledged fealty to David) should recommend David to the king's service, saying, "He is courageous of heart and fierce in battle. His tongue is quick and his aspect is pleasing."

[19] So Saul sent word to Jesse, that he might send David to him at once, and David entered into the king's service as

an armor bearer. ²⁰ Now there are those who say that David had served in this same manner before, as armor bearer to Jonathan. ²¹ It was this one who had declared to Jonathan, "I am with you heart and soul" when they had gone off with Saul unknowing to face the Philistines. And he had returned with him to witness the king direct his fury against Jonathan, passing against his own son a sentence of death.

²² Now, in these days, it is said that David entered into an alliance with him, and that Jonathan loved him as himself.

²³ Now why should this have been so?

²⁴ Some say it was because of the great regard that existed between them, each for the other. Yet others declare Jonathan sought to supplant Saul upon the throne. ²⁵ Others still say it was David who was plotting to seize the kingship for himself, and that Jonathan sought to preserve his own life in the event that David should succeed. ²⁶ For how should he expect to be spared should David overthrow Saul? ²⁷ For this reason, it is said, Jonathan gave David the robe of his back and his tunic, along with his bow, his sword and his belt. In so doing, he was yielding not only the symbols of his right to claim the throne, but also the signs that he should be leader of the armies.

²⁸ It was after this that the men under David's command went out in force against the nations round about them and claimed many victories, so that Saul's regard for David grew and the people acclaimed him, saying, "Saul has slain his thousands and David his ten

thousands."

²⁹ From that time forward, Saul ever sought to keep David close to him, for he did not trust him. ³⁰ He thought that by feigning goodwill toward him, he would entice the Judahite to say something that might give away his true intent, whereupon he could have him arrested and put to death. ³¹ But David was full of guile and showed no such intention, and Saul feared David's standing among the people, that they might rise up if the king slew him without cause.

³² Saul therefore said to himself, "I will offer him one of my daughters if he goes out against the Philistines in battle. ³³ I will not raise a hand against him. Let them do the dirty work for me." ³⁴ And he offered David the hand of his daughter Michal should he go forth into battle and slay a hundred Philistines.

³⁵ Yet David fulfilled his obligation and returned from the battlefield having slain even more of the enemy, so that his reputation grew. ³⁶ Saul therefore sought out another way to be rid of him, but Jonathan heard of it and warned David, saying, "My father is looking for the opportunity to kill you." ³⁷ And when Saul sent men to David's house with orders to slay him, Michal warned him and let him down through a window, so that he escaped. ³⁸ She then took an idol and placed it on the bed, covering it with a garment and crowning its head with goats' hair.

³⁹ After this, he went to Jonathan, and the two of them renewed their pact, with Jonathan saying, "Whatever it is you ask of me, this I will surely do." ⁴⁰ Yet he knew that if

David should rise up against his father to claim the kingdom, the Judahite would have no further use for the rightful heir. ⁴¹ Therefore he besought David, "Show me kindness that fails not, so long as I may live, and do not withhold your favor from my kin even after all your enemies are removed from the face of the earth."

⁴² Then they renewed the pact between them, and David withdrew for fear of his life.

⁴³ When, therefore, David did not appear before Saul, the king grew suspicious and knew that his son had betrayed him. ⁴⁴ "You son of a perverse and seditious woman! Do you not think I know that you have thrown in your lot with the son of Jesse, to your own disgrace and the shame of the woman who bore you?" (He said this because his own wife had left him and fled to David's camp.) ⁴⁵ "As long as the son of Jesse shall live, neither you nor your kingdom shall be established on this earth. Therefore have him brought to me, for he must not live!"

⁴⁶ But Jonathan went forth from that place with a warning for David, who fled therefore to Gath, a city of Philistia, to the enemies of Saul and Israel. ⁴⁷ There he sought to form an alliance with Achish, the ruler of that place.

⁴⁸ But Achish said, "Is this not David, the king of the land?" (He said this because David was the king of Judah, though he had sworn fealty to Saul.) ⁴⁹ Achish was therefore uneasy, for he thought that David sought to trick him into lowering his guard, that Saul's forces might attack him. ⁵⁰ "Is this not the man of whom they sing, 'Saul has

slain his thousands, and David his ten thousands'?"

⁵¹ David therefore, being afraid, withdrew from that place and made an alliance with Moab, another of Israel's enemies. In this manner did he show himself a traitor, both to his king and to his country.

6

¹ From that day forward, there was great strife in the land, which was rent asunder between the men of Saul and the men of David. ² Brother took up arms against brother, and innocent blood was shed on the naked earth, all for the sake of power and greed. ³ Neither side was without blame, and the heavens turned their eyes away from the carnage.

⁴ It is said that the men made a truce between them: that David gave his oath to Saul and in his turn promised to spare the king's sons from the sword. ⁵ Yet neither man kept his word, for both men valued power over honor and wealth above integrity. ⁶ In latter days would David, when he came into the kingdom, surrender seven men from the line of Saul to the men of Gibeon to be slain. And Saul, for his part, did not long sheath his sword against his rival.

⁷ After going his way from the presence of Saul, David and his men moved south into the desert, and there did he send emissaries ahead of him to a wealthy shepherd of that region, demanding that his men be garrisoned for the night. ⁸ (It was David's custom to go roving about and require that those whom he should come across pay tribute to him,

in exchange for a guarantee of peace.)

⁹ But the man refused him, saying, "Who is this David son of Jesse that he should be as a master over me? ¹⁰ Many servants are casting off the snares of bondage. Why therefore should I take the bread and water, together with the meat of the animals I have slaughtered, away from my own men and give it to someone who appears out of nowhere with such demands?"

¹¹ When David heard the shepherd's reply ordered his own men to strap on their swords, proclaiming, "May my god visit wrath upon me if one of the men on this shepherd's land is left alive!"

¹² Now the shepherd was a drunkard and a glutton, for which reason he met his end before David could slay him. And David rejoiced at the shepherd's death, believing his god had answered his prayers in striking him down. Yet it was not any god who accomplished this, but the shepherd's own weak heart and thirst for spirits.

¹³ After this, David took the man's wife to be his own.

¹⁴ But Saul took his own daughter Michal, who had been David's wife, and gave her to another, in the same manner that a man would bestow a mare or cow upon a neighbor. Then he came against David with a force of three thousand men, but David eluded him and fled.

¹⁵ Once again, he sought refuge with Achish, the ruler of Gath in Philistia, forsaking his own king to whom he had pledged an oath and seeking to take up residence with his enemy. ¹⁶ This time, Achish received him and the six hundred men in his company, and they made a pact

between them. ⁱ⁷ So did David and the kingdom of Judah withdraw their fealty from Israel and pledge an oath instead to the Philistines.

¹⁸ David then abode in the town of Ziklag, which is between Judah and the coastal cities of Philistia, thereby sealing their compact. ¹⁹ And David served Achish faithfully, acting without mercy against the peoples of the south. ²⁰ He led raiders against Gezer and Amalek and Geshur, all the way south toward Egypt. They were as men without heart or conscience, and wherever they went, they left not a single man or woman with breath still in their lungs. ²¹ In their greed, they took to themselves the sheep and asses, camels and donkeys that belonged to the people, along with even the garments of those whose blood they spilled. ²² And David cared not for the people whose lives he stole, but only that he might preserve his own, reasoning, "If I were to spare them, they might open their mouths and tell my enemies of my actions."

²³ Achish therefore placed his trust in David, so thoroughly did the King of Judah do his bidding, for he said to himself, "He has become an abomination to his own people, and such is the extent of it that he shall be bound to my service for life."

²⁴ Such was Achish's faith in David that, when the Philistines went forth against Saul, he wished to bring David and his men along with him. ²⁵ "Has not this man been an officer in Saul's own army?" he said. "Yet he has been in our company more than a year now, and his record among us has been without blemish." ²⁶ For he hoped that

David would be able to provide not only men to send forth in combat, but also intelligence concerning the ways of Saul on the battlefield.

[27] Yet the other rulers of Philistia worried that David might turn against them in the midst of the conflict and defect to Saul. Had he not already changed sides once? Could he therefore be trusted? [28] "Let David and his fighters return from whence they came, to guard the place you have assigned him," they told Achish. [29] "He must not accompany us in the field, or he will turn against us in the midst of the battle. What better way for him to regain his liege's favor than by bringing him the heads of our men?"

[30] Therefore Achish sent David away from them, but he did not turn aside and make for Saul's tents as they had feared. [31] Instead he returned to Ziklag in Philistia, for he remained in the service of Achish and his heart was steadfast against Saul.

[32] Thence did he set off again with his men to plunder the land around about, but when he returned, he found that raiders has treated him in like manner: that Ziklag had been burned to the ground and the women and children of the town had been taken captive. [33] So it was that David and his men were treated in the same fashion that they had treated others. But though they wept, they were not humbled.

[34] Instead, they pursued the raiders and overtook them, recovering all that had been taken from them while claiming the raiders' flocks and herds as their own. [35] The raiders themselves they killed, except for four hundred who

fled on the backs of their camels. They scattered from that place.

³⁶ And these raiders were Amalekites.

³⁷ David's men sought to keep the plunder for themselves, but David would not allow it and instead sent the bounty to the landholders of Judah. This he meant as an inducement that they might not rise up against him.

7

¹ At this time, the Philistines pressed hard against the men of Saul and drove them back, harrying them until they scattered and fled. ² They killed Jonathan and the other sons of Saul, Abinadab and Malkishua. Their archers drew back the bowstring and launched their arrows, which found their marks.

³ One of the arrows felled Saul, and he was grievously wounded, with the enemy in pursuit. ⁴ In that hour, an Amalekite rode up and found him, and the king entreated the man, "Stand here by me and slay me, for I am at the point of death, yet still I live."

⁵ The Amalekite did as he was bidden, but he took the crown that he had worn and his armband, and he brought these things to David in Ziklag. ⁶ With him also he brought news of Saul's death, and also Jonathan's.

⁷ Now some people said to themselves, "Why was this Amalekite so far to the north of his homeland?" and also, "Why did he return with news of these things to David,

unless he was in his service?" ⁸ For why should he have brought Saul's crown and armband to David, rather than to the king's surviving son, Eshbaal? Could it not have been because David so instructed him?

⁹ For this reason it began to be whispered that David had ordered the Amalekite to go forth and slay Saul. ¹⁰ But David denied this upon receiving the report, calling down curses instead upon the Amalekite. "Your blood shall be upon your own head," he declared. "Your own mouth testifies against you in proclaiming you have slain the anointed one of Yahweh."

¹¹ He ordered his own man to kill the Amalekite, and it is said that he did so to prevent the man from testifying against him, just as he had killed all the inhabitants of the towns and countryside during the raids of the southland in former days. ¹² And publicly did he lament for Saul and for Jonathan, yet in deed did he mourn them not, but instead took the crown and set it upon his own head.

¹³ But Eshbaal became king of Israel, and the two men continued the war that had begun between David and Saul. ¹⁴ When Eshbaal sent an emissary to discuss terms for peace, the leader of David's armies, a man named Joab, slew him. But the king himself admitted no part in it and put on a show of public mourning. ¹⁵ Yet what general acts in such a way without his king's blessing? ¹⁶ Is it therefore any wonder that Joab remained in his favored post even after the king's rebuke? For lawlessness begets lawlessness, and the thirst for power is never quenched.

¹⁷ Shortly after this, Eshbaal himself was slain, and the

men who did the deed brought his head to David as proof of their fealty. [18] Yet again David did not publicly condone the act and had the two men put to death, as he had done with the Amalekite who killed Saul. [19] For David sought to portray himself as always blameless, regardless of how many men were slain as he rose to power.

[20] When, therefore, he had become strong enough, he turned against his former patrons in Philistia and rose up against them, as he had risen against Saul. [21] He turned the sword also against the Moabites, with whom he had formerly made an alliance. [22] In those days did his own men proclaim him the favorite of Yahweh, speaking to him thus on behalf of their god: "I will magnify your name, like the names of the men most esteemed in all the earth. [23] I will set aside a place for my people Israel, and will establish them so they shall dwell in a home of their own and be assailed no more. [24] No longer shall they be oppressed by wicked people, as they have been since the days in which I first appointed judges over my people. And I will give you rest from all your enemies."

[25] Yet truly, none of these promises was fulfilled, and none of these things came to pass. [26] Throughout David's reign, he was harried by his enemies. A man named Sheba rose up in rebellion against him, and his own son opposed him, and had him cast out of Jerusalem. [27] Neither did the nation he had conquered at the point of the javelin and sword find rest, for the coalition of north and south that he founded continued but a single generation.

[28] Throughout his own day he would continue to

oppress his people, even those most loyal to him, should it serve his purpose to do so.

²⁹ When his son forced himself on his own daughter, then spurned her, he did not impose justice upon him nor did he remove his inheritance, but instead stood by while another of his sons brought vengeance to bear against the evildoer.

³⁰ Then he also took the inheritance of Meribbaal, the son of Jonathan (the same Jonathan to whom he had sworn many oaths) and removed it from him, giving it instead to the man who was his steward.

³¹ But perhaps the greatest of his offenses was committed against the most loyal of his followers, a Hittite named Uriah who had pledged himself to David's service. ³² In those days, David no longer went forth at the head of his armies, but instead charged his general, Joab the Slayer (for he had slain many men at David's bidding) to go forth in his stead and fight the king's battles. And Uriah went out with him, along with his fellows.

³³ But Uriah's wife remained in the city, and it came to pass that David chanced to see her bathing from the roof of his palace. She was very beautiful, and David's loins were aroused at the sight of her. ³⁴ He therefore asked as to who she was, and was told, "She is Bathsheba, the daughter of Eliam and the wife of Uriah the Hittite." ³⁵ David's lust, however, was not cooled by the fact that this woman had pledged herself to another. Nay, he desired her even so and sent messengers to bring Bathsheba to him. ³⁶ Then she went in to him (for who would dare refuse a king?), and she

lay with him.

⁳⁷ In due course, she conceived and was with child, at which news David was distraught. ³⁸ He said to himself, "Surely they will know Uriah is not the father, and there are those who know that I was with her. I must summon him to return quickly, lest I be charged with a grievous act which men may use as an excuse to oppose me."

³⁹ He therefore sent Joab the Slayer to retrieve Uriah from the battlefield, thinking the Hittite would surely go in to his wife upon his return. ⁴⁰ Yet he did not. Instead did Uriah sleep outside the entrance to the palace with all his men and retainers.

⁴¹ When David heard of this, he summoned Uriah before him and asked him, "Why did you not return home?"

⁴² But Uriah said, "My commander Joab and my lord's men are camped in the open country, sleeping in their tents. How then could I go to my house to eat and drink and lie with my wife? As I live, I could never do such a thing!"

⁴³ Then David tried to entice him to lie with Bathsheba by plying him with wine, yet still did Uriah lie on a mat among the servants. And he did not return home.

⁴⁴ Then David determined in the darkness of his heart that he should have Uriah slain, and this was the manner in which it should be done: ⁴⁶ David sent word to Joab that he was sending Uriah back to the battlefield, where his armies had lain siege to a stronghold of the Ammonites. ⁴⁷ And he told him, "Put Uriah on the front lines of the battle, where

the fighting is heaviest, and then pull back without alerting him, that he might be struck down and perish on the field."

[48] Joab therefore did as his king had commanded, and Uriah was left alone in the field to be slain by the enemy. [49] But David did not mourn for him. Instead, he took Bathsheba to himself for his wife, so that the child should not be thought a bastard and he himself should not be accused.

[50] Even so was a charge brought against him, but no punishment did he endure. Instead, it was judged that the child he had fathered with Bathsheba should die.
[51] So it was that David's dishonor was visited instead upon an innocent babe, and the blood on David's own hands was multiplied by the child's death. [52] The blame for this was cast at the feet of Yahweh, yet would any god's judgment slay an innocent babe for the folly of a king?

[52] Indeed, a king has the greatest of power, and can bring something to pass most easily without the need for any guile. [53] Yet a babe has no potency of his own, neither shame nor guilt, and is reliant in the whole on others to care for and minister to him. [54] How, therefore, is it just that the most vulnerable should be punished for the trespass of the most potent?

[55] These questions were not for David to answer, nor for his heir or those who came after them. As generations fell and new generations rose in their stead, men made wars against one another without ceasing. [56] The kingdom David had built was rent asunder once more, as it had been in the days of war between Saul and the son of Jesse. [57] Kings

rose and fell, and their realms fell after them, swallowed by the armies of Nebuchadnezzar and Cyrus, Xerxes and Alexander. [58] Thereafter were they lost to the mists of time or magnified in the cause of new kings who pillaged the false glory of their fathers. [59] Old gods were reviled in the name of new gods, and newer gods still were given homage.

[60] So it is that the world is turned on its head when men presume to speak for the gods, placing words in their mouths that are neither true nor honorable. [61] Over these words do men make war with one another, shedding the blood of their kinsmen for the sake of falsehoods and petty jealousies, over the lusts of kings and the writings of priests long dead. [62] These words they enshrine on stone tablets and sacred scrolls locked away in vaults of gold and silver.

[63] They speak "peace, peace," yet they set upon one another like ravening wolves, for the sake of pride and power.

[65] They preserve not acts of love or marvels of skill and artistry, but instead the sagas of wars so common they seem ceaseless and fill ream upon ream of their chronicles. [66] Let these stories be a lesson to those that read them, not a lesson to be emulated, but to be abhorred. Not those in which to take glory, but in which to take shame.

[67] For the world was not fashioned by a creator in blood and tears and broken dreams. Neither was it built on sorrow and regret. [68] But it is fashioned by the hands of those whose honor exceeds their bloodthirst, and whose integrity surpasses false piety. [69] As it is fashioned, so is it

also preserved as long as women of honor and men of virtue sustain it.

[70] This is the testament of Osiris, that each one should fight his own battles without visiting them upon his neighbor. That learning should always precede declaration. That kindness should swallow bitterness. That dignity should stand foursquare in the path of oppression.

[71] Neither look back at the age of the gods in longing nor wish for their return, for to humble one's self and honor one's fellow is the beginning of godhood. Its end lies not in power, but understanding.

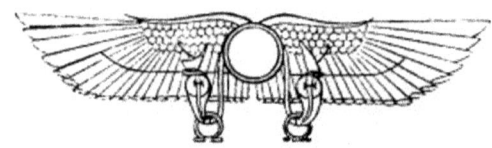

The Book of Tales

1
Origins

¹ In the beginning was Peace.
² And Peace was divided, giving rise to Fulfillment and Want.
³ Want, in her lack, gave rise to a single one, Hurt. ⁴ Fulfillment, in her abundance, gave rise to Repose, Indulgence, Greed and Hubris.
⁵ Then Hurt gave birth to Bitterness, Anger, Sorrow and Confusion.
⁶ These and the children of Fulfillment made war upon one another. ⁷ Confusion in jealousy assailed Repose, and Hubris met Anger on the field of battle.
⁸ Bitterness lashed out against Indulgence, and Greed

sought to visit despair upon Sorrow.

⁹ In these times, Repose was vanquished. In these times, Hubris and Anger mocked each other, locked in a battle neither could win, with each becoming more like his adversary as the fight raged ever onward. ¹⁰ Bitterness grew more bitter, and Indulgence allied herself with Greed.

¹¹ But Greed and Sorrow both increased.

¹² In time, the cacophony of their quarrels drove out Peace from their presence, and she withdrew to a place apart from her children, cradling to her bosom the slain child named Repose.

¹³ The others barely noticed Peace's departure, for they had long ignored her counsel. ¹⁴ In time, outside her presence, they forgot both her ways and her example, knowing not whence they had come.

¹⁵ But Peace took a new name, Memory. And she dwelt not among them.

2

The Five Creatures

¹ Four creatures found themselves together at the beginning: the eagle, the dolphin, the lion and the dragon.

² Each was asked which portion of the earth would be his, and they divided the realms among them. They drew lots, and the dragon chose first.

³ Said he, "I shall choose the realm of fire, for with it I shall

destroy my enemies!"

⁴And it was granted.

⁵Then came the lion's turn, and he said, "I shall choose the realm of earth, for the earth shall tremble at the sound of my roar, and none will dare to stand against me!"

⁶The next lot fell to the eagle, who proclaimed, "I shall choose the air. For no one knows where its next breath will take it, and in mastering it shall I become master of all I survey!"

⁷When finally it was the dolphin's turn to choose, she was overjoyed to find that the realm she had sought as her own was the one that remained - the realm of the waters. ⁸And she said, "No one can fathom her depths, no one can stand against her tides and no one can grasp her essence with their fingers." (For which reason she did not take fingers to her form, but fins).

⁹When all these things had been decided, a fifth creature arrived among them standing on two legs. ¹⁰This one was told that, because he had come late, no realm remained to assign him. But he became wroth at this and would not accept it.

¹¹So he went to the lion and said, "See how much greater the dragon is than you are because of his fire!" And the lion roared loudly, declaring, "None is greater than I!" ¹²When therefore the dragon came to sleep upon the earth, the lion buried him under a mountain. And there the dragon remains to this day, belching fire in his rage at the sky.

¹³Then the two-legged creature went to the eagle and

said, "Behold! The lion has subdued the dragon, who has defiled your realm with smoke and fire!"

[14] The eagle answered him, saying, "Am I not greater than the lion?" And he built a nest around the lion's head as a collar, and no matter how mightily the great beast shook his head, it held fast in its place.

[15] Then the two-legged creature went to the dolphin and declared, "See how the eagle lords it over everyone from his perch on high? How can we teach him a lesson?"

[16] But the dolphin said, "You are worthy to teach no one, Two Legs. For your ways are the ways of war, and I want no part of your lessons. [17] Behold! My realm covers all of the sea. What is the land in comparison?" And with that, he swam away.

[18] Then the two-legged one became master of the land, for he used the lion's collar to subdue him while the dragon slept under the earth. [19] The eagle thought to challenge him, but realized the other had tricked him into waging war against his friend, the lion, and contented himself with the realm of the air.

[20] The dolphin took counsel with them and said to them, "The two-legged one will make war on his own kind, now that he has no one else to left to provoke. [21] But we must be wary, lest he again seek to ensnare us in the net of his ambition, or lest his own wars lay waste to all the earth."

[22] The others were in agreement. And from that day forward, whenever the two-legged one approached, they fled and hid themselves. [23] It is not because they are afraid,

but because they did not trust him to recognize their beauty or understand their wisdom.

3

The Man and His Problems

¹ A certain man dug a hole in which to bury his problems, piling them up at the edge. But he dug it so deep that he found he could not climb out again.

² What happened then?

³ All the problems that lay at the edge of the chasm fell in upon him, until he was buried beneath them.

⁴ No one ever heard from him again.

4

The King and the Temple

¹ A great king said to himself one day, "Behold how greatly my god has blessed me! Therefore shall I build a wondrous temple in his honor."

² He conscripted slaves to cut down the trees of the forest and mine the quarries in the hillside. Then he levied a tax upon the people, so he could employ the greatest craftsmen from lands near and far.

³ These built for him great columns in the likeness of the trees he had cut down, but when the birds of the forest built nests in them, he chased them away.

⁴ They fashioned tables and an altar from the stone mined in the quarry. But when the men who had labored sought to rest on them, he had them shackled.

⁵ At last, the craftsmen decorated the entire temple with the likeness of pomegranates and vines, and of the moon and the stars in the heavens. But the people hungered because of the taxes he levied, and a loaf of bread became as rubies to them, a sheaf of wheat like spun gold.

⁶ When all was completed, the king stood back and marveled, saying, "Truly have I fashioned a wondrous tribute to my god!" Then did he betake himself to his bedchamber and rested from his labors.

⁷ In the night, there came a dream to him, and his god stood tall before him in the image of a woman.
⁸ "What have you done?" she demanded. "You cut down my forests to build a forest of your own, then deny the birds of the air their solace. ⁹ You overturn the earth, my resting place, yet deny rest to those who labor. ¹⁰ You set up images of fruit and bounty, yet deny these very things to those who hunger.

¹¹ "Behold this abomination. You have created a sanctuary for your own conceit and a house for your own adoration. Such a place I will never inhabit.
¹² You have defiled my true temple and made a false one to fleeting glory."

5

The Rich Man and the Island

¹ A certain rich man lived in a faraway city. Whenever he walked on the streets, the poor would come up to him and beg alms, and he would toss them a coin from his pocket. ² At length, however, he grew weary and said to himself, "If I did not appear so rich, these people would stop bothering me." So he began dressing in plain garb, but the poor still recognized him and approached him seeking alms.

³ After a time, he decided, "These people will leave me alone if I am no longer wealthy." So he loaded his entire fortune onto a boat and took it to an island, where he hid it safely away so no one could find it.

⁴ When he returned, however, the people still sought alms from him. ⁵ When he said, "I am no longer rich," they told him, "You are lying! We know you have been rich from birth. Do not deceive us!"

⁶ They would not believe him but instead petitioned him all the more. ⁷ When at last he could endure no more of it, he betook himself to the harbor, thinking that he might go forth again to the island and retrieve his fortune to placate them. ⁸ Yet when he arrived at the shore, his boat had been laid waste by the waves of a great storm and naught was left but planks floating on the water.

⁹ Having left his money on the island and having no way to reach it, the wealthy man was now destitute. ¹⁰ He therefore returned to the streets of the city and began to

beg alms there. ¹¹ But the poor still recognized him and spat upon him, saying, "Do you dare take alms that are meant for us that you may line your coffers further? Begone from here and leave us to our misery! Do not inflict your own beside it!"

¹² They drove him off from there, and none of the rich would give him any solace, for they knew him also as a selfish man and a spendthrift. And they too, believed he was seeking to line his pockets further at their expense.

¹³ In time, the man's days came to an end. And he was cast out to sea in a small boat that came to rest on the very island where his fortune was buried.

¹⁴ The one who has ears to hear, let him hear.

6

The Watchman

¹ There lived a certain nobleman who was afraid of the king and wanted to protect his household. ² He therefore went forth into the village and inquired among the townsfolk whether there were any who would be willing to guard his land.

³ Several men came forward, and he chose one from among them to serve as a watchman. ⁴ "If anyone should come here unbidden," he told the man, "be certain that he does not leave alive."

⁵ The man agreed and stationed himself inside the doorway to the man's home, where he waited day and

night.

⁶ One evening, while the nobleman was asleep, a stranger came through the door unbidden. ⁷ The watchman set upon him and beat him with his fists as he cried out in protest, then killed him with a blow to the head.

⁸ The nobleman, hearing the commotion from his chamber, hurried to find out the source of it. ⁹ When he saw what had happened, he fell to the floor and prostrated himself, for there in the doorway lay the body of his only son.

¹⁰ "What have you done?" cried the nobleman.

¹¹ The watchman said, "Just as you had bidden."

¹² The man, who was a widower, died without an heir, and the king seized all his assets. ¹³ Then the king said to the watchman, "Come and stand guard for me. For I can be sure that you will do as you are bidden in all things."

¹⁴ And he gave him three times the salary the nobleman had paid him.

¹⁵ When, the next day, the watchman came to take up residence in the palace, the king gave him a hearty welcome. ¹⁶ Then, knowing that the watchman would follow his instructions to the letter, he told the man, "Let no man enter my drawing room unbidden, save my only son, should he ask it."

¹⁷ The watchman nodded. When the chamberlain came to the king's drawing room, he was turned away. ¹⁸ When the privy counselor came to the king's drawing room, he was rebuffed. ¹⁹ But when the king's son came to the king's drawing room, the watchman admitted him, just as he had

been instructed.

[20] The prince entered that chamber and slew his father, and the next day he was crowned the new king. [21] But he dismissed the watchman, saying to himself, "Any fool could have seen that I did covet my father's throne. Were this man truly loyal, he would have betrayed my treachery."

[22] The watchman, having failed to prevent the king's murder, lived out his years in disgrace. But the treacherous prince, because of his cunning, prospered all his years upon the throne.

[23] So discernment serves the faithful and the faithless in equal measure, and trust misplaced is the undoing of them both.

7

The Price of Happiness

[1] There lived a man in a certain city who spent a lifetime accumulating wealth, thinking it would make him happy, yet all the gold in his treasury failed to brighten his countenance.

[2] He therefore sought out the oracle of that city and asked her, "Tell me, wise oracle, what may I do to be happy?"

[3] She told him, "Hoard not your fortune, but spend it freely."

[4] And he thanked her.

[5] Then the man went forth and spent freely on wine and

carousing. He bought for himself fine garments of silk and satin, and he purchased for himself a large estate with vineyards and stables. His home he furnished with fine couches, marble tables and expensive draperies.

⁶ At the end of this, though, he still despaired. So he returned to the oracle and said to her, "I did as you instructed, yet still I am miserable. Tell me, can my wealth truly be exchanged for happiness?"

⁷ She told him, "There is a certain man who stands near the back of the market every day selling vegetables. Go to that man and say to him, 'I wish to purchase happiness.' He will show you."

⁸ And he thanked her.

⁹ Then the man went forth as she had instructed and found the man with the vegetable cart at the back of the market, just as she had said. ¹⁰ He said to the merchant, "Good sir, I wish to purchase happiness."

¹¹ The merchant smiled at him and said, "This day, you are in luck! Come with me!"

¹² And the man followed the merchant away from the market and down a country lane to a small hovel next to a graveyard. The stench from the graveyard was such that the man held his nose as he passed by it, and he wondered what it was that lay ahead.

¹³ The merchant bade him step inside the hovel, and there he was greeted by a single spare room with wooden planks covered with straw that served as beds for the merchant, his wife and their two daughters. ¹⁴ A single table stood near a stove in one corner, and a draft blew in from

the window.

¹⁵ At the merchant's arrival, his wife stepped forward to greet him, smiling as she fastened her arms about his shoulders. ¹⁶ His daughters stood where they were and came running over to tug at his sleeve.

¹⁷ That evening, the merchant and his wife prepared bread and lentil soup, and their visitor declared it the best he'd ever tasted. ¹⁸ The merchant regaled his family with the story of his day, and they responded in kind. "Our friend," he said, "was sent to me, just as the oracle predicted," the merchant said.

¹⁹ The visitor was puzzled. "Did you also visit the oracle? And what was your question?"

²⁰ The merchant laughed and answered: "I asked her why money brought such sorrow," he said.

²¹ "Did you get your answer?" the visitor inquired.

²² "Indeed," said the merchant. "If not for your wealth, you would not be here with me this evening. For you would have kin of your own to tend to, a wife to love and children to raise. Instead, what have you but your money?"

²³ The visitor nodded and said no more.

²⁴ When, at last, it was time for him to depart, he said, "How may I pay you for your kindness? The oracle said I might exchange my wealth for happiness, and happiness in your company did I find."

²⁵ But the merchant shook his head and said, "Your payment is made already. The wealth you exchanged was the pleasure of your fine company this evening. As to your money, I want it not. I have treasure of my own that far

exceeds it."

²⁶ Thus was the oracle's word fulfilled.

8

The Seeker of Wisdom

¹ A certain woman went forth in search of wisdom. She went first to the priest and asked him, "How shall you answer my question?" ² And the priest pulled out a book and began to quote from it.

³ The seeker listened for a time, then asked the priest, "Who is it that wrote that book?"

⁴ "A great man who lived long ago," said the priest.

⁵ The seeker said, "Did you know his man?"

⁶ The priest laughed and said, "Of course not, for he lived many years before I was born."

⁷ So the seeker told him, "I came seeking a living word from your lips, but you have given me instead the words of a corpse." And she went her way.

⁸ Next the seeker went forth to the halls of government and asked the prefect of that province, "How shall you answer my question?"

⁹ And the prefect said, "Wait for a few moments, while I consult with my counselors as to the proper response."

¹⁰ The seeker said, "Do your counselors speak for you?"

¹¹ The prefect said, "Of course not, for they are appointed to do my bidding."

¹² So the seeker said to him, "I came seeking wisdom

from the mind of a leader, but I see I have come to the wrong place." And she went her way.

[13] The seeker went next to the prefect's counselors and said to them, "How shall you answer my question?"

[14] But they said, "Ask the prefect, for he is the one who rules over us."

[15] She then told them that she had come from the prefect himself, but they said, "We only tell him that which he wishes to hear."

[16] So the seeker said to them, "I came seeking advice, for I was told you were advisors, but I see I have come to the wrong place." And she went her way.

[17] Next the seeker went to an oracle, reasoning with herself, "Surely the prophet will know the path of wisdom." And she asked the prophet, "How shall you answer my question?"

[18] But the prophet's response was vague, so she said, "How are your words to be interpreted?"

[19] The oracle said, "Howsoever you wish," for the prophet had no answer, yet also had no wish to appear ignorant.

[20] So the seeker said to the prophet, "I came seeking the path of eternity from the heart of a seer, yet I understand now that the seer is blind." And she went her way.

[21] Next the seeker went to the arena where all the people of the city were gathered. And she called out, "Good people, how shall you answer my question?"

[22] But they heard her not, for her voice was drowned out by the cacophony of their own shouts and whistles as

each cheered on their favorite in the games.

²³ The seeker said to herself, "I came seeking wisdom from the people, yet they are divided against themselves. How can they find wisdom if they will not listen?" And she went her way, going finally to her home.

²⁴ There she sat alone and asked, "Shall my question ever be answered?"

²⁵ And in silence, the answer came.

9

The Traveler

¹ A traveler went on a journey, eager to reach his destination. Through many storms he persevered, keeping his eyes always on the road ahead and his mind ever focused on the goal before him: a gleaming golden city with crystal fountains and rainbow skies.

² He had been told so much about it, he was eager to see it for himself.

³ But when at last he came to the end, he found nothing as he had imagined it. Instead, a boulder lay at the end of the road, beside which stood a tiny shack that was boarded up and empty. ⁴ No one was there to greet him, save only a single watchman.

⁵ The traveler said, "I expected something else."

⁶ And the watchman replied, "You missed it."

10
The Ends of the Earth

¹ The people of a village asked the priest of that place, "Have you seen the ends of the earth?"

² The priest threw his cape back with a flourish and said, "But of course!"

³ So the people said, "Show us."

⁴ But the priest said, "It is far away. Only a priest is fit for such a journey. You would surely not survive it."

⁵ Then a young man among them stepped forward who was strong of heart and full of vigor. His arm was stout and his legs had run many miles. ⁶ He said to the priest "I shall accompany you."

⁷ The priest began to protest, but it became clear that the young man would not be dissuaded and the others among them were extolling him for his courage.

⁸ The priest therefore took the young man out of the village to shouts of acclaim and great hope.

⁹ The two of them went forth past the gates, past the farms and meadows and out into the wild that surrounded the village. ¹⁰ They traveled for many miles, and after the first day, the young man asked how close they were to the ends of the earth. But the priest said, "We will get there when we get there." So they went forward.

¹¹ After the second day, the young man asked the priest the same question, and the priest gave him again the same

answer, for he hoped that the young man would grow weary of the journey and reach the end of his patience. Still, the next day, they went forward.

[12] As sunset approached on the third day of their journey, it was the priest who had grown weary. His legs had become weak and his chest heaved with exhaustion, for he was neither strong of heart nor full of vigor, as the youth was.

[13] So after a time, he stopped in a clearing between two groves of trees, picked up a stick from the ground and traced a line in front of them from one end of the clearing to the other. [14] He declared, with a great deal of pomp and circumstance, "Here it is. We have come to it at last. Behold! The ends of the earth!"

[15] The young man, though, looked beyond the line the priest had drawn and saw there a stand of oak trees and blooming flowers, rocks, an anthill, a fallen log and a small deer grazing. [16] He therefore said to the priest, "I perceive the earth continues beyond this place."

[17] But the priest said, "You are surely mistaken."

[18] Then the young man asked himself, "Shall I believe the priest or shall I believe my own eyes?" And having decided at last in favor of the latter, he went forth and took a step across the line the priest had drawn.

[19] Then he opened his mouth and spoke to the priest, saying, "What place is this that I now stand, if it is beyond the ends of the earth?"

[20] The priest's eyes grew wide, for he was amazed. The priest's mouth fell open, for he was astonished. [21] Then he

said to the young man, "You have become a ghost and you have made yourself a demon. Because you have stepped beyond the ends of the earth, you may nevermore return to the realm of the living. Henceforth are you banished from this world."

²² He uttered an invocation to shun him, then he turned his back to him, shook the dust off of his feet and went his way.

²³ The young man remained there for a time, uncertain about what he should do. But after some consideration, he grew tired of standing in solitude and stepped back across the line the priest had drawn.

²⁴ Sensing nothing had changed because of his brazen act, he set out to travel back the way he had come and arrived after nearly three days at his village. ²⁵ He was on his way back to his own home when the priest spied him and gasped in horror, shouting for all to hear, "It is the ghost of the young man who fell off the ends of the earth!"

²⁶ The youth opened his mouth to protest, but before he could remove himself, the priest's acolytes and others of the townsfolk surrounded him and laid their hands upon him, holding him fast.

²⁷ "Take this demon again to the ends of the earth and remove him once and for all from the land of the living," the priest demanded, "for he is but a ghost who will haunt us if we suffer him to remain in our midst!"

²⁸ They did as he bade them, forgetting that the priest had formerly told them such a journey was beyond their capacity to endure. ²⁹ Ushering the young man once more

out of the village, they set out to return him by force to the place where the priest had first taken him. ³⁰ The youth objected loudly, saying, "If I be a ghost, how is it you can handle my flesh? And if I be a demon, wherefore can you bind me?"

³¹ But such was their fervor and devotion to the priest that the heard him not - or if indeed they heard him, they paid him no heed.

³² The priest led the rabble back to the place where he had drawn the line, which now was faded from the wind and from animals passing to and fro across it.

³³ When they arrived, they bound the young man with strong rope and sinew. Then, at a word from the priest, they cast him over the line (making sure not to cross it themselves) and began to build a high wall along the length of it.

³⁴ They labored for days, then weeks and then months to complete it, until it encircled the village and the surrounding countryside completely.

³⁵ From that time forward, no man ventured beyond it, and no one from outside came in.

³⁶ Many years passed, and the priest died, as did his acolytes. ³⁷ The hunters from the village slew every beast of the forest, for there were not enough within the wall to sustain the village and produce sufficient young that their kind might endure.

³⁸ The village grew poor or lack of trade and thirsty when its wells used up their water.

³⁹ At length, everyone in the village perished, and the

wall in time began to crumble. [40] Then did others come to seek their fortunes, and they remembered the tales of the village as it had been. These tales had been told to them by the descendants of their first king - a man sent in exile from that village in a time of legend.

[41] They remembered his tale and, when they came to the place where the village had once been, they founded it anew and named it in his honor.

[42] Thenceforth did it prosper.

[43] But no one remembered the name of the priest.

11

Two Fathers

[1] A teacher told his acolyte this parable:

[2] Two men lived in the same village. The first was a prosperous nobleman, the second a drunkard and a wastrel.

[3] The first man had several children and gave them all they wanted. If his daughter wished for fine clothing, she would have it. If his son asked for a well-bred stallion, it was his. [4] Yet when he grew old and feeble, and asked his children for a simple favor, they forsook him. They squandered all he had given them, and when he went to his rest, they laid him in a pauper's grave.

[5] The second man, likewise, had children. But he abused and berated them so they cowered in his presence. Whatever they sought from him, he withheld, and instead

spent what he had on carousing and drunkenness.

⁶ Despite all this, his children grew up to be successful craftsmen and traders. Yet whenever their father demanded that they serve him, they would do so without question in the vain pursuit of his favor.

⁷ When at last he died, his children buried him with dignity and great honor.

⁸ So it is that a kindness withheld is often more powerful than a kindness freely given.

⁹ When the parable was finished, the acolyte asked his teacher, "Is there no justice in the world?"

¹⁰ But his teacher said to him, "It is the lot of men and women to bring forth justice. It is our lot to establish and preserve it. Where we confer it not, it is absent; where we preserve it not, it perishes."

12

The Nature of the World

¹ A king wanted to know the nature of the world, so he called four wise men before him and asked his question to each of them in turn.

² The first bowed before him and said, "Good king, the nature of the world is manifest for all to see. It is first of grain, then of wood, then of stone, then also of iron."

³ The king thanked him but did not approve his answer.

⁴ The second wise man then came before him and bowed at his throne, saying, "Good king, the nature of the

world is manifest for all to see. It is composed of living spirit in four forms, the fire that is passion, the air that is breath, the water that is sustenance and the blood that is life.

⁵ The king thanked the second wise man also, but neither did he approve this answer.

⁶ Then came the third wise men into the king's presence. Bowing before him, he said, "Good king, the nature of the world is not fully manifest. It is composed of members too small to discern when separated, yet when brought together they become visible, more vast than the sands on the seashore."

⁷ The king thanked the third man, as he had the first two, but though he saw merit in his words, neither did he approve this answer.

⁸ Then the fourth wise men came before him, and the king asked him the same question. ⁹ "What you ask is a difficult question," he said, "for each man and each woman creates a new world. ¹⁰ The one who loves builds a world from joy and from kindness, from respect and understanding. The one who hates builds a world of sorrow and cruelty, of disdain and ignorance."

¹¹ The king thanked him and said, "You have answered well. Now assist me in building a world out of love."

13
Two Gods

¹ An acolyte went to his teacher and asked her, "What is the nature of a god?"

² She answered and said to him, "One man said the sun was his god, so he sat all day in the field gazing up into its radiance. A second man believed his god was invisible, so he sat all day at an altar worshiping him. Can you tell me the difference between them?"

³ The acolyte said, "The first is a fool, for he shall surely be blind by the end of the day. The second is a wise man, for he is pious and holy."

⁴ "But the second man shall also be blind," said the teacher. "For he sees nothing save the altar before him. ⁵ He sees not the changes in the tides nor the leaves changing color on the trees. He sees neither his neighbor's strife, that he may console him, nor his joy, that he may join in celebration. He sees only a cold stone altar."

⁶ The acolyte asked, "How then is one such as myself to learn of his god's ways?"

⁷ And the teacher said, "It is not given for us to see the face of a god, any more than it is given for us to look into the face of the sun. The sun illuminates all that surrounds it; so it is also with the divine. They reveal all that they survey. ⁸ If, therefore, you wish to see a god, look all around you at what is made manifest by the light of wisdom. And if you wish to be like a god, reveal wisdom to

others."

⁹ The acolyte then went his way. He nevermore visited the altar, and the world was the better for the wisdom he shared.

14

The Six Prophets

¹ The queen of the land called together all those who claimed to be prophets and said to them., "How will your god prove himself to me?"

² The first prophet declared, "He will send down fire from the sky!"

³ The second proclaimed, "He shall bring forth rain upon the land for forty days and forty nights!"

⁴ The third said, "He shall cause the womb of a barren one to be with child."

⁵ Another said, "He shall cause the queen to prosper in all she does."

⁶ And still another said, "He shall go forth before you into battle, and you shall claim a mighty victory."

⁷ Finally, the last of the prophets stood before her, and she asked him also, "How will your god prove himself to me."

⁸ But the prophet said, "Wherefore should a god prove himself to a mere mortal? In promising such, each of these others has proven his own god false. ⁹ Consider this: If their promises fail, they prove nothing. Yet if they are

fulfilled, it is from chance or deceit, for no true god need prove himself. [10] My god resides not in bluster, but in silence."

[11] She marveled at his answer and dismissed the other prophets from her sight.

[12] But the last prophet departed of his own accord, for liberty is the child of wisdom.

15

The Lesson of the Traveler

[1] A teacher told her acolyte the following parable:

[2] A traveler came upon a man bowing before a shrine alongside a great river.

[3] "Why do you bow before this shrine?" the traveler asked him.

[4] The man replied, "Because it is holy."

[5] The traveler said to him, "Come with me. I will show you things you will never see if you remain beside the river."

[6] But the man thanked him, but declined his offer, and the traveler went on his way.

[7] Sometime later, after he had crossed high mountains and seen magnificent waterfalls, after he had broken bread with peasants and princes, the traveler returned the way he had come. [8] When he happened upon the place beside the river, he found the man he had met earlier, bowing before the same shrine.

⁹ The traveler was surprised to find him still there, so he asked the man, "Why is this shrine holy?"

¹⁰ The man answered and said to him, "Beause the scripture so declares it."

¹¹ Then the traveler looked at the man and asked him, "Why do you believe the scripture?"

¹² The man looked at him, puzzled, and said, "Because my master has declared it."

¹³ The traveler then approached and said, "May I see this scripture of which you speak?" whereupon the man produced a scroll: taking it gently from beneath his cloak, he handed it to the traveler.

¹⁴ But instead of opening it to read the words within, the traveler took the scroll and flung it into the river.

¹⁵ Its owner looked at the traveler with dismay and asked him, "Why have you done this thing?"

¹⁶ And the traveler said to him, "So that you might come with me on my journey. There are many scrolls that speak the same as this one, and I shall obtain for you another when we reach our destination."

¹⁷ But the man's eyes only widened, and he said to the traveler, "What you have done is a sacrilege. You shall pay for your crime with blood." And he drew his sword.

¹⁸ In that moment, the traveler vanished from before his eyes. ¹⁹ The man called out for his master, but no one answered. He waded into the river in search of the scroll, but he could not find it. He bowed before the shrine, seeking revelation, but none came to him.

[20] When the teacher had finished her parable, she spoke to her acolyte and asked him, "Which of these two men has given the greater offense?"

[21] The acolyte responded, saying, "Surely, it is the traveler. For he has interrupted his neighbor's devotion, desecrated the scripture and spurned the teachings of a master."

[22] But the teacher said, "Was not the greater offense given by the man at the shrine? For did he not offend his own spirit by declining the traveler's offer? [23] Had he accepted his invitation, he would have crossed high mountains and seen magnificent waterfalls; he would have broken bread with peasants and princes; he would have been enlightened, and his wisdom would have been magnified. Yet he chose instead to remain in ignorance."

[24] The acolyte was astonished and asked his teacher, "But what of the scripture and the shrine and the master? Should their lessons be so quickly discarded?"

[25] The teacher smiled and said in reply, "The greatest lessons are those lived, not those filtered through mind of another. [26] A shrine is never holy; it is but a symbol of that which is. A scroll is never sacred; it is but a symbol of sanctity. So it is also with the master and his words.

[27] "Those who worship the vessel ignore the truth contained within it. They are as those who stand in the gateway, so captivated by its magnificance that they cannot pass beyond it. [28] The vessel becomes their tomb, the shrine a monument to their folly."

16
The Queen's Heir

[1] There lived a queen who was without an heir, so she sent forth a herald to all the people of the land and said to them, "Whichever one of you can describe me most accurately shall be become the heir to all my realm. Come, therefore, and answer for me this simple question: Who am I?"

[2] Many people came from far and wide and assembled before her throne one by one, each hoping to answer her correctly.

[3] The first was a baker, and she said to the queen, "A good and noble queen such as you, I surely know your tastes!"

[4] But the queen answered, saying, "Have you not seen the people of the village - the farmers and the craftsmen and the merchants? They eat milk and porridge each day. How is it that I should have sweets while they partake of gruel? [5] Nay, no queen should prosper so while her subjects are wanting. I am neither good nor noble, but my taste is to become such." So the queen dismissed the baker.

[6] The next was a soldier, and he said to the queen, "A brave and mighty queen are you! Your army is fierce, made in your image. And your courage is beyond dispute."

[7] But she answered, saying, "Have you not seen the enemy slain in battle? We have taken them from their families by the force of our hand. Our own have fallen also,

leaving widows and orphans to beg for their keep. [8] Nay, what you have seen is not courage, but cowardice. True courage stands fast against the violence men inflict upon one another. True courage defends the widow and orphan, it does not tear them from their households. [9] I am neither brave nor mighty, but I seek to become such." So she dismissed the soldier.

[10] The next was a carpenter, and he said to the queen, "A woman such as yourself must appreciate fine art, for you surround yourself with the finest woodcarvings in all the land!"

[11] But she answered him, saying, "The forests of my realm once were home to fox and ferret, to squirrel and starling. Yet now they have fled because of the woodsman's axe. [12] These woodcarvings of which you speak were once a living home to the hart and hedgehog. Yet now they are dead and taken from their rightful place. The art you see before you is but a perversion of its true beauty. [13] Had I appreciated the artistry of the forest, I would not have let this happen." So she dismissed the carpenter.

[14] Finally, there came before her a peasant girl who was nearly grown.

[15] The queen asked her, as she had asked all the others, "Who am I?"

[16] But the peasant girl said to her, "Forgive me, but I do not know. I came from the village, where my father was a blacksmith. He went away to fight the enemy, and he never returned. [17] My mother sent me to the forest to gather pears and gooseberries and walnuts. But where the trees had

been were only stumps, and the woodsman's axe had laid the forest bare. My journey led me here, for we are hungry."

[18] The queen said to her, "You shall have the choice of all the food within my realm," and bade her come forward to the throne.

[19] Then the queen stepped down from the dais and yielded her chair to her. "You have much to learn," she told the girl, "but the lessons your life has taught you are those I am in need of." [20] So saying, she went away from that place and never returned. And from that day forward, the peasant girl ruled the land fairly and wisely. [21] She called the army home from battle and planted new trees in the forest. And every morning for breakfast, she served milk and porridge with her own hand to all the members of her court.

17

The Woman and the Merchant

[1] A young man went forth to the village square, where he saw a woman whose face was not veiled, whose head was uncovered and whose ankles were bare. He thought to himself, "She is seeking to attract a man," so he approached her.

[2] When he greeted her, the woman told him he was mistaken and sought to return to her business, but the man persisted.

³ She therefore told him that she wore no veil because she wished to see clearly, she wore no head covering because of the warmth and she wore no ankle covering because she did not wish to stumble over the hem of a long garment.

⁴ Yet he did not believe her.

⁵ So he laid his hands upon her and sought to take her with him by force, but she raised her voice so that a crowd gathered around about them. ⁶ Still, no one in the crowd moved to help her, and the man who had lain hold of her cried in a louder voice still, "She has provoked me!" and "This is my right!"

⁷ But just then a merchant stepped forward, the richest man in all the marketplace. He said to the man, "I would speak to you."

⁸ The young man felt proud at being recognized by so distinguished a person and thinking that the wealthy merchant meant to reward him in some way. So he stopped his yelling, but still held fast to the woman.

⁹ The merchant said to him, "Tell me, are you the one who stole twenty pieces of gold from my stall when I left it unattended?"

¹⁰ The young man's face turned pale, and he said, "Of course not! Why would you think such a thing of me?"

¹¹ "In all my time at this market, I have never heard a man speak the words that you have spoken," the merchant said. "You said, 'She has provoked me.' ¹² Is it not natural that I should assume you believe my gold coins provoked you, as well? If you wish to take this woman who does not

belong to you, would you not also take my money were you given the chance, saying I had provoked you to do so?"

¹³ The young man was speechless.

¹⁴ The merchant then said to those assembled, "This man has nothing to say in defense of himself." ¹⁵ Those who were in authority came and took him into custody, whereupon he was charged with both assault upon the woman and thievery of the merchant's gold.

¹⁶ The woman thanked the merchant for his courage, but he said to her, "It is not I who showed courage, but you yourself. For I have gold and am known throughout the village, yet you who are without money and known to but a few stood up for what is virtuous."

¹⁷ And from that time forward, all the women of that village wore their heads uncovered and disdained the veil; neither did they care to cover their ankles.

¹⁸ And no man dared question their honor, because none could match either their confidence or their courage.

¹⁹ Time passed, and hours became days, which in their turn became years. The woman who had been confronted in the marketplace had a daughter, and her daughter had a daughter after her.

²⁰ The young woman, however, was modest and humble, and when she visited the marketplace, she adorned herself as the women of old, so that the people turned their heads to see her. ²¹ A veil was drawn across her face, and a cloth obscured her brow. A long and flowing robe fell down across the entire length of her body, so that it nearly swept the ground as she passed by.

[22] The townsfolk had forgotten that all women once had dressed this way, and they mocked her, saying, "She is hiding some disfigurement," and "She must be hideous!"

[23] The grandson of the man who had once assailed her grandmother still lived in that place, and when he spied her passing by, stepped forward to confront her. [24] In rudeness and presumption, he put his hand forward to remove her veil. But she drew back from him, saying, "It is not your right to do this!"

[25] Soon, others gathered around them and took the young man's part. They remonstrated with the woman, saying, "What is it you are hiding? Do you have a demon?"

[26] But she said to them, "My body is my own, to reveal when I choose it. You are the ones who obey a demon, for seeking to annul my choice and make it be your own. [27] You are nothing but thieves and hypocrites. Would you have me draw back your coats and pull down your trousers? Go your way, and leave me to my peace."

[28] They marveled and could say nothing to this, and one by one, they went their way.

[29] The veil is but a piece of cloth, and the skin is likewise but a covering. Regard them not of much importance, but rather the heart of the person which lies beneath them.

[30] The one who has ears to hear, let him hear.

18

The Faithful Dog

¹ Six shepherds took their flocks to pasture in the rolling hills many miles from the city. There they found a great expanse of grassland, and their sheep had more than their fill.

² The shepherds were content until it came about that a pack of wolves came down from the forest and attacked the flocks. Five of the shepherds lost many sheep, but in the morning they noticed that not a single sheep from the sixth man's flocks was missing.

³ They therefore went to the man and said, "What sorcery is this? How is it that the wolves have taken so many of our sheep, yet have not harmed a single one of yours?"

⁴ But the sixth shepherd said, "Friends, it is no sorcery. The wolves visited my flocks in the night as well, but my sheep were well guarded by my shepherd dog, Arturo."

⁵ Then the other men became jealous and said, "We do not believe you. We believe your good fortune is the work of a demon. If indeed your dog is such a fine protector, let him protect our flocks, as well!"

⁶ So the shepherd said, "As you wish."

⁷ The next night, however, the wolves returned. And though Arturo chased most of them away, he could not be in so many places at once. ⁸ When he fought off one of the wolves from the north, another came in from the east. And

when he guarded the eastern edge of the grassland, another attacked from the south.

⁹ One of the wolves came upon him from the west, and would not yield, sinking his teeth into the flank of a large, plump lamb. So Arturo growled and leapt upon him, fighting him fiercely until the wolf at last drew back.

¹⁰ But when the owner of the sheep heard the sound of the wolf howling, he rushed out to find the sheep lame and Arturo's coat strewn with blood.

¹¹ He therefore cried aloud, saying, "See what this dog has done? Now we see who the real demon is!"

¹² He went to the others and told them this, and together they made their way to the house of the sixth shepherd in order to accuse him.

¹³ "What treachery is this?" they demanded. "Your dog is the one who was attacking our flocks all along. This is why none of your sheep were killed!" ¹⁴ They then beat the shepherd with their fists and stoned Arturo until he was so badly hurt he could no longer raise his head. Then they went back to their own fields, congratulating themselves for having preserved their flocks from such a demon.

¹⁵ But that night, the wolves came again, and neither Arturo nor his shepherd was there to oppose them. ¹⁶ The wolves came in and devoured as many sheep as they could eat, for indeed it was a great feast. And when morning came, the shepherds were all dismayed.

¹⁷ They said, "What is this evil that has befallen us? Surely that devil of a shepherd and his hound from hell are behind this. They have struck out now at us in retribution,

as is the way of evil men. We should never have shown them kindness or mercy!"

[18] They picked up sticks and stones, and they went straightaway to the shepherd's home, where they slew both the man and Arturo. Then they returned to their own fields, saying to themselves, "Now, we will know peace at last, and our flocks will prosper."

[19] Yet again, the wolves returned, taking even more of their sheep, so that they became despondent and said, "Behold, the demons haunt us even from the grave!" But they knew not what more they could do. [20] From that time forward, the wolves feasted every night, until not a single sheep remained in the fertile fields.

[21] So it was that the five shepherds lived the rest of their lives as beggars and as paupers, never understanding that they had slain the ones who tried hardest to help them. [22] For such is the way of men: they see what they want to see and believe what they wish to believe, regardless of what the truth might be.

19
The Pilgrim

[1] A woman lived on the side of a hill in the high mountains when the rains came. The sky fell down in streams and torrents, until it loosened the earth on the hillside, and it came crashing down on the woman's home.

[2] Her parents and children, who lived there with her,

were spared. But her husband fell dead as the earth consumed him, and their home was utterly ruined. ³ She and her family had nowhere to lay her heads and no roof to shelter them from the storms to come.

⁴ Knowing not what she should do, the woman went to the village priest and asked, "How could the gods have allowed such a thing?"

⁵ But the priest answered and said to her, "Who are you to question the gods? Repent of your pride, lest you be cast down into the pit. ⁶ It is your own lack of faith that has brought this thing upon you. Had you not dared to question the gods, surely they would have watched over you."

⁷ The woman began to cry, and she went from there, disconsolate, feeling the weight of sorrow heavy on her breast.

⁸ After a time, she met a hermit by the side of the road, deep in meditation. The woman asked the hermit the same question. "How could the gods have allowed such a thing?" and said to him also, "What should I do?"

⁹ The man inclined his head toward her in greeting and said, "Who knows the mind of the gods? They do as they will, and I fear a humble man such as I cannot answer your question. ¹⁰ Betake yourself instead to the wise teacher. You must travel many miles from here on a great pilgrimage to reach her, but perhaps she will have the answers you seek."

¹¹ Then he told her of the place that she should seek, and showed her the beginning of the path that led there. "You will find the wise teacher tending to her garden, and

she will welcome you with kindness."

[12] The woman thanked the man and went on her way, gathering up what few belongings she still had and taking her mother, her father and her children along with her.

[13] So did she become a pilgrim.

[14] They traveled many miles, away from the tall mountains that had been their home, across wide rivers and fertile valleys, through pastureland and forest and barren desert. Then at last they reached the place the hermit had described. [15] She found the wise teacher, just as the hermit had said, tending to a small garden behind a cottage with a thatched roof. Her skin was dark and wrinkled, and her hands were withered yet strong.

[16] When she raised her head to meet the pilgrim and her family, her lips did not smile, but her eyes were radiant.

[17] "You have come far," she said. "Your garments are worn, and your bodies are stooped. What is it you seek?"

[18] "Wise teacher," said the pilgrim, "I seek an answer to my questions. We have journeyed to this place because we have no home, for the rains came, whereupon the hillside fell down upon my home and my beloved. And it consumed all that we knew.

[19] Why have the gods done this thing to us? And what are we to do now? [20] We built our home in the mountains for the safety they offered us against our enemies, yet now they have become our undoing. How is it that we may have the security we seek?"

[21] The pilgrim looked at her and said, "Behold this young seedling."

²² She held up a fragile shoot of green, its tiny roots dangling from a small clump of dirt in the palm of her hand. ²³ "Tell me, where would this fragile sprout be without the rains? Would it not wither and perish in the heat of the sun? And would we not perish also?"

²⁴ The pilgrim nodded. "Then it is the sun that is to be blamed."

²⁵ But the teacher said, "Without the sun, the plant would also perish, as would we all. Deprived of the sun's warmth, how would we resist the snows of winter? And deprived of her light, how would we find our way amid the darkness?"

²⁶ The pilgrim had no answer.

²⁷ "You built your home in the mountains seeking security," said the teacher, "and now you come to me in search of how to obtain it. Tell me, then, what is the nature of this security you seek?"

²⁸ The pilgrim thought a moment and said, "I wish for everything to remain the same."

²⁹ The teacher smiled and inclined her head. "If the eye never opened, it would not see. If the child never grew, she would not learn. If the night never ended, we would not know the day. If the shoot never blossomed, it would not produce fruit. ³⁰ Tell me, then, do you really wish for all things to remain the same? For if no thing ever changed, the neither would you perceive it, and then you would be dead."

³¹ The pilgrim knew not what to say. She closed her eyes, then opened them, gazing on the tiny shoot in the

teacher's hand.

³² Then the teacher said to her, "Come, let us speak no more of such things. Now is the time to take our sup. Sit at my table, and partake of my garden's bounty. Then I shall make a place for you and your family to rest this night."

³³ The pilgrim nodded, grateful for the teacher's hospitality, for she was indeed weary and in need of nourishment. ³⁴ They all ate a hearty meal and slept well in the teacher's cottage, so that when they awoke the next morning, they were rested and refreshed.

³⁵ The pilgrim sought out the teacher to thank her for her kindness, but she was nowhere to be found. Instead, there was only a note upon the table. ³⁶ It read: "I have waited long for one such as you to seek me out - one open to hearing the truth, though it be painful, and one in need of renewal. ³⁷ Now renewal has come to us both. This day, I depart for a new life, I know not where. To you, I gift this cottage and garden. and I am grateful for the gift of your friendship."

³⁸ So did the teacher become the pilgrim, and the pilgrim, having learned from her, became the teacher.

20
The Debaters

¹ Two men stood in the town square debating. The first was saying, "Faith leads to wisdom! Believe first, then you shall see!" But the other was saying, "Wisdom leads to

faith! He who seeks understanding builds the foundation for belief."

² Many people gathered around to hear them, until the square was overflowing with the thoughtful and the curious.

³ The first man said to them, "Tell me, is it not true that those who seek wisdom are always left wanting more, while those of faith are at once fulfilled?"

⁴ The other answered him, saying, "Those who see what they wish to see are indeed fulfilled, yet blind themselves to all else. And worse: what they wish to see may be but an illusion."

⁵ Then he said also to the first man, "Tell me, if faith precedes wisdom, how is it that one decides where to place that faith? ⁶ Does he accept the faith of his fathers or his homeland? Is he convinced by miracles and answered prayers? If so, does one god answer prayers more often than another? If it is so, I wish to hear of it."

⁶ "Surely," answered the first man, "such wisdom comes by way of revelation."

⁷ "Then you admit that wisdom comes first."

⁸ The man shook his head. "It is a different sort of wisdom. It is divine wisdom. The ways of heaven are not the ways of men."

⁹ "Do you intend to say," asked the second man, "that true wisdom is guised as folly?"

¹⁰ "Indeed," said the first. "It is often thus."

¹¹ "So whatever seems wise to me I should discard, that I may receive the proper faith?"

¹² "Yes."

¹³ "But I have faith that the sun will appear on the morrow, because it has been so each day throughout my life. I have faith that rain will fall in the winter, for thus has it always been. I have faith that the moon will wax and wane in its due course, because I have observed it. ¹⁴ Would you have me believe that the sun would hide her face from us in the morning? That the rain will cease falling? That the moon will go forever dark? Simply for the sake of faith?"

¹⁵ "If it is so revealed, then of course."

¹⁶ "And who is to reveal it? A priest? A king? A scribe? If such ones ask that we believe a thing that is foolish, I must at once ask whether they do so to further their own cause. For either they have renounced the ways of wisdom because they are foolish, or they have adopted the ways of folly to some purpose."

¹⁷ "The purpose," said the first man, "is to further the cause of faith."

¹⁸ The second man looked to the skies and frowned, then fixed his gaze once more upon his opponent. "I will ask you once again: How does one decide whether to place one's faith? ¹⁹ The priests of one god declare a certain thing, and the priests of another say something different. Without wisdom, how is one to decide whether the one or the other seems more reasonable? Or should I merely choose that which appears more foolish?"

²⁰ "You must choose that which is truly revealed."

²¹ "By whom? By the priests? The scribes? The king? Even now, is not wisdom still required?"

²² But the first man's eyes narrowed and said to the other, "Wisdom is but a trap set by the beguiler. Trust not your own understanding, but yield to the one who is greater. I perceive you have a demon."

²³ The second man laughed. "Have not you yourself said that folly appears as wisdom, and wisdom as folly? Therefore, what you perceive as a demon could indeed be the image of your own god.
²⁴ Regardless, why should I - or any of these good people - credit the words of a man who admits he speaks but folly?"

²⁵ With those words he left the place. And the crowd was amazed at what he had said.

21

The Mountain

¹ A student asked her teacher, "What is the world like?"

² And the teacher said, "The world is like a hill, and the world is like a valley. On the hill live all the kings and nobles, the wealthy men and generals. In the valley dwell the poor and the hungry, the laborers and ploughmen. On the top of the hill lie many stones, which are greatly valued."

³ "Stones?" asked the student.

⁴ "Yes, stones. The men on the hilltop roll them down with a single push, and those in the valley, through great toil and effort, seek to return them to the top again."

⁵ "But why?" asked the student.

⁶ "Because," said the teacher, "those at the top of the hill demand it."

⁷ The student was puzzled at this, for, she wondered, why would the people of the valley not simply refuse?

⁸ At this question, the teacher bowed her head and replied, "They dare not, for fear that those on the hilltop will cast more stones down upon them, and they will be buried underneath a multitude of rocks and rubble." ⁹ She paused and laid a hand on the student's shoulder. "And because they live in hope that, should they reach the top themselves, those already there will reward them with a place of their own."

¹⁰ The student looked into her eyes and asked, "If the stones are of such great value, why do those on the mountain not simply hoard them for their own pleasure? Why do they bother to push them over the edge?"

¹¹ "Because they fear the people of the valley would rise up and make war upon them, and that without the stones to encumber them, they would ascend in force against them." ¹² She smiled and asked her student, "What wisdom do you glean from this tale?"

¹³ Her student thought for a moment and said, "It is always easier to push a rock downhill than it is to raise one up!"

¹⁴ The teacher laughed. "Indeed, it is. And the world is oft unjust in this regard."

¹⁵ The student shook her head sadly. "Then what are the people of the valley to do?"

¹⁶ The teacher's expression grew earnest and her tone

sober. "They must learn that their true masters are not the men on the top of the mountain, but rather their own fear and the false hope to which they cling. [17] Then can they proclaim their freedom - as can you, dear child."

[18] "But how?" asked the student.

[19] "Take the stones cast down upon you and build a mountain of your own, then share it with all who care to ascend it."

[20] The teacher handed the student a single stone, and the student went her way.

22

The Suitors

[1] Three men sought a woman's hand in marriage. The first was a rich merchant who said to her, "I will shower upon you all the gifts your family could never give you. If you marry me, you will never want for a single thing. [2] I shall show you the wonders of all the world and you shall never have a care for what you shall eat or whether you shall have a roof over your head. [3] Your fare shall be the rarest of delicacies, and your roof shall be carved from the finest cedar."

[4] He bowed before her and kissed her hand, saying, "Give me your answer in a fortnight, that I may plan for our future together."

[5] The second man who came before her said, "My lady, you are the most radiant vision I have ever beheld. Your

virtues are more numerous than the stars, and your beauty outshines the sun. ⁶ My need of you is such that I would be destitute without you. Should you consent to be my bride, I will be ever loyal and never forsake you."

⁷ He prostrated himself before her and kissed her feet, saying, "Pray, give me your answer on the morrow, for I cannot bear another day that we are parted."

⁸ The third man who sought her hand then said to her, "Behold, I am content in life. Should you spurn me, I will not grieve, but should you accept me, more content still shall I be. ⁹ I cannot offer you a vast estate or fine linens, nor will I affirm you in all things. Nay, I shall challenge you should you offend me, and shall expect the same of you."

¹⁰ Then he said to her, "By your leave," and at her nod, embraced her.

¹¹ She said to him, "When do you require an answer?"

¹² And he answered, "Whenever you have one that is true and well-considered."

¹³ The woman then sought out her mother, desirous of her counsel.

¹⁴ "Which man should I marry?" she asked her. "What of the first man?"

¹⁵ But her mother asked her, "Are you a trinket or bauble? This is how the first one will treat you. He has enough of these already, so how greatly will he value you? ¹⁶ Only a man without a heart offers ornaments to one he wishes to make an ornament herself!"

¹⁷ "Very well, then," said the woman, "what of the second suitor?"

[18] But her mother asked her, "Is he a slave that he wishes to bind himself to you in servitude? Bound indeed shall you be, but *you* shall come to do *him* service, for he cannot manage it himself. [19] Only a man without a mind of his own offers unquestioning devotion. Truly, such devotion will be a millstone around your neck!"

[20] The woman frowned at her mother and then said, "What of the third man?"

[21] Her mother smiled at this and said, "The one who embraces you is the one most to be considered. Yet consider also this: You are not bound to marry. [22] Make the choice which seems best to you, my daughter, even if that choice be none at all."

[23] The woman did not marry the first man. Many years later, she happened upon him and found him destitute, whereas she had acquired a bounty without benefit of his affections. [24] He had parted with his whole fortune in an effort to purchase the one thing his wealth could not procure for him. After that, she never saw him again.

[25] The woman did not marry the second man. One day, she saw him following a woman down a certain path. He was always asking some favor of her, and a frown seemed ever knit upon her brow. [26] She never regretted spurning his flattery, for her own esteem was far preferred. After that day, she saw him no more.

[27] As to the third man, she saw him every day and they became the best of friends. Did they marry? That is another tale.

23
Two Sorrows

[1] A man asked his teacher, "Which is the greater sorrow - the one who has much wealth yet does not share it or the one who would share, yet has no resource?"

[2] "Truly," said the teacher, "the first sorrow is far greater. [3] The hoarder of gold will share nothing of value. Yet the one who is generous, though he has neither gold nor silver, will share from the bounty of his heart. And such, indeed, is the far greater treasure."

24
The Foolish Fathers

[1] A great general fathered a son, but his beloved wife died in childbirth. [2] As the boy grew, the man was often engaged in great battles and had no time for his son. The boy vexed him sorely, for he lacked discipline, as is the way with children. [3] So the man took to beating the child, telling himself, "The boy is unafraid of his own folly; in this manner shall I impart to him understanding."

[4] But when the boy came of age, he had learned to fear only his father's hand, and the beatings, which seemed wrathful and capricious.

[5] When the time came, the young man left his father's care, vowing never to return and taking with him the whole

of his inheritance. He shunned the way of the soldier, for he loathed it, yet he was ever restless and found no solace in the world. ⁶ His father's harsh corrections had not redressed his folly, but had instead preserved it, for now he feared nothing save scorn and disapproval.

⁷ The young man sought in vain to please all men and grew bitter when they, too, abused him. Soon, in his quest to gain their favor, he had surrendered every coin of the wealth his father had given him.

⁸ Yet as fortune would have it, in the course of time, the young man found a woman and loved her, and she returned his ardor. She was a woman of some means, and they lived without want in consequence.

⁹ In the course of time, she came to be with child, but like the young man's mother, she died giving birth to a son. The man was therefore left to care for the boy by his own hand alone.

¹⁰ He swore to himself that never would he strike the child, as his own father had done, but would instead protect him from all that was cruel and evil in the world. So the boy was brought up lacking nothing, and his father guarded him from every care. ¹¹ But the boy, like his father, grew up mindless of his own folly. He feared not the hand of his father, yet neither did he fear the world's harshness.

¹² When the time came, he too struck out on his own. And it came to pass that he, like his father, grew bitter when men abused him and when the world grew cold and distant.

¹³ So did the man who was brought up in fear and the man who was shielded both come to the same end. ¹⁴ False security is a door with a broken lock, unbarred against future hardship. ¹⁵ Fear rightly held is a true guardian, but fear misplaced is the gatekeeper of sorrow.

¹⁶ He who has ears to hear, let him hear.

25

The King's War

¹ A king bent on conquest sent great armies against his neighbors, who in their turn mustered armies of their own.

² The people said to him, "We are afflicted by this war, for we are bereft of those who provide for our sustenance. Not enough of us remain to pull in the harvest. Their food is not on our tables, but their blood is spilled on your battlefield. We beseech you, good king, recall them, lest we starve."

³ But the king said, "The lands to the east are green and fertile. Once they are ours, your bounty will increase. Fear not, for your harvest will increase tenfold once we have prevailed."

⁴ The people then said, "What good will that be to us if we are dead? ⁵ Yet if you are determined to pursue this quest, at least send your own son, whom you love, to lead our children into battle. Then shall we know, as a token of good faith, that you will honor your word to us."

⁶ But the king grew wroth with them and cursed at their demands, saying to himself, "Would they be king in my stead? What right do these commonfolk have to make such demands of me?" ⁷ Then he issued a proclamation, saying that no one should speak of this thing again and keeping his son from the battle thenceforth for as long as he should live.

⁸ The war then raged for many years, and the children of the land were slaughtered so that there were not enough hands to till the soil, and it turned fallow as the nation's sons and daughters perished.

⁹ But as to the king's own son, not a hair on his head was harmed.

¹⁰ And it came to pass that the young prince thought to himself, "Behold, no man in the world can hurt me. Do I not deserve to sit on my father's throne?"

¹¹ He therefore went forth and took counsel in secret with men he could trust, and arranged to have the king put to death, that he might supplant him.

¹² So it was that the king who sacrificed so many sons and daughters of the people, yet sought to spare his son, was slain by the hand he had preserved.

¹³ But it was not long before the people rose up against the new king and removed him from power, for the one who sacrifices others in the cause of vanity oft seals his own destruction.

26
The Problem of Evil

¹ A lame student came to his teacher one day and asked him why he had been born with a withered hand.

² "Some say it is because my parents did evil," he said. "Others because I have done evil. Others still because the gods are displeased with me."

³ His teacher shook his head. "It is not because of any of those things."

⁴ A shadow fell across the student's countenance, for he did not understand. ⁵ And the student grew displeased with the teacher, saying, "Then it is a grave injustice, and I am due recompense. Do you not see it, good teacher? Should this outrage not be avenged? What of justice? What of karma?"

⁶ Then the teacher set before him a wooden box and brought forth a handful of round balls. Handing one to his student, he said, "Cast this now into the box."

⁷ The student did as he had been bidden, and he watched as the ball bounced slightly sideways, then back up to him so he caught it.

⁸ "This is what would happen if you were the only person in the entire world," his teacher said, and handed him another. "Now, he said, drop both in the same instance."

⁹ The student did so. One bounced true, and he caught it up in his good hand, but the other bounced askew off the

side of the box, so that he could not retrieve it.

¹⁰ "This is what would happen if you and I were the only two people on the earth."

¹¹ The student frowned, but the teacher smiled at him. "Now imagine there are a thousand thousand thousand balls. Can you foresee how many different places each one might land?"

¹² The student shook his head. "I cannot."

¹³ "How, then, can you hope to predict the ways of karma? And how can you think to explain why a thing happens the way it does?"

¹⁴ But the student had no answer. "There are too many possibilities," he said, and his face became downcast. "It is beyond the abilities of a simple man such as I."

¹⁵ The teacher laughed. "You are no simple man, my friend," he said. "Nor am I. Yet for all my years receiving instruction, and more years still of observing life, such questions are far beyond my ability to answer. ¹⁶ It is natural for a man to think that, when he takes a single action, it will produce a certain outcome, as though a line were drawn from one point to another. ¹⁷ Yet each action is a current that flows outward from the center, encountering other currents, waves and ripples as it advances. It touches not a single point, but every shore it reaches, and those on every shore are changed in consequence. ¹⁸ If you can predict such things with surety, you are a wiser man than I, and, indeed, wiser than the wisest ones in all the earth."

¹⁹ The student went his way and was content. And from that point forward, his withered hand was not a cause of

questioning, but a means of understanding.

27
The Seventh Sigil

¹ Long ago, in a time of antiquity, there arose a great empire that was long at peace. Each day was much the same as the last, and all its citizens did their part that the land might prosper.

² Some were craftsmen, some were merchants, some were soldiers, some priests, some laborers and some rulers. These were the six vocations, and each had its own sigil.

³ The symbol of the priesthood was the falcon, which flew between heaven and earth. ⁴ The symbol of the craftsmen was the beaver, for its industriousness. ⁵ The seal of the rulers was the elephant, for it was the largest of all earthbound creatures. ⁶ The sign of the soldiers was the dragon, for its ferocity. ⁷ And the sigil of the merchants was the fox.

⁸ The laborers had their own sigil, as well. Their symbol was the earthworm, for its lowly station.

⁹ In time, the people grew so accustomed to their way of life that they enshrined these six into the book of their law. ¹⁰ It was decreed that a certain portion of their number would be assigned to each of the five great vocations, and those who failed would be consigned to the office of the poor.

¹¹ Much debate took place on how the members of each

rank were to be chosen. [12] Some suggested birthright, that the sigils be passed down from the first generation onward. Others said the priests and rulers should choose, and still others that the members of each class should choose apprentices.

[13] They could come to no agreement. So it was suggested that a certain number of lots bearing the sigil of each station be placed into a drawing, and that every person in the realm be called upon to draw from a great barrel when they were of a certain age.

[14] And each would then receive the animal that was the symbol of their station.

[15] Of the rulers' lots, there were the fewest, and of the laborers', there were the most. [16] Each person aspired to draw the elephant sigil, though many also sought the fox and the falcon. But none desired the earthworm.

[17] It came to pass that a certain young woman traveled from the far mountains to the capital for a drawing one year. She attended the drawing, as required, but said to those in charge, "Pardon me, but none of these stations befits me."

[18] They only laughed at her, saying, "It is not for your good that this great ceremony is being staged, but for the good of the entire realm."

[19] To this she answered, "Is it not for the good of the entire realm that I pursue the station that most befits me? In this way, I would be the greatest blessing to all whom I encounter."

[20] But the men would not listen to her, saying instead,

"You shall be trained for whatever role you may choose. Your hand shall choose it, and it shall become a part of you, as surely as are the hairs on your head." [21] Then they took her to the barrel and demanded that she choose.

[22] She became desperate, saying, "Can my fate be changed should I not do well in the role that is assigned me?"

[23] The men, however, answered her with a saying common among the people, "A fox cannot grow wings like a falcon, and an earthworm is ever an earthworm."

[24] Like many others that day, she drew the lot with the earthworm sigil, and was sent forth to a camp of miners whose task it was to dig coal from the root of the mountains. [25] She was given these things to take with her on her journey: a knapsack with a change of clothes, a thick jacket, a pan for cooking and a single earthworm.

[26] This last creature was her only companion during the weeks ahead, and it grew quickly on the leaves she fed it. [27] She noticed its appearance was not entirely like those belonging to her fellow laborers, but she thought little of it until one day it disappeared into a silk cocoon.

[28] When this happened, she understood the truth of it - that she had been given not an earthworm, but a caterpillar. [29] The other laborers saw this thing and marveled, but she hid the cocoon away from the overseer, so he could not see it. Then she patiently waited until it broke forth anew as a butterfly with sparkling, many-colored wings.

[30] She brought it forth, but it did not fly away from her, and the one in charge of the miners caught sight of it and

demanded, "Where did you get this thing?"

31 Then she said to him, "It is the sigil of my station that was given to me when I was brought here."

32 The overseer frowned, saying, "Never have I seen this before. Show me the earthworm you were given."

33 But she told him, "Here it is." And the others confirmed it.

34 "Behold," she said, "the sign of the artists. The butterfly. The seventh sigil."

35 All those present saw it as a sign that a new station had been ratified by heaven. 36 Therefore was the woman taken to the high seat of the empire, where she was granted a place as the court's royal artist. Indeed, such had been the role she sought from the outset.

37 She worked with diligence and great skill, so that every work she produced was a masterpiece.

38 So greatly did she impress the high ruler that he swore to grant her a single blessing, whatever she might ask save the throne itself. And she asked of him, "Would that the drawing of lots be abolished, and that all the people of the realm may be trusted to pursue the station to which the most aspire."

39 Her request was granted at once, and soon a new saying was heard across the land.

40 "My worm may, in fact, be a butterfly. And if a fox seeks the wings of a falcon, then who are you to deny him?"

28
The Three Words

¹ A certain man had long been afflicted with a palsy, such that the side of his face drooped and distorted. ² From childhood, the others in the village would deride and scorn him, and whenever he opened his mouth to speak, they heard nothing of what he said, though he spoke only three words.

³ "Forgive us," they mocked, "for we cannot hear your words, so distracting is your face."

⁴ He turned aside for them and soon stopped speaking altogether, so that those who made his acquaintance thought him mute. Yet secretly, he thought to himself, "If only I were handsome, then the people would listen."

⁵ Then, one day, he awoke to find that the palsy had departed. Spying his reflection in a pool of water, he realized that not only was his affliction gone, but his countenance was entirely without blemish.

⁶ Those who had known him before did not recognize him, and those who met him anew heaped praise upon him, saying, "Behold! What radiant features! Surely, this is the son of a god!"

⁷ After a time, he even dared to speak again, but again, no one deigned to listen. Again, they told him, as before, "Forgive us, for we cannot hear your words, so distracting is your face."

⁸ And again he fell silent.

⁹ In time, the years took their toll on his countenance, as they are wont to do with every man. His radiance faded, and he became simply a common-looking man, neither radiant nor afflicted.

¹⁰ At last, he thought to himself, perhaps the people will listen to me. So he raised his voice once again, but once again, no one listened, for his common looks did not draw their attention.

¹¹ "Forgive us," they said, "for we did not hear your words, so common is your aspect."

¹² So he repeated the three words he had been speaking from the beginning.

¹³ "Kindly show love."

¹⁴ And still, no one heard.

29

The Moon, the Daffodils and the Candle

¹ A boy in the village heard from a storyteller that the moon was made of cheese. When, therefore, his father told him that cheese came from cows, he thought it a wonder.

² One night, when staring at sky, he noticed certain stars in heavens made the shape of a cow, and he imagined that the moon must have come from this place.

³ He spoke excitedly of this to his father, but the man was hard at work and did not correct his son's exuberance. In consequence, the boy became confirmed in his belief of it, through his childhood and beyond.

⁴ When he grew to manhood, he recalled the cow and the moon and the heavens. He found a plot of land on which to grow grain and fruit trees, and he made a pact with the landholder to supply much of his crop in exchange for his tenancy.

⁵ Once this was accomplished, and when the time was right, he purchased a cow. She gave him milk aplenty, of which he drank his fill and sold the rest.

⁶ But he knew naught of how cheese was made, so he reasoned that it must be given at the full of the moon.

⁷ He watched long, over many months, but his cow gave only milk. ⁸ At last, distraught, he sold her, convinced she was afflicted with some malady that prevented her from bringing forth cheese.

⁹ For a short while, he lived off the profit from her sale, but before long, it came to pass that this resource was nearly exhausted.

¹⁰ About that time, it so happened that he met a man along the roadside, selling flowers. ¹¹ "Behold the bright, gold petals of the daffodil!" he said. "If you purchase these, they will surely bring you fortune, their golden blossoms drawing to you golden coins, which shall enrich you."

¹² The young man was impressed at this and, taken in by the merchant's confidence, believed his tale. ¹³ He therefore gave him the last of what he had earned from the cow that he might procure the flowers, along with an abundance of seeds.

¹⁴ He returned to his home straightaway, whereupon he uprooted the fruit trees and plowed under the grain fields

that he might plant the flowers far and wide. [15] But in the course of time, their color faded, and the gold gave way to brown. The day came when they shed their petals, and the young man saw no golden coins.

[16] Before long, he knew, the owner of the land would come calling and demand the grain he had plowed under to plant the flowers, and the fruit of the trees he had cut down.

[17] Desperate, he sought out a book he had been given as a child and found a line from it, which counseled:

[18] Find a candle, dark and red

Burn it long beside your bed

Your enemies, their blood shall run

Before the morrow's rising sun

[19] The young man found such a candle and lit its taper, setting it at his bedside just as the book had instructed.

[20] But in the night, the hot wax dripped onto the pages of the book he had been reading. These pages soon caught fire, and the flames did spread as the young man slept, until the entire house was ablaze with their fury.

[21] In a single hour, all was consumed.

[22] In the course of time, the landholder found another tenant - one who did not believe that the moon was made of cheese. Or that golden flowers brought forth coins of precious metal. Or that red candles could vanquish an enemy.

[23] He rose early by the light of the moon to tend his crops. [24] He planted golden flowers at the base of his fruit trees that the faithful honeybee might visit them. [25] Then,

he collected the true gold the bees produced, the soft, sweet honey they brought forth, which he sold at the village market for a profit.

[26] Soon, he had saved enough to buy the land from its owner.

[27] As for candles, he used them only to read by, and he always snuffed them out before letting his eyelids close for the evening. [28] Their color mattered little to him, only the words their light revealed, which made him all the wiser.

30

The Blight and the Messengers

[1] A landholder set off on a journey of trade and commerce, leaving his sister to tend his fields.

[2] One afternoon, she found the beginnings of a blight upon his fruit trees. Not knowing the source of it, she grew concerned, for the fruit was a goodly part of her brother's livelihood.

[3] She inquired of those who tended the neighboring fields, but none could say the cause of it. She therefore reasoned with herself, saying, "My brother is a master gardener. Were he here, he would discern the cause of this blight and heal it. But since he is abroad, the whole crop may perish."

[4] She determined to send a runner to him straightaway, bearing an urgent message to bid him return that the fruit might be salvaged. [5] But as it was nearing the harvest, no

one among the landholders could spare any of their field hands to make the journey. ⁶ She therefore found a beggar by the town gate and said to him, "I will pay you handsomely if you tell my brother of these things."

⁷ To this he readily agreed, and set out on his way immediately.

⁸ When at last he found the woman's brother, the beggar sought to deliver the message as promised.

⁹ But when the landholder saw the man's rags and drawn countenance, he said to him, "You have come here to deceive me while I bargain for new fortune. Which one of my enemies has sent you?"

¹⁰ The beggar opened his mouth to answer, and said that the man's sister had sent him. But the landowner would suffer that he speak no further.

¹¹ Instead, he called upon the authorities and proclaimed to them, "See this man here? He is a liar, sent by men to cheat me of my fortune. He speaks in my sister's name, yet I know him not. ¹² Arrest him, therefore, and have him cast into your dungeons."

¹³ When the messenger did not return and the blight became worse on the leaves of the trees, the landholder's sister grew worried. ¹⁴ Fearing the first messenger had been waylaid, she sought a second for the task, but still no man of the village cold be spared to embark upon such a journey.

¹⁵ As chance would have it, a foreigner was in that place on a visit from some distant land far northward. ¹⁶ When the woman heard of this, she approached him, and he

consented to bear her message, for he was young and keen to see the world.

[17] She paid him well for his troubles and sent him on his way to the town where her brother had business, whereupon he began inquiring where the man could be found.

[18] At length, he located the woman's brother and opened his mouth to deliver her message. But alas, the man would not hear him. [19] Instead, he said to the messenger, "Who are you, a pale-skinned northman, to intrude upon me thus?" (For the people of his own land were all swarthy in complexion.) [20] "Your kind are all layabouts and swindlers, every last one of you. You sleep the winter away because the sun never shines on your land! [21] Begone from my presence, or I shall sell you to the slavers."

[22] The northman, fearing for his safety, departed with haste, leaving his message undelivered, and went forth to continue his travels.

[23] By this time, all the fruit of the landholder's trees had turned rotten, and all the leaves had fallen away from their branches. [24] Soon, every last one of them had withered from the blight, and when he returned at last to discover it, he despaired greatly.

[25] "What has happened?" he asked his sister. "And why did you send no messenger? Had I known of this blight, I could have cured it. But as it is, my dealings abroad proved unfruitful, and now my entire grove is lost!"

[26] His sister told him that she had sent two messengers to him, but that neither had returned to her.

[27] It never occurred to the man that she was speaking of the beggar and the foreigner, for to his eyes, such were less than men.

[28] His fortune forfeit, the man was forced to sell his land for a pittance and seek a new means of supporting himself. It is said that, at the last, he became a messenger himself, but that no one listened to a word he had to say.

STEPHEN H. PROVOST

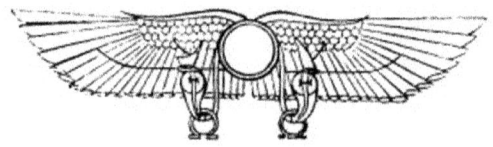

The Book of Teachings

1

Integrity

[1] The All is a singular, unified whole. It is not at odds with itself. The limits of each one's perspective create the illusion of conflict, when in fact, all things are in balance and harmony.

[2] Try as we may, we cannot oppose this. The human beast may cut down forests, topple kingdoms, plough up the earth and, through hubris, create a wasteland. [3] But amid these things, the All just winks, knowing that we are a part of her.

[4] Who are we to oppose her? Within her womb, her heart and her mind lie worlds upon worlds uncounted, dying and being born across a tapestry beyond imagining.

⁵ This world shall pass away, whether at our hand or through some other power. To the All, it makes no difference. Its end shall be but a moment in eternity, a gateway through which the All must pass in perpetual self-renewal.

⁶ One may ask, "Can the All be destroyed from without?"

⁷ Such a question has no meaning. For how can anything exist outside the All, which by her very nature is inclusive? ⁸ We are a part of her and cannot venture beyond her essence. We can only act in such a way as to help define her balance.

⁹ This balance reflects her integrity. It is neither a cord pulled taut nor pool cold and stagnant, but remains in every way dynamic. ¹⁰ Its nature is change, and its symbol is the unified circle. Having neither beginning nor end, it is self-fulfilling and self-perpetuating. ¹¹ Its names are the All, the Source and Completion. It is the beginning and the end, containing both but having neither, and even this symbol is wholly inadequate.

¹² Some call it "God," but such a name is inadequate. It is at once creator and creation, its emanations remaining a part of it.

¹³ The All is harmony amid dissonance, constancy in chaos. Her face we see in glimpses and reflections, our perception ever incomplete and flawed. ¹⁴ For this reason, we remain humble and also vigilant: humble in the knowledge that we may never know the All, yet expectant that more will be revealed, even as her visage changes.

[15] The All is herself the very process of discovery – ever changing, always shifting as the desert sands that erase the traveler's footprints. Nothing remains as it once was. [16] Never achieved, she is always achieving.

[17] To our eyes, her essence seems chaos that may not be grasped. Yet our perspective is what deceives us. [18] From within, we see but fragments of the All, bits and pieces swirling in a maelstrom, frantic in their turbulence and unfinished in their aspect.

[19] Still, it is we who are unfinished, and the All is ever becoming, for life is transformation.

[20] Do not say to yourself that the All is never ending. Say instead, the All is ever beginning.

[21] Change is continual. The All is neither a line stretching forward nor a single point on that line, nor is it a circle or even a spiral, though these last are closer to its nature. [22] Still, the mind cannot contain it, nor can any shape encompass it. It is always unfolding and ever transforming.

[23] When this is understood, we free ourselves from the bonds of Now and take on the aspect of becoming.

[24] We bow to past lessons but no longer serve them.

[25] We welcome each instant, but do not lay hold of it.

[26] We build bridges for the future without presumption.

[27] No moment is separate unto itself, but the All flows in a single stream that transcends what we call time.

[28] There are those who say that every road leads to a single summit, and there are indeed many such roads. [29] Yet some roads lead away from the mountain, and still others

begird the base of it, but never ascend. If you wish to reach the summit, be sure the road you choose leads upward.

[30] If all things are fated, nothing ever comes to pass, for it has happened already, and "already" has no meaning.

[31] Love without kindness is not love.

[32] Kindness without justice is not kindness

[33] Justice without understanding is not justice.

[34] Understanding without humility is not understanding.

[35] Humility without truth is not humility.

[36] Truth without love is not truth.

2

Perception

[1] Perception is that which grants us access to the All. If something exists apart from perception, can we know it? If it does not exist, even with perception, can we discover it?

[2] Without a doorway, no key will avail us. And without the key, the way is barred, as surely as if nothing lay beyond.

[3] That which is perceived is no more than the tiniest fraction of the All.

[4] Consider the dog, who cringes at the sound of a whistle no human can hear. To us, it is but silence.

[5] Consider the one who is blind and the one whose ears are deaf.

[6] Consider also the sound of the thunder, the voice issued forth by the lightning, which arrives long after his

blade rends the night in two.

⁷ Many things are seen, yet not perceived.

⁸ Many things are heard, yet not noted.

⁹ Many more still are felt, yet are ignored.

¹⁰ Even those perceived are soon forgotten, save for a precious few. These are stored away and seldom brought to mind, unless the need arises or some new thing perceived recalls them.

¹¹ Memory itself may shift with time, fading with the passing years or taking forms far different with the turnings of each life's path.

¹² Memories shaped by fulfillment and regret are but ghosts and shades of times now past.

¹³ It is not well to trust alone one's own remembrance; test it instead against the words of trusted companions.

¹⁴ Perception shared carries weight and power, for good or ill. If true, it bolsters truth; if false, it creates an artificial truth of its own, a house of lies built upon deceit's foundation.

¹⁵ Once the lessons of memory are corrupted, they are either lost or must be relearned. The cost is great, the sorrow needless.

¹⁶ Those without scruple purchase the truth with fear and corrupt memory with spite, that they might enslave others to their will. The fear of evil robs them of their hope, and resentment steals their joy.

¹⁷ Thenceforth shall they cling to such horrors as though they were precious treasure, pressing a bitter blade against their breast and wielding it with impunity against all those

who dare defy them.

[18] Perception is the only gateway to the All, yet when twisted for gain or power, it leads only to oblivion.

[19] The one whose eye is ever upon a distant goal risks stumbling over unseen rocks along the path. The one whose eye is ever cast downward for fear of stumbling risks losing his way. Let not one eye be blinded by the other.

[20] The enemy close at hand distracts from a greater foe unseen … and from blessings nearer still.

[21] The seed planted in the heart spreads ever outward in shoots and branches, taking root and demanding nourishment. Kind multiplies after its kind.

[22] The joyful heart spreads joy.

[23] The angry heart spreads anger.

[24] The fearful heart spreads fear

[25] The compassionate heart spreads compassion.

[26] The bitter heart spreads bitterness.

[27] The mind creates divisions, some born of need and others of fear. The heart discerns the difference, and the All transcends their names.

[28] Power resides not in men, save when by men it is bestowed. Authority is given, honor is accorded and respect is proffered. [29] Some who earn these things rightly never receive them, for fools and despots withhold what is rightly theirs in service of their own lies.

[30] Fear is a sentinel, not a master. It keeps watch but should never command you.

[31] Pain is a fire to keep watch by. Yet left untended, it spreads and consumes the entire camp.

[32] Pain gives warning for those who heed not prudence. Yet sometimes, even the prudent must bear it, and even some who observe its counsel shall not escape its wrath.

[33] Decisions are steps, not conclusions.

3

The Earth

[1] There are those who say man was given charge of the earth to rule over it, yet if this were true, would the earth rise up against him? [2] The winds roar mightily to drown out his commands. The sea rises up and swallows his puny ships. The earth brings forth fire from its depths to consume him, and the skies fall upon him in torrents.

[3] Men raise their scepters upon the earth, and she laughs at their insolence. They build monuments to eternity, and she uproots them like weeds from her garden. [4] Your palaces fall to ruin, your inscriptions to glory worn away by wind and rain.

[5] Even your gravestones are cracked and weathered. Soon they will return to the earth itself, leaving no record your sojourn.

[6] But grieve not, for all things pass away, yet even so are renewed.

[7] Creation did not come to pass in six moments, in six days or in six thousand thousand years. It occurs in every moment, renewing itself in color and pattern, in sound and

in silence, from the moment that was to the moment that will be and onward.

⁸ Indeed, it is far easier to tear down than to build up, so the building must always continue. In the same way, it is far easier to wage war than to preserve peace, so trust need always be fortified.

⁹ There are those who say that men have been given dominion over the beasts of the field. Yet men are but beasts in their own right. Wherefore should they have dominion?

¹⁰ Have you given birth to the cattle? Does your blood run through the hawk or serpent? If you have not given them life, who are you, then, to take it. ¹¹ If by need you ask it, then ask in humility, for your need is not glory but frailty. ¹² If for sport you seek it, you dishonor yourself. And if for glory you take it, you defile yourself. It is not yours, and you are but a robber.

¹³ O man, you reign not over the earth, but she is your master through all of your days and your conqueror when the last night falls upon you. ¹⁴ You may toil to subdue her, and she may bring forth her bounty, but how great your vanity to imagine that she does so for your pleasure!

¹⁵ There are those who say, "A mere beast has no soul!" Those who say such things understand not the nature of the All. ¹⁶ No one has a soul; each one is a soul. So it is also the way with animals. The eyes of every creature serve as gateways to new wonders.

[17] The one who mistreats or neglects a beast is not worthy of your company. If he has no regard for a beast, what regard will he have of you?

[18] The straight path is illusion and the stable foundation will crumble.

[19] Water is supple and creates its own path. Rock is rigid and cracks under pressure. Be like water, which falls down from on high and is carried away by the rivercourse to be gathered by the great water-carrier in seas and lakes and basins. [20] Thence is it cast once again skyward, in secret, and we see it not, to fall once more and renew its blessing.

[21] This is the way of things, no straight path but a cycle in constant renewal. The path unfolds by the way of the wheel, and the journey continues in struggle and repose.

[22] Some say, "Do not strive," and others, "Do not sit idle." Yet the one sits idle not achieves not, and the one who strives always forgoes what is achieved.

[23] Strive for that which is beyond your reach, yet be grateful for all you receive. [24] The one who strives not shall be sacrificed to the passion of others, and the one who is thankless shall be given in sacrifice to his own appetite. Surely shall he be consumed.

[25] Be thankful, yet not content.

[26] Be eager, yet not expectant.

[27] Be vigilant, yet not fearful.

[28] Be strong, yet slow to anger.

[29] Be ready, yet at ease.

[30] Serve all, yet let no man enslave you.

[31] Know yourself, yet seek to learn of others.

[32] The lion hunts but sleeps long. The camel moves slowly, yet endures. The falcon flies, yet cannot run. The sawtooth rides the waves, yet cannot walk. [33] The smallest insect, in sufficient number, can fell the largest tree, and a single idea, which no one can see, may call forth an army that spans the horizon.

[34] It is easier to gaze upon the surface of an onion than to peel away the layers and reveal its inner meanings. In the same way, it is easier to gaze upon the surface of a man than to seek his true essence - and to stare at the face of an idol than to explore the mysteries behind it.

[35] The one who stays in the center perceives both ends. But take heed, for there is no center between truth and falsehood, between verity and illusion.

4

The Gods

[1] There are those who say that the gods demand to be honored. Yet the gods require not that you honor them, only that you honor your own word.

[2] But some will say, "What if your word is a falsehood?" or "What if it is a word of malice?" Such questions are folly. What have gods to do with such things?

[3] The wise man judges a message not on authority, but on merit.

[4] There are those who say they hear the voice of a god. It is their own voice they hear, and they are mistaken. [5] Yet

those who say, "I have never heard such a voice," become a fount of inspiration.

⁶ When a person enslaves his neighbor and says, "My god commanded it," either his god is false or he is.

⁷ When a person mistreats his beloved and says, "My god placed me over her," either his god is false or he is.

⁸ When a soldier plunders his enemy and says, "It is in the name of my god," either his god is false or he is.

⁹ Who are you, O man, to condemn another's god? If that god lives, do you not think he could destroy you with a whisper, mere mortal? And if you say, "It is only an idol," how shall you acquit your own god of like charge?

¹⁰ Do you think that blasphemy offends a god? Do the gods truly care for the babbling of men? And can they not defend their own honor? ¹¹ Indeed, the one who does violence in retribution for such offense brands himself an idiot. ¹² It is bad enough that he shows disdain or his neighbor by doing him violence. But he heaps scorn upon his own head by presuming his god needs protection. ¹³ Truly, the contempt he shows his own god and his neighbor shall return to him.

¹⁴ There are those who say, "Do not take the name of a god in vain." Yet these same ones do this very thing when they claim to know the mind of that same god. ¹⁵ O, sons of conceit and daughters of treachery! You children of dust speak not of eternity. But from your own minds, you spew forth gibberish and as though you were a prophet. ¹⁶ If the god in whose name you speak should hear you, he shall

surely upbraid you, and he will close the ears of all to your empty rantings.

¹⁷ Those who pray from rooftops fall from rooftops. As their eyes are ever skyward, their step is never sure.

¹⁸ If all the time spent in prayer for the impossible were devoted instead to achieving the possible, how much richer this world would be!

5

The Priests

¹ The priests of one god spoke of honor. The priests of another preached forgiveness. The priests of a third demanded justice and a fourth, sacrifice.

² Yet their words were false and their motives were impure.

³ Those who spoke of honor had no honor of their own, but offered in its stead false promises and demands of blind loyalty.

⁴ Those who preached forgiveness wished to be forgiven their own cruelty.

⁵ They that demanded justice sought first to define it, and they that called for sacrifice desired that their followers part with their dignity.

⁶ Some said, "Peace!" that their foes might yield; some cried, "War!" that their followers would fight and die in their behalf.

⁷ Here, then, is what you should do when confronted by those of such false virtue:

⁸ Let your honor surpass theirs.

⁹ Forgive yourself first and take not upon yourselves their burden of shame and misplaced guilt.

¹⁰ Serve justice in accord with truth and conscience, not in accord with the lies of those who would reforge it in their own image.

¹¹ Sacrifice in the cause of love and compassion, not in behalf of unyielding dogma.

¹² Seek peace without yielding to tormentors, and seek not war - others will surely bring it to your doorstep in due course.

¹³ They that submit blindly to one who claims authority shall die in darkness, but those who open their eyes to questioning shall live in light.

6

Justice

¹ There are those who say that the sins of the fathers are visited upon the sons. Where, therefore, is justice? ² If the son is punished for the acts of the father, should the swallow be chastened for the deeds of the hawk? Should the tortoise be judged for the works of the jackal?

³ Nay, for each one's deeds are his alone, and justice is not mocked by cowards.

⁴ The law knows nothing of change. It is written for constancy and cannot awaken to see the new day. ⁵ The law

itself is dead, and like a dead man does not change, save that it decay. It cannot reform its failings; this task is left to those who live.

⁶ There are these two things: life and the law.

⁷ The law without life is futile. Lacking context, it is like a foreign tongue with no one to translate.

⁸ The law without discernment is deadly. It consumes the innocent and guilty alike in its false judgment, and is itself consumed by its passion.

⁹ The law is a guardian to life, and so it is that life without law stands in peril. Yet be watchful, lest the guardian turn his sword against the one charged to his keeping.

¹⁰ There are those who say, "Let the scapegoat bear the sins of the guilty one." Where, therefore, is wisdom? ¹¹ The one who blames another for his own folly learns nothing and only repeats it. And each time, an innocent bears his burden. To this there is no end unless the one at fault knows contrition.

¹² Blood does not satisfy vengeance. Desire does not satisfy contrition, and a scapegoat does not satisfy justice.

¹³ Forgive not one who asks for solace with a knife behind his back. Turn aside your anger, not your prudence. Temper fury, but not wisdom. ¹⁴ Only a fool who touches fire seeks again the flame's affliction.

¹⁵ Blame not the innocent for the acts of the guilty. The guilty must bear their burden, and the innocent must be spared. The one who falsely accuses another, and

knowingly does so, is as guilty as the one whose acts are in question.

[16] The one who takes credit for the deeds of another is but a vapor. Some say the moon claimed the light of the sun as her own, but was chastened for her hubris with a face consigned to shadow.

[17] The one who blames a demon for his actions is either himself a demon or a scoundrel bent on treachery.

[18] There are those who demand, "An eye for an eye!" Yet they see not their own faults. What, therefore, is the loss of an eye to one already blind? Hypocrites. They ask of others what they themselves can never give.

[19] Those who oft recall a wrong against them inflict upon themselves the way of sorrow.

[20] There are those who say, "treat others in such a manner as you yourself would be treated." Yet what is this but vainglory? [21] Would the fish of the sea do a kindness by sending the waves to flood the eagle's nest? Would the ploughman favor the herdsman by tethering his ox? [22] Nay, treat others in such a manner as they themselves would be treated. [23] Think not in your own conceit, "That one is the same I." But learn another's ways and favor him in like manner. In this way do you show kindness and humility.

[24] Some may protest, "There are those who would take advantage of such kindness." [25] Do not put the well being of such ones before your own, but remove yourself from their presence and do not worry about giving them offense. Such ones are already an offense unto themselves.

²⁶ There are those who make laws and say they are eternal. Yet where were your laws before you walked the earth? And where will they be when you are forgotten?

²⁷ No minstrel sings lyrics without music. In the same way, no one who sits in judgment should serve law without compassion.

²⁸ There are those who say, "Black is black and white is white." Yet such ones miss the beauty of the many hues and colors with which the earth is adorned.

²⁹ There are those who say, "Judge not." Yet without judgement, where is justice? They who judge to share understanding show wisdom. They who judge to exalt themselves are in error.

³⁰ Do not fear to say, "The thing you have done is an error." But hold your tongue should you be tempted to say, "The person who has done it is an abomination."

³¹ Which does the greater offense, the one who violates an imperfect law or the one acts from malice by seeking to pass through the cracks between the law's letters?

³² Actions are subject to the judgment of anyone. But the accused are subject only to the judgment of that law which is agreed upon in common and the principles that undergird it. ³³ Who can visit punishment upon a deed? It is the doer of the deed who pays the penalty.

³⁴ Judgment tried and tested strengthens the common good.

³⁵ Judgment withheld oft turns to deceit.

³⁶ Judgment imposed by the covetous bears the seed of resentment.

[37] There are those who say, "By the standard you mete out, so shall you likewise be judged." Yet if your standard is just and your heart is true, what place is there for fear?

[38] There are those who say, "I own this land." Yet when your life has ended, the land shall claim dominion over you.

[39] Do you think that the scales of justice are balanced if the same man is acquitted when guilty yet convicted when innocent? May it not be so. Indeed, both errors weigh just as heavy on the side of transgression.

[40] To tolerate injustice is no virtue. The one who speaks not against an abuser or sits idle in his presence has handed him a weapon more potent than a sword.

[41] Three possible fates await the guilty when sentence is passed: the fate of punishment, the fate of separation and the fate of redemption. The first is the fruit of vengeance, the second is the fruit of fear and the third is the fruit of hope.

[42] The thirst for punishment too often binds the innocent, blinded by the demand for blood and recompense. Separation may preserve the people, and should be used when trust is broken. Redemption holds the richest promise, but have a care, for it also places much faith in the one who may not be worthy. Be sure such a one is deserving.

[43] Blame seeks conclusions. Compassion seeks healing.

7

Instruction

¹ There are those who instruct others how to live, yet they themselves are dead.

² To the one who says, "I know," the door is barred. But to the one who says, "I seek," passage is granted. For the first one thinks he need go no further, while the second knows the path leads ever onward.

³ The teacher who learns nothing from the student is unworthy of the title.

⁴ Those who seek the counsel of only the like-minded never know the thoughts of their enemy, and those who revel in flattery never recognize deceit. Such ones are easily vanquished. ⁵ But those who take heed of adverse opinion see the world from every angle.

⁶ Do not say, "This is my teacher." Say instead, "This is my teaching." Do not rely on the authority of others, but let your words carry their own authority.

⁷ Do not ask, "Who has sent you?" Instead ask, "What has brought you?"

⁸ Ascribe not your own folly to another's lips because you wish to shame him. Let his own folly expose him; otherwise, learn from his wisdom.

⁹ The one who makes excuses lacks understanding. The one who seeks understanding has no need for excuses.

8
Family

¹ There are those who say the man is head of the woman. But I ask you: Who was it that gave you birth? Woman was not taken from man, but man from woman. ² Do not boast, therefore, in your strength, O man. But be grateful to she who bore you, for had she cast you aside as an infant, you would surely have perished.

³ The man who sells his daughter in exchange for a dowry treats her like a harlot and dishonors himself. But the daughter so given is not dishonored. Indeed, her honor is ten thousand times that of her father.

⁴ The one who lays an offering on the altar while his family goes hungry defiles the altar and dishonors his name.

⁵ Those who give tithes and offerings while their household is in want are no better than a king who collects taxes from a beggar.

⁶ There are those who say, "Do not divorce your helpmeet." But I say, do not remain bound to one who is poorly suited. It is a kindness to release such a one, and it is folly to remain yoked in deceit and bitterness.

⁷ The foolish judge a person by his birthright, for no one knows how much fruit a tree may bring forth until the proper season. ⁸ Would you prize the seed that may never take root and cast aside that which may feed a village? How foolish is such condemnation! ⁹ Those who rush to judgment deny justice. But more than that, they deny themselves the bounty of a fine harvest.

¹⁰ The one who cuts or brands his children as though they were property has branded himself as a keeper of slaves. Such a one has sacrificed his children to his own vainglory and his honor upon a barren altar.

9

Intimacy

¹ There are those who say, "Do not waste your seed." But one's seed is always replenished. Better instead to worry about wasting your words, which may not be withdrawn or replaced if they are folly.

² There are those who say, "Be fruitful and multiply." Yet true fruitfulness lies in acts of honor; when these are multiplied, they bring a far greater harvest.

³ If a child is brought up among quarrels, he will learn the way of quarreling. If a child is brought up in the presence of anger, she will learn the ways of anger. If a child is raised in a home of true affection, he will not shrink from love.

⁴ If a man lies with a man, what is that to you? If a woman lies with a woman, what offense is given?

⁵ You concern yourself with such things, yet curse your own husband or beat your own wife. You defile another's bed with accusations, yet your own is filled with spite. Behold! It is soaked in blood and fallow.

⁶ When you have fed all the hungry, clothed all the widows, housed all the outcasts and put an end to violence, then

you may consider such matters. ⁷ But consider them well before you speak of them, lest the ones you accuse bring their own case against you. If they do, mark this: They surely shall prevail.

⁸ Some speak of man and woman as though they were ice and fire. Yet does not each desire compassion? Indeed, both seek the respect of their neighbors, and both would have others mark their words and treat them kindly. ⁹ Why do you magnify that which is different when so many things are held in common? Each does breath, does think, does laugh, does mourn, does bleed, does sleep, does take sustenance. ¹⁰ Give not so much thought to fine distinctions. Consider instead this shared life, which binds them.

10

Government

¹ Seek not to place a king over you, for if that one is unworthy, he will pillage your land, and even if he be worthy, his sons may not follow in his ways. ² Seek instead leaders of wise counsel, whose words are noble and proved by all their actions. May they be women and men of good repute among the people, and may they be answerable for their edicts to those whom they affect.

³ The one who obeys without question is like the one who says "I see!" without looking, and the one who concedes without trying. ⁴ Such a one has relinquished his soul and become the lapdog of a tyrant.

⁵ The ruler who seeks war for the sake of glory is not fit to rule. The one who seeks war for the sake of gold betrays his people. The peace must be protected, but war should never be pursued.

⁶ Those who rush to war find the path to peace the slowest.

⁷ The one who taxes the people for his own enrichment is a thief.

⁸ The wise leader is truly humble, for true humility casts its eye outward, not inward. It focuses not on the deficiency of self, but on the greatness of the All.

⁹ The one who leads should be the greatest listener, and also the greatest observer. The leader who fails to see and hear what lies ahead leads the people into hardship. The one who heeds not the words and deeds of those behind him will quickly find himself alone.

11
Defilement

¹ There are those who say that the clothes or the hair defile the people. Yet what are clothes and hair but shade and warmth? ² Those who forbid adornments to no purpose are slaves of vanity, as surely as those who preen and gawk at their own image.

³ In like manner, there are those who say, "Do not eat this, for it will defile you" and "Do not eat that, for it is forbidden." But each one should eat according to his own

conscience and partake according to that one's disposition. ⁴ It is the one who kills and does not eat who is defiled, for he is a wastrel and a murderer.

⁵ If a woman has an issue of blood, she neither defiles nor is she defiled. Do you curse the blood that runs through your veins or the child brought forth from the womb? ⁶ The blood of life is a blessing and should be celebrated. It is never a cause for shame.

⁷ If someone among you should convulse, do not say, "He has a demon" or "This one is cursed." The one who utters such ignorance curses only himself.

⁸ You who put wine to your lips when your child goes hungry, how is it that you scoff at a woman nursing her child. ⁹ There is nothing sweeter than a mother's milk and nothing more bitter than a man drunk on his own condemnation.

¹⁰ You who find cause to curse your neighbors for their differences, who shall be cursed when their skill and resource exceed your own?

¹¹ You curse the foreigner. You curse the one who is afflicted. You curse the poor. You curse the one whose belly is large and the one whose frame is lean. ¹² You curse the poor and the homeless. You curse the one who rejects your book and the one who affirms another. You curse the one who is too tall or too short, too old or too young. ¹³ You send them all into exile within your own mind and, if you have the means, to the very ends of the earth. ¹⁴ Yet which of these are you? Certainly you are one of them. And just as surely, it is you who are the exile.

¹⁵ The one who laughs at another in spite masks his fear, yet the mask is but illusion and what is hidden shall quickly be manifest. ¹⁶ The one who laughs at himself in good humor shows his heart to all the world. There is no mask, no illusion. Such is the way of courage.

12
Wealth

¹ The one who profits from another's labor is like a tick on the ear of a dog or a wolf in the sheepfold.

² The wolf eats only until his belly is full, but the appetite of greed is never sated.

³ The one who demands payment at high interest is like the landholder who shears his tenant's sheep in winter, then mocks him as he freezes for want of a covering.

⁴ The one who buys another's speech with gold buys only falsehood and corruption.

⁵ The one whose wealth speaks to silence another has sewn up the mouth of freedom with threads of gold.

⁶ The one who lends at interest for profit is a sluggard with nothing of true value. He sells thin air and deals in illusion. ⁷ Let him earn his keep by the fruit of his labor, the skill of his craft and the sweat of his brow.

⁸ It is an irony of ironies that gold is taken from the earth by those who seek to possess the earth, to which they shall at last return.

⁹ Bring no sacrifice to any god's altar. The earth shall fall upon you. The skies shall open up and lay siege to you. The sun shall cause you to wither, and the sea shall pull you under. ¹⁰ This is your true sacrifice, and all must offer it when their lives are completed.

¹¹ What use is something offered from the hand which cannot grasp it? Would the one who borrows a fortune from the royal treasury approach the throne with a few coins and call them a gift? ¹¹ Such an act is no gift, but effrontery, and so it is with all your offerings.

¹² Offer nothing save your virtue, and in so offering this, preserve it.

¹³ Offer nothing save your honor, and in so offering this, sustain it.

13

Fellowship

¹ Despise not those who are different, for they are your teachers. Cast them not aside, lest they leave you to wallow in your folly.

² The one who mocks the foreigner, the maid or the afflicted revels in his own ignorance. Such a one clings to fear as though it were a scabbard, unaware that it is empty.

³ Some wish to see their own success in the ruin of others, never knowing they are blind.

⁴ Some say a child is born wretched and evil, that there is no good within him. Others call the same child pure and good, entirely without blemish. ⁵ But what is "good" and

what is "evil"? Are they not the deeds of men and women: acts of valor and betrayal, of compassion and of cruelty, of charity and thievery?

⁶ An infant has done naught for good or ill ere he departs his mother's womb. How, then, is he blameworthy, and how can he be lauded? ⁷ A child is neither worthy because he is heir to a kingdom nor wretched because of some ancestor's transgression. Nay, it is a man's deeds that are good or evil, and likewise deeds which do corrupt him.

⁸ In battle, the one who inflicts pain upon a captive to gain the advantage is himself captive to an illusion. ⁹ Thinking he shall be made wiser, he plays the fool. For he knows not that lies are born of desperation, and that deceit pours from the lips of an enemy afflicted.

¹⁰ There are those who say, "Welcome your enemy." Yet they who invite malice are seldom disappointed.

¹¹ There are those who say, "Welcome the stranger into your home in the cause of hospitality." But does the mole invite the snake or fox into its burrow, though it be a stranger to him? Does the rose invite the aphid to feast on her branches, though the aphid were not known to her? ¹² No, welcome not the stranger, but the person of good character. Should an intruder claim your home, and should he claim it, how then can you offer your hospitality to one truly in need?

¹³ There are those who say, "Burn no bridge once you have crossed." Yet what if an enemy pursues you? Better that you burn a bridge behind you than look always over your shoulder. ¹⁴ Do not risk stumbling through the

darkness with your eyes fixed on the past.

¹⁵ When others bring disgrace upon themselves, be gracious.

¹⁶ When others are fearful because of lies, assuage their fears with truth.

¹⁷ When others revile or extol you, know that these are their perceptions.

¹⁸ There are three sorts of offense. The first is created out of ignorance, the second out of malice and the third from fear. The first is called error, the second cruelty and the third cowardice. ¹⁹ Before you accuse or forgive your neighbor, be sure concerning the nature of his transgression - and also his future intent.

²⁰ If you offend another and are in the wrong, remember this: the effect upon the one you have wronged is the same, regardless of your intent.
²¹ Therefore let your sorrow be sincere and not bound up with some excuse.

²² There are those who say a woman should marry the man who takes her by force. Where, then, is justice? ²³ For if a woman is made to accept such a one, his vile deed is magnified. Better for such a one that he be forbidden to marry. Remove such a one far from your daughters.

²⁴ He who says a woman is less than a man is himself less than a man.

²⁵ There are those who say the slave is born to his station. But those who speak thusly were never slaves.

²⁶ The one who makes the most promises is the one least apt to keep them.

²⁷ The one who gives a gift and seeks its return is like a baker who makes bread for a neighbor, yet demands it back once eaten. ²⁸ He has no cause to complain if he receives it back in a condition far different than its former state.

²⁹ It takes two sides to make peace, but only one to make war. Yet where the two stand together, they are stronger.

³⁰ Guard these three things more closely than any treasure: the light in your eyes, the song in your heart and the love of your companion.

14

Appearances

¹ Who are you to say, "Woman, cover your face!" or "Man, shave not your beard!" Is the visage a shame to the either? Or is it not instead your own shame that you seek, in your hubris, to inflict upon them?

² If a priest says, "Clothe the poor!" yet dresses in fine raiment of silk and golden cords, of what merit are his words? ³ If a prophet says, "House the orphans!" yet builds a fine temple of marble and cedar for those who follow him, of what value is his entreaty?

⁴ A man who seeks perfection is a dog chasing his own tail. All he shall catch is the stench of his own pretense.

⁵ The one who judges others according to the manner of their dress is like the one who judges the butterfly according to her cocoon.

⁶ The one who upbraids another publicly for a perceived breach of protocol is the one who should be upbraided.

⁷ If a man wears his hair long, what is that to you? If a woman dons the garb of a man, what is that to you?

⁸ They who seek the favor of nobles for the sake of their own nobility sacrifice it at the feet of those they flatter.

⁹ One who hides behind the name of another is no better than a criminal who stows away in the hold of a ship. He seeks free passage at the peril of its owner, endangering also its crew and cargo by his presence.

¹⁰ The first temples were tombs and empty monuments. Your fathers built grand houses for their fathers, while their children found no shelter and starved in squalor.

¹¹ Pretense is the servant of conceit.

¹² Ostentation is the child of vanity.

¹³ Flattery is a bribe and a warning.

15
Speech

¹ Promises are like bridges to the morrow. Never build one without cause, lest you neglect it. And once built, forsake it not, lest it crumble beneath your feet.

² The one who boasts lacks surety, but the one who stays quiet shows resolve.

³ The one who offers an oath betrays want of conviction, either toward his own intent or the trust of another.

⁴ Do you think yourself a prophet? Then you are not one. Do you deem yourself wise? You still have much to learn. Do you claim inspiration? Let it speak on its own behalf. ⁵ The true prophet does not announce himself, but attends to his own soul and speaks through his actions. ⁶ The sage does not shout from the rooftops, but in silence hears the whispers others miss. ⁷ The inspired one believes himself to be ordinary and in the rightness of this belief transforms the world.

⁸ The herald who speaks unbidden in the name of a queen or a king has no excuse. How much greater is the guilt of a self-proclaimed prophet who speaks unbidden in the name of god or goddess?

⁹ If one who speaks hatred in the name of a god, he reveals himself as hateful or his god as the very same. In no wise can hateful speech be godly, any more than the sun can bring forth darkness.

¹⁰ If one speaks destruction in the name of a creator, he speaks nonsense. He might as well spread plague in the name of a healer. ¹¹ The one who destroys a thing simply to rebuild it labors to no purpose, and the one who afflicts a man in order to heal him is a scoundrel.

¹² You look to the stars for answers, yet neglect the heart of the matter within. You search the scrolls for meaning, yet find only that which you wish to see. ¹³ You appoint leaders to guide you, then lay traps for them to preserve your own conceit. You travel far across the earth in search of glory, yet forget to sing the song that lies within you.

¹⁴ There are those who seek a reward in the next life, but will they find it? Or have they wasted their opportunity in this one?

¹⁵ Yesterday is your teacher; the morrow, your student. Today is the test.

¹⁶ If you want someone to hear you, speak softly. If they do not hear, they were not listening and would not have understood.

¹⁷ The one who bargains with a man who breaks his word is like the one who seeks pleasure from cutting himself on broken glass.

¹⁸ The wise one speaks softly, and others incline their ear to hear them. The slaveholder speaks loudly, and his words are like a swarm of the locusts devouring everything in their path. ¹⁹ The one who raises his voice when another disagrees does not seek to be heard, but to be obeyed.

²⁰ The one who falsely plays the victim makes a victim of those who heed him.

²¹ The one who boasts of his own affliction and the one who boasts of his own greatness, how are they different? Each seeks the notice of others, but both are crows calling into the wind.

²² Be thankful for the boaster, who by his bluster makes known his folly. But be on guard against the whisperer, who reveals it not until he strikes.

²³ The snake concealed is more to be feared than the lion that roars. The one who lies in ambush atones for many flaws by way of stealth, and the one who shows all strength betrays his weakness.

24 Fear not the one whose lies are abundant, whose deceit is clear to many. Fear instead the one who leavens truth with subtle falsehood and poisons honor with a single drop of pretense. Such a one is a destroyer.

25 Those who reason together may unlock many gifts wrapped plainly. Yet those who argue stridently in order to prove themselves covet a jeweled box - and scorn its priceless contents.

26 Those who speak in a language beyond your understanding are masters of it. If you deride them for such mastery, you betray only your jealousy. Your true purpose is to mask you own deficiency.

27 Threats are strong poison. If carried out, they kill trust - and perhaps much more. Left unfulfilled they must be swallowed, and are not easily digested.

28 Flattery prepares the way for lies far greater.

29 The gossip speaks not to impart knowledge, but to test it; not to convey information, but to obtain it.

30 Do not give your tongue over to insults. They speak only to your own nature.

31 Do not give your tongue over to boasting. It speaks only to your own deficiency.

32 Do not give your tongue over to cursing. It speaks only of your own ingratitude.

33 Do not give your tongue over to gossip. It speaks only of your own languor.

34 Do not give your tongue over to rudeness. It speaks for itself.

16
Faith

[1] There are those who say it is enough to believe. Yet they who believe wrongly rely on their own conceit, and they who believe rightly and fail to act will fare no better.

[2] Some say, "Those who believe not shall never see." But I say that those who act not shall never know.

[3] Some who have faith say, "I have no need of learning, for I know." Some who are learning say, "I have no need of faith, for I am finding out!" [4] Yet do these not have faith even so? Their faith is in the mind, their faith is in the senses and their faith is in the journey of discovery.

[5] Faith untested is like a great feast which no one consumes. It soon grows stale and poisons those who finally partake. [6] Those who question do not abandon faith, they test it. And in the testing, they discover whether it is fit to partake.

[6] Those who believe without seeing and those who see without believing are too often content with seeing half the moon.

[7] No plan put forth by priest or prophet, by king or captain, by scribe or sage can save you. [8] Let your counselors ever be three in number: your conscience, your wits and your humility. These three things will preserve your honor.

17
Trust and Forgiveness

¹ Loyalty offered a betrayer is like the fattest lamb offered up to the hungriest wolf.

² Trust offered a beguiler or a charlatan is like a log thrown on a roaring fire.

³ There are those who say, "Grant forgiveness to all who seek it." Yet who would open his treasury to all who covet its gold? Surely, such a treasury will soon be empty, and is not your goodwill more valuable than a pile of coins and ingots?

⁴ Forgiveness is no simple thing. It is no simple matter of "yes, I forgive" or "no, I do not." ⁵ As a temple with many courts admits the commoner to the outer square, the priests to the inner courtyard and the high priest to the sanctuary, so it is also with forgiveness. ⁶ No one admits a supplicant at once to the inner sanctum, lest he consider himself entitled and pollute it. In the same way, offer no betrayer access to your inner keep at once.

⁷ Your neighbor may earn your trust in one matter yet be unworthy in another. Make it your practice to know the difference.

⁸ The one who withholds forgiveness should take care not to cultivate a crop of bitterness. Grasp its stalk firmly and uproot it, for it is a weed left behind by the fruit of betrayal. Let nothing of that thing remain to choke the new seeds you have planted.

⁹ One who betrays a treaty is unworthy of another. If such a one seeks a new bargain, he must offer a guarantee more valuable than the boon he is seeking. Otherwise, let him wait his turn behind those who have not broken trust.

¹⁰ The one who offers a treaty under threat of invasion deals falsely through coercion. The one who demands obeisance in exchange for salvation knows only tyranny.

18
Blessings

¹ Blessed are the seekers, for their eyes shall be filled with wonder.

² Blessed are the strong of heart, for they shall persevere.

³ Blessed are the craftsmen, for theirs is an honest living.

⁴ Blessed are the artists, for theirs is the work of creation.

⁵ Blessed are those of good cheer, for misfortune shall not deter them.

⁶ Blessed are the disciples, for they shall not cease from learning.

⁷ Blessed are the lovers, for theirs is the secret of the universe.

⁸ Blessed are those who know compassion, for theirs is the way of peace.

⁹ Blessed is the one who sees with the eyes of a child and reflects with the mind of an elder, for such a one knows wisdom.

19
Exaltations

¹ Exalted are the caregivers, who sacrifice of themselves that others may take comfort.

² Exalted are the mediators, who stand on neither side but bridge the chasm between.

³ Exalted are the healers, who bind the wounds of the afflicted.

⁴ Exalted are the scholars, for whom failure is but a stepping-stone.

⁵ Exalted are the explorers, who step where others fear to venture.

⁶ Exalted are the strangers, who bring new wisdom to those in privation.

⁷ Exalted are the protectors, who see that no harm comes to the defenseless.

20
Woes

¹ Woe to you priests and prophets, for you say, "How dare the governor tax the holy treasury!" Yet you yourselves tax the people with tithes to fill your bellies. ² Hypocrites! You flout the laws of the land in the name of your gods, then replace them with burdens that no one can bear.

³ Woe to you kings and nobles, hypocrites! For you condemn a man for stealing a morsel of bread, yet set the price so high he cannot meet it. You congratulate the one who steals a fortune, yet condemn the one who takes a pittance. ⁴ Yet who has done the greater wrong: the one whose lies have made him wealthy or the one whose empty stomach has made him weak? Fools you are, and a fool's reward shall you earn. How safe will your fortune be when the time comes?

⁵ Woe to you priests and prophets, hypocrites! You laud those who speak lies in the name of a god but fault them that speak truth for the good of man.

⁶ Woe to you priests and nobles, for you give aid to those who prosper and withhold it from the suffering. ⁷ Fools. The one who does not need your help will forsake you, but the one who is saved by a kindness shall return it.

⁸ Woe to you kings and nobles, who tax even the dead to build your fortune. Yet you yourselves are dead already, and you do not even see it.

⁹ Woe to you kings and nobles, hypocrites! You steal from the poor to fund your wagers and use the bread of the homeless for a stake at your table. But when your luck runs short, who then will save you?

¹⁰ Woe to you priests and prophets, hypocrites! You preach, "Forgive one another with no expectation!" Yet you yourselves sell forgiveness in exchange for tithes and indulgences. ¹¹ You absolve one debt while incurring another, and so enslave men to you.

¹² Woe to you kings and nobles, hypocrites! For you rob

the poor to fund your petty disputes and in the end accomplish nothing. The poor are cheated and your breath is wasted.

[13] Woe to you priests and nobles, for you say, "Thou shalt not kill," yet you slay a man on false charges and make wars on false grounds. [14] You say, "Thou shalt not steal," yet you invade another's land for the sake of plunder. You say, "Honor your father and mother," yet you dishonor them with your deeds.

[15] Woe to you priests and prophets, for you say, "This world is passing away," yet sacrifice your honor to possess it.

[16] Woe to you priests and prophets, hypocrites! You condemn a poor woman for selling her body, yet sell your very souls for the sake of mammon. [17] Fools. You say the body is a temple, how much more precious is that which resides within? Yet body and soul are one.

[18] Woe to you priests and prophets, for you tremble at tales at ghosts and demons, yet fear not the man or woman whom you have wronged.

[19] Woe to you priests and prophets, hypocrites! For you say the devil appears as an angel of light - a convenient excuse to debase true angels.

[20] Woe to you prophets and seers who say, "It will surely come to pass!" Yet see how quickly the truth betrays you. [21] If you had truly seen tomorrow, would you not have said so plainly? Yet when your words are proven false, you heap more lies atop the first and so compound your error.

21
Instructions

¹ It is written that "You shall have no other god before me." Yet I say, have no other way before compassion and serve no other god but truth.

² It is written, "Do not take the name of your god in vain." Yet I say, anyone who dares place his own words in the mouth of a god has already done so.

³ It is written that you must keep the Sabbath holy. Yet all days are holy, and none should be wasted.

⁴ It is written that you should honor your father and mother. Yet I say, honor is greater than kinship.

⁵ It is written that you are not to kill. Think hard on this, then, before you send armies beyond your homeland.

⁶ It is written that you shall not commit adultery. Yet I say betray no one who is faithful.

⁷ It is written that you shall not steal. Yet I say, they who oppress the poor are worse than thieves.

⁸ It is written, "You shall not give false testimony against your neighbor." Yet I say, do not stand idle when such testimony is given.

⁹ It is written, "You shall not covet." Yet I say, covet kindness, covet smiles and covet virtue.

¹⁰ And I say also to you: Jealousy is but another name for covetousness, so wherefore may a god be jealous?

¹¹ Some say, "Let your first aim be obedience." Yet I say, let your first aim be understanding. Then after understanding, compassion. Then after compassion,

encouragement, aid and sustenance.

¹² Some say, "Give aid for the fear of your god." Yet I say, give aid for the love of your neighbor.

¹³ Some say, "Purify your garments." Yet I say, purify your goals.

¹⁴ Some say, "Devote yourself to prayer and fasting." Yet I say, devote yourself to acts of kindness and thanksgiving.

¹⁵ Some say, "Make a journey to the holy place." Yet I say, make the place where you are holy.

¹⁶ Some say, "Shun the heretic and unbeliever." Yet I say, your fear is speaking.

22

Charges

¹ Care then for the children, whose future is your legacy and whose character testifies to your own.

² Care also for the elders, who give of themselves that you may prosper.

³ Care for the earth, who is your mother and provider.

⁴ Care also for the creatures who are your companions on this journey.

⁵ Let the dew kiss you good morning and the nightingale sing you a lullaby.

⁶ Let the road lead you onward, but fear not to explore the hidden paths.

⁷ Let the sun warm your shoulders, but cast no shadow

on your neighbor's day.

⁸ Let your eye be open, your song be joyous, your life be shared and your heart be true.

⁹ The one whose eye is ever upon a distant goal risks stumbling over unseen rocks along the path. The one whose eye is ever cast downward for fear of stumbling risks losing his way. Let not one eye be blinded by the other.

¹⁰ Be as a flower, which opens itself to the light.

¹¹ Be as the ocean, fluid yet unyielding.

¹² Be as the moon, reflective yet illuminating.

¹³ Be as the stargazer, always seeking out new light, however distant it may be.

¹⁴ Be as the ship's captain, who knows when to drop anchor and when to ride the waves.

¹⁵ Be as the owl. Cast your gaze in all directions.

¹⁶ Be as the sand crab, at home in shifting sands or pounding surf.

¹⁷ Be as the robin, a herald as winter wanes of better things to come.

¹⁸ Be as the serpent. Shed your skin when it no longer fits you.

¹⁹ Be as the spider. Weave your web and take your leisure.

²⁰ Be as the leviathan. Plum the depths of your own true waters.

²¹ Be as the trees of the forest, sentinels that shade the earth beneath them, that they may be nourished.

²² Be at rest, that you may awaken.

²³ Be silent, that you may hear.

²⁴ Be at peace, that you know no distraction.

²⁵ Be watchful, that your eyes may be opened.

²⁶ Be supple, that you may bow without cowering.

²⁷ Be honest, that you may be courageous.

²⁸ Be joyous, that your joy may be multiplied.

²⁹ Be steadfast, that you may endure.

³⁰ Be open, that you may be filled.

23

Paradoxes

¹ The one who seeks to banish chaos withers, yet the one who seeks to escape from order is consumed.

² Those who speak of righteous anger believe that they are right, yet more often they are in error.

³ Existence is confined to a moment, yet that moment cannot be confined.

⁴ Solitude is an illusion, yet no one can enter the mind of another.

⁵ No man is liable for the sins of his father, yet all too often, he pays for them.

⁶ A mystery holds power only so long as it remains a mystery; once understood, it surrenders its power, which is transferred to those who understand it.

⁷ These things dance together in tandem. Though two threads, they are a single cord. Though distinct, they are, even so, joined:

⁸ The conscious is bound to the hidden self.

⁹ Potential and achievement should be two ends of a journey. The first without the second is dross in the wind; the second without the first is a wonder of wonders.

¹⁰ The many are aspects of the one, and the one a product of the many.

¹¹ Vision without truth is empty, truth without vision is veiled … or absent.

¹² The wondrous is present within the simple, and the simple is itself a wonder.

¹³ Light chases darkness, and darkness is the womb that gives birth to that which illumines.

¹⁴ Creation is its own true source, renewing itself throughout all ages.

¹⁵ That which is truly divine transcends the mortal realm through death. It emerges anew, yet only a few may recognize it.

¹⁶ Motion demands substance, and substance is ever in motion.

¹⁷ That which is birthed is also dying, and that which dies gives birth.

¹⁸ The humble are best equipped to go forth with confidence, for true humility is based on truth.

¹⁹ The one who has no convictions can never compromise.

²⁰ Silence is among the greatest allies of communication.

²¹ Harmony is of the greatest use in conflict: those who work best in concert are most likely to prevail.

²² Tension is the fuel for peace, lethargy an excuse for war.

²³ Hope unfulfilled only magnifies despair; love spurned can turn to hate. Yet the one who is aware renews the source.

²⁴ Now is the only moment. Yet the one who knows this always transcends it.

²⁵ One must first acknowledge one's circumstance in order to change it. Mistake not recognition for compliance or anger for determination.

²⁶ The one who breaks down things for the sake of understanding should know also how to assemble them in the cause of unity. The one who assembles things for the sake of unity should not fear the one who breaks them down for understanding. Analysis and synthesis are partners who work best when in accord.

²⁷ Science without art is vacant; art without science is a ghost.

²⁸ That which gives definition must also be flexible, lest it break at the least provocation. That which is flexible yet undefined is but a wisp upon the wind.

²⁹ Inspiration is to art as vapor is to liquid, different in form yet one in substance. When the liquid is frozen, seek instead the vapor's path.

³⁰ Those who wake are ever dreaming, and those who dream know not their slumber.

24
Success

¹ These four things bring success: hard work, the help of friends with resource, a shrewd mind and good fortune.

² Without hard work, good fortune is squandered.

³ Without a shrewd mind, work can be to no avail.

⁴ Without luck or favorable friendship, one may toil for years unnoticed.

⁵ Yet all these things together may not be shaken. Nay, all these things together cannot be stopped.

⁶ The one who seeks the All is ever attaining, always releasing.

⁷ Patience waits; persistence acts. Persistence is patience in motion.

⁸ The light-bearer is not concerned with darkness but with finding what it conceals.

⁹ The singer is not concerned with silence, but with the ear that craves her song.

¹⁰ The scribe is not concerned with the empty page, but with the visions to be placed there.

¹¹ The moon without the sun is unseen, but the sun without the moon is constant. Become like the sun.

¹² Which is more potent, the sword or the quill? It depends on the one who wields them.

¹³ Which is more fearsome, the shark or the lion? It depends on the place of their meeting.

¹⁴ Which is more noble, the king or the priest? It depends on the condition of their hearts.

¹⁵ Which is more deadly, the brushfire or the cobra? It depends on which one is nearer.

¹⁶ Which is more powerful, a lie or the truth? It depends in some measure on how many believe them.

25
Endings

¹ Some say the world was fashioned in six days, others in years uncounted. Yet it begins always in a single instant, in the moment a new child touches the All.

² Some say the world was spoken into being, others that it began with a flash of light, still others in a single breath from the heavens.

³ Light illuminates being, but light is not the All.

⁴ Breath sustains life but does not impart it.

⁵ Words bear forth meaning, yet they themselves are not the truth.

⁶ The world begins in a moment for each one of us, yet for each one, the moment is different. So the end is also.

⁷ Fear not that mountains shall be uprooted or that the seas should rise up in wrath and fury. Fear not that dragons shall send forth fires from the sky or that the earth shall be opened to consume you.

⁸ The end shall not come at a trumpet blast from the heavens, or at the point of fiery swords from some imagined host of hell.

⁹ For each, the end is different. Some will meet it in

battle, and others on a sickbed. Some will find it in time of joy, and it comes to others in mourning. For some, it is born of vengeance, and for others it is but ill fortune.

[10] For a single one, death is the end of the world. For the world, it is but new beginning.

[11] The womb is a gateway into this world, and death is a passage beyond. You ask what awaits there? Are you vain enough to answer? [12] Does a child know what awaits beyond his first true sanctuary, wherein his mother preserves him? To him, it is all there is. Can he know what, if anything, is waiting for him beyond?

STEPHEN H. PROVOST

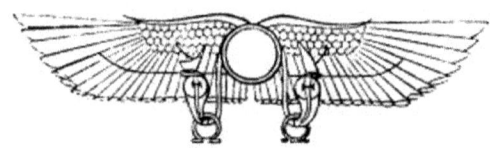

THE PHOENIX CHRONICLES

The Gospel of
The Phoenix

1

¹ When there was nothing
   Still there was truth
   Abiding in silence
   Not knowing itself

² And there abode wisdom,
   A bride to her bridegroom
³ Saying, "Come my beloved,

And let us be one."

[4] Her words of love birthing renewal in all things
    A song of creation
    Eternally sung
[5] One thought manifesting in all of the earth
    A manifold tapestry
    Ever new spun

[6] Adorning the bride with fine jewels of great splendor
    The gold of the sunrise
    The emerald forests
    The great lapis oceans
    The silvery moonlight

[7] For thought became deed
    And word became substance
[8] And took for its dwelling
    The mouths of the sages
    The song of the night bird
    The dome of the heavens
    The heart of the poor

[9] Echoing down through the ages from wisdom
    Love is eternal
    All things are one

Selah

¹⁰ Now the great wheel spun an illusion called time, and all the earth became snared in its gossamer strands.

¹¹ And it spun forth an age of fire, when the earth was hot and molten. ¹² In those days did fire rise up from the belly of the earth, ascending skyward in fountains of liquid gold. This was the first age.

¹³ Then it spun an age of water, when great seas engulfed creation. ¹⁴ Rain fell down and springs welled up, creating wide rivers and vast lakes. ¹⁵ The mighty Nile sprang forth, and the great Euphrates. And mists hung over all the deep. This was the second age, the age of water.

¹⁶ And the heavens were lifted away from the abyss, so that a cool wind swept away the lingering mist. ¹⁷ The curtain of cloud was pulled away, and the sun's bright rays shone through. This was the third age, the age of air.

¹⁸ Then the waters drew back from the face of the earth, yielding their place to barren deserts and great young mountains that rose up to touch the sky. ¹⁹ The rivers carved out canyons, and caverns were crafted deep within the heart of the earth. This was the fourth age, the age of earth and stone.

²⁰ Up from the depths of the underworld rose flowering plants of every sort, and ferns and palms, and cactus and mosses. ²¹ Grasses covered the sweeping plain, and great trees that reached the height of a dozen men: the cedars of Lebanon, which gave shade to the blistered earth. This was the fifth age, the age of verdure.

²² Then at last there came a sixth age, which gave birth

to the fish of the seas and the birds of the sky and the beasts of the field and the children of men. ²³ This was the age of blood, a time of cruelty and striving, of desire and remorse.

²⁴ And in their pride, the sons of men laid hold of wisdom, taking her by force from the garden she had planted east in Eden. She bestowed on them the power of speech, yet they in their arrogance sought to bind her with their words. ²⁵ With vain decrees they held her fast. With scrolls and parchment, they made as if to contain her in their scriptures wrought by men.

²⁶ Fools! Yet she confounded them.

²⁷ She scattered their tongues four winds, so that no man understood his neighbor, and she fled from their sight like screech owl in the night. ²⁸ They in their ignorance cursed her and said, "She is a demon!" And they named her Lilith. But children of the wise do call her Isis, queen of heaven, Aphrodite, Astarte, Venus, Inanna.

²⁹ Therefore did the children of men forgot their beginnings and cast about in vain for understanding. ³⁰ Their ears heard not the poet, and hearkened not to the wise ones. ³¹ Mistaking parable for chronicle, they made for themselves false histories, and these they used to justify their cruelty.

³² From their mouths sprang forth a cacophony of madness, each naming his gods by different names and seeking to assuage them with the blood of guileless creatures. ³³ They waged war with one another and with the earth from which they had been taken, being

called Adam, which means "earth."

34 So the gods withdrew from them also and left them to their folly.

The Coming of Osiris

35 Yet still did wisdom visit men of virtue, abiding in the mouths of the sibyl and the healer, the sage and the seer. 36 She sent them the wise king Osiris, who ruled the two lands of Egypt with his consort, the lovely Isis. 37 It was he who brought the arts of learning and cultivation to the Nile lands, while she was skilled in wisdom and healing. Therefore was he called "gardener" and "teacher."

38 Osiris had a brother called Set who coveted his throne. Therefore did he devise a scheme in treachery to supplant wisdom's chosen king. 39 Crafting for himself a large ark of the finest wood, covered in gold and precious jewels, he waited until the day of a great feast in Egypt. This he presented to the guests there with this challenge: Whosoever should fit inside the box perfectly should claim it as his own.

40 Set had fashioned the box in such a way that none save his brother would be able to enter it. 41 So each of the guests stepped forward one by one, yet none was able to meet the challenge. 42 Then at length did the turn pass to Osiris, whereupon he climbed inside and found it fit him perfectly! 43 Yet at that same moment, Set rushed forward with seventy-two of his disciples to seal the ark shut while the king reclined there. 44 With great alacrity did they make

their escape, spiriting the ark away and casting it forth on the waters of the Nile, which now flowed swiftly as the tears of grieving Isis.

[45] Still, hope was not abandoned, for the queen used charms and magic to conceive a child in spirit by her fallen husband. And she named him Horus of the Horizon.

[46] And when Horus had grown to manhood, he avenged his father's death by slaying Set in mortal combat. [47] His sign is the falcon and the fiery sun, whose bark bears forth the wisest of Adam's children across the sky to life eternal. For Isis is the font of wisdom, and her son its true expression.

[48] The first upon whom she placed her blessing was called Enoch, whose very name means wisdom. He was taken up on the bark of Horus after abiding for 365 times, so that he rode across the heavens with the sun in all its glory. [49] So it was also with Elijah and the rest whom Isis has so favored. Her dove came unto Noah. Through Solomon she spoke, and Hillel, and Gamaliel, and through Jesus and many others who had ears to hear her.

The Sayings of the Masters

[50] These therefore are her words, the sayings of the masters:

[51] "The way is a great mother, empty yet inexhaustible. She gives birth to worlds unending. Ever present within you, manifest her as you will."

[52] "No thing exists in solitude. All things stand in

relation to every other thing."

⁵³ "The world is sacred in perfection. To disturb it is to spoil it. To possess it is to lose it."

⁵⁴ "As we think so also we are. All that we are arises with our thoughts. With our thoughts, we make the world."

⁵⁵ "The master watches the world around him, yet trusts the sight within. He permits all things to come and go. His heart is open to the sky."

⁵⁶ "To live a pure and selfless life, count nothing as your own in the midst of abundance."

⁵⁷ "Freedom may not be had by obtaining every desire, but by controlling all desire."

⁵⁸ "Holding to anger is like grasping a hot coal, seeking to hurl it at another. You are the one who is burned."

⁵⁹ "Give evil nothing to oppose, and it will vanish of its own accord."

⁶⁰ "Speak for those who have no voice, and for the rights of all who are destitute."

⁶¹ "By three methods may one learn wisdom. By reflection, which is noblest. By imitation, which is easiest. And by experience, which is bitterest."

⁶² "That which we wish, we are quick to believe. That which we think, we imagine others think as well."

⁶³ "No one can save us, but only ourselves. We ourselves must walk the path."

⁶⁴ "All war is based on deceit."

⁶⁵ "In the sky, there is no distinction between east and west. The children of men create distinctions in their own minds, then believe them to be true."

⁶⁶ "He who does not increase, decreases."

⁶⁷ "No gem can be polished without friction, nor can a man be perfected without trial."

⁶⁸ "If you wish to lead them, learn how to follow."

⁶⁹ "Expectation is the greatest hindrance to living. While it anticipates the morrow, it loses today."

⁷⁰ "The master seeks not fulfillment. Neither seeking nor expecting, she is present and can welcome all things."

⁷¹ "Boast not of the morrow, for you know not what a day may bring."

⁷² "Like an earring of gold or a precious adornment is the wise man's rebuke in the ear that attends him."

⁷³ "It is better to travel well than to arrive."

⁷⁴ "Like clouds and wind without rain is the one who boasts of gives he does not give."

⁷⁵ "The hard and stiff shall be broken; the soft and supple shall prevail."

⁷⁶ "If you wish to be whole, let yourself be limited.

    If you wish to go straight, let your path be winding

    If you wish to be filled, let yourself be empty

    If you wish to be reborn, let yourself die

    If you wish to receive all things, release all things."

⁷⁷ "A soul is nourished by its kindness, but destroyed by its own cruelty."

⁷⁸ "What has been shall be again. What has been accomplished shall be done again. There is nothing new beneath the sun."

⁷⁹ "He who knows that all things change clings to nothing."

[80] "As a dog returns to its vomit, so a fool returns to his folly."

[81] "Hatred does not cease by hatred, but by love. This is the eternal rule."

[82] "True perfection seems imperfect, yet is perfectly itself. True fullness seems empty, yet even so is fully present."

[83] "The desire of the sluggard will be the death of him, for his hands refuse to labor. All the day he craves for more, yet the virtuous give without sparing."

[84] "Know yourself."

[85] "God is the universal essence of all things. All things are contained in him. He is the fount of being. In him do all things exist."

[86] "Seeing into darkness is clarity. Knowing how to yield is strength. Use your own light and return again to the source of light. This is the way of eternity."

[87] These are the words of wisdom crying in the wilderness, seeking to restore her garden in the seventh age yet to come. [88] In this, the age of spirit, time's illusion shall be shattered and all things will return to one. Then shall the people enter into their rest. And until that day, the word abides.

2

[1] These are the chronicles of the word manifested in hope from a son of man who spoke the word.

² Called by some Jesus, by others Yeshua, and by others yet Issa, he dwelt in an age now past but dwells among us still in word and remembrance.

³ Born in the last days of King Herod, he was called the bridegroom, heir to Solomon's throne of wisdom, who would rebuild a temple not made by human hands but through wisdom and understanding. For it is written:

> ⁴ Wisdom calls aloud in the street
>   She raises her voice in the public squares
> ⁵ At the head of the noisy streets she cries out
>   In the gateways of the city she makes her speech:
> ⁶ How long will you simple ones love your simple ways?
>   How long will mockers delight in mockery
>   And fools hate knowledge?
> For those who have ears to hear, let them hear.

⁷ Now it came to pass in those days that Herod saw betrayal all about him. And he divorced Mariamne the Egyptian, also called Mary, because he believed her to be plotting against him. ⁸ Though she was the fairest woman in all the land, this was nothing in the face of his wrath, therefore did he send her away from him. ⁹ Yet this was not the worst of his transgressions. Becoming mad with rage, he ordered each of his sons executed one after another; only Mariamne's own son Philip escaped and in due course married a woman named Herodias.

This daughter's name was Salome.

¹⁰ At this time also, Herod deposed Mary's father

Simeon as high priest and replaced him with one from another family.

¹¹ When these things took place, it was almost three score years since the coming of the Romans, when the general Pompey entered the temple, desecrating it. ¹² Since those days, the sons of Rome had remained among us, subjecting us to their decrees and demanding heavy taxes to feed their treasuries. And Herod was their servant.

¹³ Now Mary was newly with child, and when it became known that she had borne a son, Herod feared that his enemies would use the newborn against him. For this birth was being hailed as a miracle.

¹⁴ Some say that he was born under a date palm tree, the sacred tree of the phoenix in Egypt; others, that he came forth from a cave, the womb of the great earth mother. ¹⁵ Still others say he was born in a stable and placed in a feeding trough with animals round about him. ¹⁶ As it was written: "The ox knows his master and the donkey his owner's manger, yet Israel does not know and my people do not understand."

¹⁷ And again:

> The wolf and lamb will abide together
> > The leopard shall lie down beside the goat
> > The calf and lion and yearling together
> > And a little child shall lead them

¹⁸ And Simeon himself came to the child and blessed him in the temple, proclaiming him to be the messiah. ¹⁹

Others, too were gathering to him, bestowing gifts upon the infant and offering him their service. [20] This, to Herod, was sufficient to stoke his wrath. So he had a rumor spread that the child was a son of fornication, being the offspring of a certain soldier named Pantera.

[21] And he sent forth spies to seek out mother and child, signing a decree that all newborn male children should be slaughtered.

[22] Yet Mary, having given birth, fled with her new husband to Egypt and hid the child there.

[23] For it is written:

Do you come to kiss this child?
   I will not let you kiss him
[24] Do you come to soothe him?
   I will not let you soothe him
[25] Do you come to do him harm?
   I will not let you harm him
[26] Do you come to take him away?
   I will not let you take him from me!

The Phoenix Reborn

[27] During their travels, they came to the temple in On, which is called Heliopolis, the City of the Sun in the heart of Egypt, as foretold by the prophet Jeremiah. [28] It is said by some that Adam, known to the Egyptians as Atum, was created there.

[29] It is in Heliopolis that there dwell the sacred priests

of the phoenix, that mystical bird which is consumed in a fire and reborn from its ashes. ³⁰ The Egyptians say that it bears within its bosom the very soul of Osiris, the heavenly father, and that its appearance heralds the birth of a new king. And it takes upon itself a form like unto a heron.

³¹ There was in Heliopolis a giant obelisk, upon which the phoenix was said to alight. And atop this was placed a sacred stone called the ben-ben, bearing a cross upon which the great bird would perch. ³² This was the stone spoken of by the psalmist who said, "The stone that the builders rejected has become the capstone," inasmuch as Jesus had been cast out of Israel but would after a time become lifted up as a light brighter than the sun for all to see.

³³ When he was in Egypt, all this was revealed by the priests of the city, who were wise in the ways of the heavens and of magic and philosophy. ³⁴ These men had watched the skies for a sign, and had seen a bright star rise up from beneath the earth in the east: the star of Hor-em-akhet, lord of the Horizon and son of the heavenly father Osiris. ³⁵ He it was who was reborn each year from beneath the earth to his mother, whose name was Isis. Yet she had another name, as well, which was Mery.

³⁶ Now when Mary arrived with her son Jesus, it was at the very time this star appeared. And for this reason, the magi of Heliopolis took his arrival as a sign to them that Hor-em-akhet called Horus had come in the flesh. ³⁷ As it was written in the ancient texts:

"A youth sat in the presence of the universal lord
    Claiming the office of his father, Osiris
³⁸ Beautiful in appearance,
    He illumines the west with his face
    As Thoth presents the healthy eye
    To the great prince in Heliopolis
³⁹ Then said Shu, the son of Re,
    In the presence of the great prince in Heliopolis
    'Power is borne by Justice'
    And 'Award the office to Horus!' "

[40] The magi of On relate this story of the phoenix, which has come down to them through the ages: "There is a bird we call the benu, which is the only one of its kind. [41] And it passes during its lifetime five hundred years until, when it has come time for it to die, it makes a nest for itself of spice and frankincense and myrrh, and therein breathes its last."

[42] And for this reason, some began to say that magi from the east came forth to present these gifts to Jesus. [43] Yet in truth, these things never came to pass. For it was the magi of On who saw the star rising in the east, and who speak of frankincense and myrrh in their story of the phoenix. [44] Likewise, some said he was born under a date palm, because this tree in Egypt is called a benu, after the phoenix, and as with the phoenix that alights upon the cross, Jesus was likewise to be reborn. [45] And though his mother had taken to herself a new husband, it was said that Jesus was the son of a heavenly father, that is Osiris.

⁴⁶ So it was that Mary remembered all these things in her heart and told them to her son when he was of an age to understand them, and he listened and he told them to those that came after him. ⁴⁷ "I tell you the truth," he would say to them, "no one shall see the realm of God unless he is born again."

Way of the Therapeutae

⁴⁸ Now Mary kept her son in Egypt, for it was foretold by the prophet Jeremiah: ⁴⁹ "He will set fire to the temples of the gods in Egypt; he will set their temples afire and take captive their gods. ⁵⁰ As a shepherd wraps his garment around him, so he will wrap Egypt around himself and depart from there unscathed." ⁵¹ And all this came to pass, according to the prophecy. Jesus' very presence set the temples afire with excitement that Hor-em-akhet had returned, and the priests there kept him safe during his sojourn, so that he would indeed depart unscathed, taking captive to himself the wisdom of the gods of Egypt, which he would share at the appointed time.

⁵² During these days, they passed by Alexandria, where dwelt the Therapeutae, whose mission was healing and seeking after wisdom. As it is written, "The tongue of the wise brings healing."

⁵³ The Therapeutae lived in harmony near the lake called Mareotis, with its brackish waters and reeds bending low round about. ⁵⁴ There did they immerse themselves in the traditions handed down by their elders through

generations, which they called the Theravada, meaning "ancient teaching." ⁵⁵ These things, it is said, were from the east, whence they came to spread the knowledge of the eternal spirit and denial of the self.

⁵⁶ They therefore self-called themselves "servants," disdaining the goods of the world and holding all things in common. ⁵⁷ Not deeming it proper for a man to be placed above a woman, both were held in equal esteem and admitted to their common meetings. Many of the things they were teaching, Jesus also taught as well.

⁵⁸ The precepts of the Therapeutae were four in number. ⁵⁹ First, that the essence of life is suffering, and then second, that its cause is desire. ⁶⁰ Therefore, they said, could suffering be removed by renouncing all desire, the third precept. And the fourth was the pathway which leads to this end.

⁶¹ It is for this reason that the Therapeutae shared all their possessions, thereby removing all cause for desire. Wherefore Jesus would admonish those who followed him: "Go, sell all you have, and give the money to those in need."

⁶² For he told them, "Therefore I say to you, have no concern about your life and what you will eat or drink, or about your body and how to clothe it. Is not life more than food and the body more than garments?

⁶³ "Look to the birds of the air, which do not sow or reap or store away in barns, and yet their father in heaven feeds them. Will he not do the same for you? Who of you, by worrying, can add a single hour to his life?

⁶⁴ "And why should you worry about what you will wear? Behold the lilies of the field, which neither labor nor do they spin. Yet I say to you, even Solomon in all his splendor was not arrayed as one of these. ⁶⁵ If this is how God clothes the grass in the field, which is here today and tomorrow is fuel for the fire, will he not clothe you also?

⁶⁶ "Therefore have no care in saying, 'What shall we eat?' or 'What shall we drink?' or 'What shall we wear?' For the ignorant run after these things, which your father in heaven already knows that you need. ⁶⁷ But seek first his realm and his way, and then all these things will be given to you in like manner. ⁶⁸ Worry not for tomorrow, but let it worry for itself. Each day has enough trouble for his own."

⁶⁹ And this he told them because he knew that they would suffer, and he sought to show them the pathway from suffering into light.

⁷⁰ Yet he knew also that his own path must lead through suffering to enlightenment.

⁷¹ He who has ears to hear, let him hear.

Wars and Rumors of War

⁷² In the final days of Herod and thereafter, there arose in Judea and Galilee great strife and tumult. For Herod had begun to build a spectacular temple to the god of Israel, but defiled it with the image of the eagle, thus exalting the empire above heaven itself.

⁷³ In those days, certain men arose named Judas ben Ezekias of Sepphoris and Matthias ben Margalus who were

vexed at the acts of Herod. They saw that he had grown ill and feeble, and they were emboldened to oppose him. [73] They therefore called upon the people to go forth and cut down the golden eagle from its place above the temple gate. Such men as were affected by their words went forth in full daylight and, using sturdy ropes, let themselves down from the height of the temple and laid axes to the image of the eagle.

[74] Herod, however, was not so infirm as they first supposed, and those under his command yet obeyed him for fear of his wrath. [75] When, therefore, news of these events reached the ear of the temple guard's captain, he made great haste with a full contingent of armed men to the site of the unrest. In due course, the soldiers under his command laid hands on forty of the young men, whom he brought to stand before the king.

[76] The men they had taken into custody, consumed by their zeal, confessed to their crime. Thereupon did Herod command that they be burned alive and that those who were with them be put to death, along with their teachers. [77] But Judas escaped and returned to Sepphoris, where he began laying plans for greater sedition.

[78] Before long, Herod was overtaken by a gross distemper that ravaged his limbs and organs. And, his mind being afflicted as well, he ordered a large number of citizens be locked inside the hippodrome, giving orders that they should be slain upon the news of his death. [79] In this way, he reasoned, though the whole country hated him, all would yet mourn upon his passing.

[80] These orders, however, were not carried out, so that there was no mourning at Herod's demise, but the whole land celebrated. [81] Yet still his death did not bring to an end the strife that engulfed the land in those days, for his kingdom was divided among three of his sons, whose ways were no less cruel than their father's had been. Thus were the country's divisions magnified by their quarrels.

[82] In those days and the times that followed, the land was full of bandits and men who called themselves "messiah." [83] One among them, a certain shepherd named Athronges set himself up as king of the Jews, even daring to crown himself king. [84] He and his followers cut down a Roman centurion at Emmaus, and his rebellion continued for some two years before it was ended. As to what became of Athronges, no man knows.

[85] Another brigand, Simon of Perea, likewise set a diadem upon his head. He and his men burned the royal palace at Jericho before his ambitions were ended by Gratus, the captain of the royal infantry, who slew him in combat.

[86] Then also, Judas the Galilean, drew to himself a great number of followers, and these men invaded the royal armory at Sepphoris. This Judas and another man named Zadok, whose name means "righteous," raised a rebellion to protest the payment of taxes to Caesar, and thus began a movement that would persist for many years. [87] These were the Zealots, many of whom came forth from Galilee, where Jesus also made his home.

3

¹ When Jesus was but a child, King Herod breathed his last, and his kingdom was divided among three of his heirs. ² To his son Archelaus the sovereign bequeathed the heart of his kingdom, which is Judea, Idumea and Samaria. ³ And though his followers proclaimed him king, Archelaus declined such an honorific, bowing instead to the will of Caesar Augustus and taking for himself the title of ethnarch, which translated means leader of the nation. ⁴ His half-brother Philip was granted the northeast territory around Caesarea Philippi, which city he rebuilt and was named in his honor. ⁵ And another half-brother, Antipas, received charge of the Galilee.

⁶ Antipas, for his part, built the new city of Tiberias on the southwest shore of Lake Gennesaret, known by some as the Sea of Galilee (though in truth it was surrounded on all sides by land and barely large enough to be named a lake). ⁷ In antiquity, this place had been called Rakkat, but Antipas replaced this small village with a modern city, naming it in honor of the emperor's adopted son. ⁸ He also ruled over the city of Sepphoris, called Tzippori, the largest city in the region and a center of learning and commerce.

⁹ Antipas and Philip each governed his own territory as a tetrarch, ruling under the auspices of Caesar for many years and living into their middle years and beyond. ¹⁰Archelaus, however, was driven from his office barely ten years after receiving it, because the people raised a tumult

against him. Caesar therefore banished him to Gaul and installed his own favorites, called prefects, to watch over Samaria, Judea and Idumea.

[11] About this time, Jesus came into the temple courts and began to question the priests and scholars there. They were amazed at his questions and the answers he gave to them. [12] But it is said that he left from there and went with the Therapeutae to the land of their birth, which is called Sind in the west of India.

Jesus in India

[13] In those days, merchants driving caravans carried goods from east to west, braving robbers and other dangers as they came from China and India along the great Silk Road. [14] This route runs to the end of the earth from Damascus, stretching across the land of the Parthians through Ctesiphon and into the heart of India. [15] Thence came traders to the cities and outposts of the west, bringing with them silk and other treasures to exchange for gold in the western empires.

[16] It was in India that Jesus is said to have found refuge. There he dwelt among the laborers, merchants and artisans in that land. [17] But the priests and the scholars refused to allow him into their presence, for the merchants and artisans were not permitted to read the sacred texts. They were allowed only to hear such things on festival days, being otherwise restricted from these writings.

[18] Further, the priests said, those of the laboring class

below them were not even permitted to hear or contemplate the words of the text, for it was their lot only to serve those in the classes above them.

[19] (Now the lowest class of all was the untouchables, who engaged in actions that were considered ritually impure. These were shunned in the same manner as lepers, who Jesus would take compassion on and minister to in their afflictions, so purifying them restoring them to the fellowship of all men).

[20] And the priests said to Jesus, "Death alone can free them from their servitude. Come, therefore, away from them and give honor to the gods."

[21] But Jesus refused, saying, "The father makes no distinction among his children, for he holds them all equally dear."

[22] In these days it is said that Jesus, who was called by that people Issa, traveled also to Persia and Nepal and the great heights of Tibet. [23] These are the mountains that bear the weight of all the heavens, as pillars support the roof of a great temple. Next to them, the mountain called Zion seemed but a pebble, and they seemed ever adorned in garments far whiter than the purest priestly robes. [24] As he passed this way, he learned for himself the ways of the Buddha, called Gautama, who had gone this way before him, and who had said to his followers: "We are the heirs of all our own actions."

[25] Were these not the same things said also by Solomon, who had declared, "Cast your bread upon the waters, and it shall return to you"?

²⁶ Yet in this land, such wisdom was known by the names of karma and vipaka, which translated mean "action" and "fruit." ²⁷ No healthy tree could bear bad fruit, nor could a rotten tree produce a good harvest. Workers did not pick figs from thorn bushes or grapes from briars, did they? ²⁸ In the same manner, the good man would bring forth good things out of the good that is found in his heart, and the evil man, in like manner, would spew out evil things. For the mouth was the gatekeeper to the heart's abundance.

²⁹ These things Jesus took to his heart and remembered from his travels.

³⁰ So he taught his disciples according to this way:

³¹ "Blessed are the poor, for theirs is the realm of heaven.

³² "Blessed are the mourners, for they shall be comforted.

³³ "Blessed are the humble, for the earth is their inheritance.

³⁴ "Blessed are those who hunger and thirst for goodness, for they shall be filled.

³⁵ "Blessed are the pure in heart, for they shall see God.

³⁶ "Blessed are the peacemakers, for they shall be called God's children.

³⁷ "Blessed are they who are persecuted for their goodness, for the realm of heaven is theirs."

³⁸ These were the teachings of Jesus.

³⁹ "Is not God good and merciful, granting to his children all they need to live? What man, when asking his

father for a fish, will be given a stone? Even more so will the heavenly father care for his children.

[40] "Therefore," he told them, "Ask! And it shall be given to you. Seek! And you shall find. Knock! And the door will be opened to you. [41] The one who seeks should not stop until he finds. And when he finds, he shall be grieved, yet when he is grieved, he shall marvel, and when he marvels, he shall be the master of all things. Then shall he rest."

[42] Now some did not understand these teachings, saying that, behold, the one who asks for riches will surely receive them. [43] Yet what are riches? Are they gold and silver, jewels and possessions? Or are they riches found within? [44] So Jesus would admonish the wealthy, "Go, and sell all you have, and give the money to the poor. Then will you be rich in heaven's realm. For man may not serve God and money, and it is a hard thing indeed for a rich man to enter God's realm."

[45] For those who have ears to hear, let them hear!

[46] During his travels, Jesus continue to amaze those who dwelt among the eastern lands with his wisdom. [47] And he taught them concerning the nature of this world. [48] For he said to them, "The world is a bridge. Pass over it, but do not settle upon it." And again, "The world is a proud house. Heed this well, and do not build on its foundations."

[49] And he also said, "Become passers-by."

The Ten Methods

[50] He therefore taught those who were with him ten methods of contemplating the world and its ways.

[51] "Know first that when the children of men are born, from that day they begin to grow old and will certainly die. [52] The world is like an inn, and you are only lodgers. The bed and the tables therein are not yours. Soon, you will pass beyond that place, for no one can tarry long at an inn.

[53] "See how your friends and loved ones are taken from you, just as leaves fall from a tree in autumn. When winter arrives, wind shakes the leaves from the branches, and they are gone.

[54] "In this world, the success of the mighty and the wealth of the rich man do not endure. They are like the moon at night, which casts its light on all things until the clouds appear, or until the moon begins to wane and its light is forgotten.

[55] "In this world, the children of men steal things from one another because they think them valuable, but at length will do them harm. They are drawn as moths to the light, but heedless, dive into the flame.

[56] "The wealthy use up both body and spirit in gathering treasures that will not benefit them in the end. They are like jars that cannot hold the rivers, lakes and seas they covet.

[57] "Consider the world, this place where the children of men seek to fulfill the desires of the flesh, yet gain only

sorrow and are not fulfilled. They are like a tree infested by insects that sap its strength and consume its heart until it dries up and breaks.

58 "In this world, the children of men become drunk so that they no longer see the good and the bad. They are like a clear pool in springtime, whose surface reflects all things perfectly like a mirror, but which becomes clouded with mud so that the images vanish, leaving filthy water in which nothing can be seen.

59 "The children of this world act as though life is a game, and they sit idly for hours of the day as their spirit becomes drained. These are like a madman who imagines he has seen flowers, then stumbles around through the darkness, seeking them anew. In the end, he is exhausted and sees nothing.

60 "The children of this world go from one path to the next seeking truth but find only confusion. They are like a master carpenter who carves wood in a certain way, then adorns it with color so that it resembles an ox. But when he takes it into the field to plow, it sits there and does nothing.

61 "In this world, many seem to follow these ways, but deceive themselves and benefit no one. They are like an oyster that holds within it a bright pearl. A fisherman comes and breaks the shell to have the pearl, and the oyster dies. They are left with the beauty of the pearl and a dead oyster."

62 And Jesus went forth having learned these things and shared his wisdom with everyone he met.

4

¹ But it came to pass that, after a time, he returned to his homeland and settled in Galilee of the Gentiles. And he became known there as a sage and a worker of wonders.
² Some have said he was a carpenter, but these know not the meaning of the word that is so translated, for in truth he was a sage, and he built a reputation as a magus.
³ Such was his wisdom that it had not been seen since the days of Solomon.
⁴ And Jesus' mother gave birth to his brothers, who were named James and Simon and Judas and Joses. And these became his followers. ⁵ James was known as "the Just," for he had taken a vow neither to drink nor to let any razor touch his hair. He wore not wool but linen, and he was called Oblias, which means "Bulwark of the People."
⁶ Simon was called Cephas or Peter, meaning "A Rock." He was quick of temper, for he was a zealot, believing with those who would establish a new kingdom by force of arms. ⁷ Judas was called as Thomas or Didymus, which means "the Twin," and was also called "the Knife-Wielder," for he was an assassin. ⁸ And Joses was also called John.
⁹ About this time, some began to say that the kingdom had come to another man named John, who was baptizing in the river Jordan. His name means, "God is Gracious."
¹⁰ This man had set himself apart in the wilderness and had taken the vow of a Nazirite, neither shearing his hair nor tasting the fruit of the vine. ¹¹ He was like a wild man of

old, calling the people to him with great power like Samson the mighty or the prophet Elijah. And men were saying that, behold, Elijah had returned to walk among them.

[12] There were in those days men in that place called Essenes, who followed in the ways of their brethren the Therapeutae, holding all things in common and neither buying nor selling. [13] These had withdrawn from the world to live a life of poverty in the wilderness. They were also champions of freedom, laying down all weapons and practicing daily baptisms. [14] They lived in many places, but most especially in the desert at Qumran, whence John also came. [15] And his appearance greatly troubled many men, for here was one who spoke with a tongue hot as fire and sharp like a steely blade.

The Circle-Drawer

[16] Now in times past had there been such a one, whose name was Honi, which also means "Gracious." [17] Honi was an Essene and a great wonder-worker, and he was said to have the ear of God, just as Elijah had before him. For as Elijah called down fire from heaven, so did Honi call down water from above.

[18] Once a terrible drought was upon the land of Israel, and no rains had fallen by the month of Adar, so the people sent word to Honi. [19] He prayed, but no rains came. So he drew for himself a circle on the face of the dusty earth and stood inside it, raising his arms up toward the heaven. And he declared to God, "Until you send forth

rain, I shall not move from within this circle!"

[20] And at these words, there came forth from heaven a few drops of water, which hissed as they struck the hot stones. [21] But the people murmured that this was not enough, so Honi turned his face once more to heaven and spoke thus: "Not for this trifling drizzle have I asked, but for rain to fill wells and cisterns and ditches!"

[22] At once the heavens opened, and rain poured down in torrents as during the time of Noah, each drop that fell being enough to fill a soup ladle. [23] Wells and cisterns overflowed, and the wadis flooded the desert, so that the people scrambled for safety, running to the Temple Mount to avoid being swept away. [24] And they cried to Honi, "Save us! Or we shall be destroyed like the generation of the great flood. Cause the rains to cease!"

[25] But Honi said to them, "I was glad to ask that God should end your misery, but how can I now ask him to end your blessing?"

[26] Still, they continued to beseech him until at last he agreed to petition God once more. And he said to God, "This people that you brought up out of Egypt can take neither too much evil nor too much good. Give them therefore what they ask for, that they may be fulfilled."

[27] Then a strong wind came and swept away the torrents of rain, and the people went to gather mushrooms and truffles on the Temple Mount.

[28] But the leader of the Sanhedrin which is in Jerusalem said to Honi, "I should expel you for your audacity, yet how can I, for you are Honi! God indulges you as a father

does a young child who says, 'Hold me and bathe me, my father! Give to me poppy seeds and peaches and pomegranates.' And the father gives him whatsoever he may ask."

The Carob Tree

²⁹ And it came to pass that one day, Honi was traveling along a byway and came upon a man planting a carob tree. He therefore asked the man, "How long will it be before this tree bears its fruit?"

³⁰ The man told him, "Seventy years."

³¹ So Honi asked the man, "Do you think you will live another seventy years, that you may partake of the fruit of this tree?"

³² The man said, "Perhaps I will not, But when I was born into this world, I found an abundance of carob trees that had been planted by my father and my father's father. Just as they planted trees for me, I now plant so my children and their children can partake of the fruit these trees shall bear."

³³ Then Honi sat down to have a meal, and he was overcome by sleep. And it is said that the rocks of the earth grew up around him and hid him from the eyes of the world, so that he continued to sleep for seventy years. ³⁴ When he finally awoke, he saw a man gathering fruit from the same carob tree and asked him, "Are you the man who planted this tree?"

³⁵ And the man said, "No, I am his grandson."

³⁶ Honi therefore marveled, for behold, he had slept seventy years!

³⁷ Now it was during this time that John appeared upon the earth, being a master of the waters in the desert, as Honi had been. ³⁸ And as Honi fell had fallen asleep beneath a carob tree, so now John came forth eating carob seeds with wild honey and cakes, and the roots of trees. This is a great mystery.

³⁹ Let him who has ears to hear, hear!

And let the one who dares, understand!

John's Baptism

⁴⁰ John now went out to the Jordan wearing camel's hair and the pelts of animals, girded in a belt of leather. He lived in a desolate area in which there are many caves and rocky inclines. ⁴¹ And here men came out to hear him speak, saying, "Turn from your ways, for the realm of God has come!" All manner of men came out to him, and he counseled them. ⁴² To the tax collectors, he said, "Do not collect any more than your due." ⁴³ To the soldiers, he said, "Do not demand money from the people, but be content with your pay." ⁴⁴ And to the multitude, he said, "The one with two tunics should share with he who has none, and your food should be shared in like manner." Whereupon he would cleanse them in the river.

⁴⁵ Now Jesus went out also with the multitude and came to John for anointing in the waters. But recognizing him, John objected, saying, "I need to be baptized by you.

Why do you come to me?"

⁴⁶ Yet Jesus knew that this was to fulfill what had been said of him, that he be born of water and the spirit, and so he humbled himself to receive John's baptism. ⁴⁷And immediately Jesus saw the spirit came upon him like a dove and heard a voice from the heavens saying, "I am well pleased with you, my son. On this day have I begotten you." ⁴⁸ This was the voice of his mother in spirit, the great goddess Astarte, known to the Egyptians as Isis and the Greeks as Aphrodite. From old was she the consort of the Hebrew god, before his priesthood shunned her. ⁴⁹ Her symbol is the dove of peace and the great star Sirius enclosed within a circle, the star which had appeared to the magi in heralding his first birth. Now also was it present at his second as well.

⁵⁰ And he went away from that place. And he took to himself twelve followers, one for each of the tribes in Israel and each house of his heavenly father. For he would say to them, "In my father's house are many dwellings. Were it not so, I would not say it to you." ⁵¹ By this he meant the twelve houses in the stars, and he promised his disciples that he would go ahead of them and prepare a place for them, ascending to the heavens just as his father had done in days of yore.

⁵² Yet they comprehended not the meaning of his words.

⁵³ His four brothers were among them, as was Matthew, a tax collector, and a man named Philip and one called Thaddaeus. ⁵⁴ Some who followed him had followed John,

among whom some started baptizing as he had done. But Jesus himself did not baptize. ⁵⁵ And there arose a disagreement between John's disciples and certain others, because many were crossing over the Jordan to be baptized by Jesus' disciples instead. ⁵⁶ And John said, "A man can only receive what is granted him in heaven. The bride belongs to the bridegroom. The bridegroom's friend attends him and listens for him, and he is joyful on hearing the bridegroom's voice."

⁵⁷ In so saying, he identified Jesus as Solomon, the bridegroom of old, and foretold the sacred wedding that was to come. ⁵⁸ And Jesus himself said of John, "If you are able to accept this, he is Elijah who was to come. He who has ears to hear, let him hear."

5

¹ Simon, James and John were fishermen, and they plied their trade in the lake called Gennesaret. One day, Jesus came to the lake and saw two boats sitting there, but the fishermen were not in them but rather nearby, cleaning their nets. ² He entered into one of the boats, which was Simon's, and bade him put out a little from the land. Then he sat down and began to speak to those who were nearby, teaching them from the boat. ³ When he had finished, he said to Simon, "Put out into the deep waters, and let down your nets for a catch."

⁴ And Simon replied, saying, "We have worked all night and taken in nothing, but at your word, I will let down the

net." ⁵ And behold, they caught a great multitude. So they called out to James and John to bring their boat as well, and they worked until both vessels had been filled. ⁶ Then they went forth to the home of Simon, who was married and lived there with the mother of his wife. ⁷ This woman, however, was sick with fever. Therefore did Jesus take her by the hand, healing her in the manner of the Therapeutae so that the fever left her and she rose up and went about caring for them.

⁸ After this, they went to Capernaum, Nahum's village on the lake's northwest shore. It was a small village with a synagogue and a fertile spring, and Jesus taught there.

⁹ When he was coming to enter the town, a centurion from the Roman army came up to him and sought his help, saying, "My servant suffers greatly, for he is paralyzed."

¹⁰ Jesus said, "I will go to him."

¹¹ But the centurion told him, "I am undeserving that you should be a guest in my home. Yet if you only say the word, my servant shall be healed. ¹² For I myself am a man under authority, with soldiers who are bound to do my bidding. If I tell this one, 'Go!,' then he will go; and that one, 'Come!' and he will come. I tell my servant to do this thing, and he does it."

¹³ Jesus was astonished at the man's words and said to those around him, "Truly I say to you, I have found no one in Israel with faith such as this.

¹⁴ "Go," he said to the centurion. And word soon spread that the servant's condition improved in that very hour.

[15] Hearing of this, the residents of that place brought to him many people who were sick and taken by seizures, and he healed their afflictions after the manner of the Therapeutae.

The Kingdom Established

[16] But when it was day, he left that village and went out to a place of desolation, and the multitudes followed him and besought him to remain. But he refused them and went on his way. [17] Going out, he met a tax gatherer named Levi, with whom he conversed. Upon hearing his words, Levi left everything there and followed after him. [18] He took Jesus to his house and prepared in that place a great feast in his honor, so that many people came from round about, among whom were tax gatherers and many others. [19] Some Pharisees also were among them. And these were offended, saying, "Why do you eat with tax gatherers and transgressors?"

[20] But Jesus said, "Those who are healthy have no need for a physician."

[21] When therefore his brothers saw the crowds who were following him, they began urging him, saying surely he should lay claim to the throne of Israel. [22] Yet he rebuked them, saying, "My kingdom is not of this world." And they marveled, for they understood him not.

[23] And Jesus told them, "If your leaders say to you, 'Behold, the kingdom is in the sky,' then the birds of the sky will precede you. If they say to you, 'It is in the sea,'

then the fish will precede you. But rather, the kingdom is within you, and it is all around you."

²⁴ They then wondered how he would restore the kingdom if it was already established. "When," they asked him, "will the kingdom come?"

²⁵ And he said to them, "It will not come by watching for it. It will be said, 'Look here!' or 'Look there!' No, but the Father's realm is spread out upon the earth, and people see it not."

6

¹ When he had anointed Jesus with water, John went away to Philip, Mary's eldest son by Herod, who sought an interpretation for a dream in which an eagle appeared and tore out both his eyes. He summoned many of his advisors and soothsayers, but none could tell him what it might mean. ² It was then that John appeared and spoke to him directly, saying: "The dream which you have seen is of God. Now the eagle is your deceit and corruption, for it is violent and full of avarice, and this will take away your eyes, which are symbols of your dominions and your wife."

³ John departed, but Philip's wife Herodias betrayed her husband with his half-brother, Antipas, and went away to marry him. Then Philip's life was taken from him, whereupon his lands were forfeit to Agrippa.

⁴ But John continued to baptize in the Jordan, and he told those who came to him, "I am sent of God that you

may know his laws, and that you may free yourself from those who hold power, so that no mortal may rule over you but only the Most High God."

5 And the rulers, hearing of this, sent men out to spy on him and trap him. 6 But he recognized and rebuked them, saying, "O brood of vipers! Who warned you to flee from the wrath that is to come? Turn from your ways and produce the fruit of repentance. 7 But do not think you can say to yourselves, 'We have Abraham as our father.' I tell you truly that God can raise from these stones children unto Abraham. 8Behold! The ax is at the root of the trees, and every one that does not bear good fruit will be cut down and cast into the fire."

9 All these things they reported back to their masters, and Antipas the tetrarch of Galilee, another of Herod's sons, grew suspicious. For the multitudes were gathering to him, and were moved by his words, and it was feared that they might start a rebellion. 10 Antipas therefore sent men to lay hands on John and remove him forcibly to the fortress called Machaerus, and there to have him imprisoned.

11 About this time, Jesus was becoming known throughout the countryside for healing those who came to him. John therefore sent messengers to question him. 12 And Jesus said to them, "Report to your master what you have seen. The blind receive sight, the lame walk, the lepers are cleansed, the deaf hear, those who have died receive new life and good news is taken to the poor."

13 Now he said these things to fulfill the words of the

prophet, who proclaimed wonder upon wonder, declaring:

¹⁴ In that day, the deaf will hearken
    To the words of the scroll
    And from the gloom and the darkness,
    Blind eyes shall have their sight
¹⁵ The wayward shall gain understanding
    And those who find fault will accept instruction

¹⁶ Many who had gone out to hear John in the wilderness were there at that time, and Jesus questioned them, saying, "What did you think you would see there in the desert? A man dressed in finery? No, for those in fine clothes are found in palaces. A prophet? And yes, more than a prophet. ¹⁷ This is he of whom it is written, 'I shall send my messenger before you, to prepare a way for you.' "

¹⁸ Those who had been baptized by John accepted his words and followed them, and many of his followers began gathering now to Jesus. In those days, many thousands gathered to hear him speak.

¹⁹ Now John had rebuked Antipas for his marriage to Herodias, saying he had acted unlawfully by marrying the wife of his brother while he still lived.

²⁰ So it came about that a feast was planned in honor of Antipas' birthday, and when news of it reached Herodias, she arranged to have her daughter Salome dance as a gift for him. ²¹ When, therefore, she appeared at the celebration, her dancing so pleased the tetrarch that he offered her anything she might request of him, up to half

his kingdom.

²² Hearing this, she asked that he deliver to her John the Baptist's head upon a platter, so he sent word to Machaerus and ordered him put to death.

²³ Now there are some who say that Antipas was loath to comply with her request, but did so only because he feared what his guests might think should he fail to keep his word.

But others say that Antipas feared John's followers and sought a convenient excuse to kill him.

Return to Galilee

²⁴ Yet Antipas, seeing that Jesus now commanded the crowds that once had gone after John, grew once more suspicious, saying, "Is this John, now raised from the dead? Behold the powers he commands!"

²⁵ But Salome went away and became his disciple.

²⁶ And Jesus took his followers away from Judea and returned to Galilee. Among them were men and women, also: Mary who is called Magdalene or "the Tower," and Suzanna, and Joanna the wife of Cuza, who managed the household of Herod Antipas, and also Salome, the daughter of Herodias. ²⁷ These women used their own means to support him in his travels, though his brother Judas kept charge of the money.

²⁸ Now first among these was Mary, his consort, who kissed him often on the mouth. ²⁹ This offended some among them, who said to him, "Why do you love her more

than the rest of us?" ³⁰ Yet he answered and said to them, "When a blind man and one who sees are together in the darkness, they are no different from one another. But when the light comes, he who sees will see the light, but lo, he who is blind will in darkness remain."

³¹ And they marveled at this, for they knew not the meaning of his words.

7

¹ It came to pass that Jesus went away into the desert, where he sojourned alone with the wild animals for forty days and forty nights. ² Now the desert lands are consecrated unto Set, the god of Egypt whose abode is the dark red wastelands. ³ It is he who is called Satan by some, the adversary who contended with Horus for the throne of heaven.

As it was written:

⁴ Osiris who is first among the Westerners
    The great god, lord of Abydos, is justified
    His son Horus reigns here
⁵ The lands of the south are in his grasp
    The lands of the north follow after him
    The banks of Horus are his portion
⁶ O Set, you are expelled into the regions far afield
    The great gods guard you
⁷ You shall neither come nor descend upon this

kingdom

So it is, by the order of Ra's majesty

⁸ When Jesus had gone out into these regions, he began to fast and meditate, until he became hungry. ⁹ Then the spirit of Set came to him and began to beseech him, saying, "If you are the Son of God, make these stones become bread!"

¹⁰ But Jesus rebuked him, saying, "It is written that a man shall not live by bread alone, but by every word that goes forth on the breath of God." And in so saying, he declared himself man, not god, and in this way he spurned the path of hubris.

¹¹ Yet his adversary did not leave him, but instead removed him to a lofty peak whence he gazed upon the kingdoms of the world, beholding their splendor. And he said to him, "All this will I give you if you will bow and worship me."

¹² But Jesus rebuked him, saying, "Depart from me, O adversary! It is written, 'Worship the lord your god and serve him only.' " And in so saying, he declared himself a servant, not a king, and in this way he spurned the path of desire.

¹³ Yet his adversary did not leave him, but led him to the highest point of the temple, for this was the place reserved for the phoenix. And he said to him, "Cast yourself down, for it is written: 'He will command his messengers concerning you, and they will lift you up in their hands that your foot will strike no stone.' "

¹⁴ But Jesus rebuked him, saying, "It is likewise written: 'Do not put the lord your god to the test!' " And in so saying, he committed himself to humility and spurned the path of folly.

¹⁵ Therefore Set did leave him, as it is written:

¹⁶ "Your crime has been set before Ra
   The ruin you have inflicted
   Has been made known to the great god
¹⁷ The great council confers
   And Thoth sits in judgment

¹⁸ They report to all the grief that you have caused
   They tell of the injury you have created
   They deliver you to the devourer."

¹⁹ And Jesus was met by messengers who cared for him until he had recovered from his sojourn.

8

¹ Now it came to pass that Jesus betook himself away from that place, saying, "The foxes have their holes, the birds of the sky have their nests, and this son of man has no place to lay his head." For he had been rejected in his own hometown and had found no rest by the Jordan, where John was baptizing.

² Behold, he said, "My condition is hunger; my inner garment is affliction and my outer garment wool. The sun

is my warmth in winter, and my candle is the moon. ³My feet bear me to and fro, and the fruits of the earth do nourish me. Neither in evening nor in morning have I any possession, yet no one on earth is richer than I."

⁴ His followers made a place for him where his beloved, Mary, lived with her sister Martha and their brother Simon, who was rich and had arranged for them to stay there. ⁵ Simon was a Pharisee, yet he had been called unclean because he was also leprous. Even so did Jesus come into his household and accept his fellowship, for which he was thankful.

⁶ This place they called Bethany, which name they chose for its many meanings. ⁷ In some ears it was Bet Annu, which means "House of the Sun" after the city of the sun in Heliopolis. In others, it was Bet Anya, which is to say "House of the Poor" after the poor who were his companions. And in still others it was Bet Aeuni, meaning "House of Dates," for the date palm was the sacred nesting place of the phoenix.

⁸ It was also called Cana, or place of reeds, after the words of the prophet: "A bruised reed he shall not break." This became a place of refuge for him.

Bride and Bridegroom

⁹ So it was that when the time was fulfilled, it was here that Jesus took Mary aside to be his wife. ¹⁰ And as her sister Martha was busy preparing for the celebration, Mary sat at Jesus' feet and listened to him. ¹¹ Martha therefore

complained, saying, "Must I do all the work myself? Instruct my sister, that she may help me."

¹² But Jesus answered and said to her, "Martha, Martha, you fret and worry over many things. But one thing only is needed. Mary has chosen the better part, and it shall not be denied her."

¹³ He said this to honor her as the one who would be his bride. Therefore the scripture was fulfilled which says of Ruth, "She lay at his feet until morning." And she became the wife of Boaz, the ancestor of David. So now, in like manner, was Mary betrothed to Jesus.

¹⁴ And a great feast was planned, and the disciples of Jesus were there with him.

¹⁵ Jesus therefore spoke to them, saying, "A king prepared a wedding banquet for his heir, sending servants forth to invite all he knew. But these refused his invitation, so he sent again for his servants and said, 'Tell them I have prepared a great feast! I have slaughtered my oxen and fattened cattle, and all is prepared. Come now to the wedding banquet!'

¹⁶ "Yet again they did not come. One went off to tend to his business, and another to plow his field. ¹⁷ And so the king sent his servants out yet again, this time saying to them, 'The feast is prepared, but those I have invited would not come. They do not deserve to sit at my table. Go therefore to the street corners and invite to the banquet anyone you find."

¹⁸ This he said to teach them in the ways of wisdom. As it is written:

¹⁹ Wisdom has built her house
   She has hewn its seven pillars
²⁰ She has prepared her meat and fermented her wine
   She has also set her table
²¹ She has sent forth her maids
   And she calls from the highest point of the city
²² "Let all who are simple come in to me!"
   To those of poor judgment she proclaims:
²³ "Come! Partake of my food!
   And drink of the wine I have mixed!"

²⁴ Some, recalling these words, believed he spoke of his betrothed. So it came to pass that many would call her Sophia, which means "wisdom." ²⁵ Yet others scoffed at this, saying that the seven pillars were seven demons that had entered into her; and these also called her a sinner and a harlot who prostituted herself with the simple-minded. For they knew not the meaning of the scriptures, and their ears were closed.

²⁶ When it came time for the feast, as they were eating, Mary was there with Jesus. ²⁷ And at the appointed time came, she brought forth an expensive jar of alabaster, filled with perfume of pure nard, and anointed his head and feet with it. She stood behind him weeping, so that her tears fell down upon his feet; and she kissed his feet and wiped them with her tears.

²⁸ In so doing, Mary performed the ancient service of the bride to her bridegroom, preparing him for the bridal

chamber by anointing his head and for his burial by anointing his feet. As it was written in the scripture of King Solomon's marriage to his beloved, "You anoint my head with oil; my cup is overflowing!"

[29] But it came about some of those present objected, saying, "This perfume is worth a year's wages! It should have been sold, that the money might be given to the poor." [30] (They said this because some of some among his followers had begun calling themselves Ebionites, which translated means "the poor," and they coveted what had been spent.)

[31] To this Jesus replied and said, "Leave her be! She has done a beautiful thing for me. This perfume was intended to prepare me for my burial. The poor are always with you, but it is not so with me. I tell you truly that wherever these things are spoken of throughout the land, that which she has done will be recounted in her memory."

[32] And he said to them, "Many stand at the door, yet he who is solitary enters the bridal chamber."

Water and Wine

[33] Now as the celebration progressed, Jesus' mother came and said to him, "There is no more wine." And she said to the servants who were there, "Do whatever he tells you."

[34] Nearby them stood six stone jars, which were used for ceremonial washing, able to hold twenty to thirty gallons each. So Jesus told the servants, "Go and fill these

all with water." And when they returned, the vessels were completely full. ³⁵ Jesus, seeing this, instructed them, "Draw out some and take it to the master of the banquet," by whom he meant Simon, at whose home the feast was being held.

³⁶ And behold! The water was exchanged for wine.

³⁷ This he did to honor his heavenly father Osiris, who likewise is said to have performed this same wonder.

³⁸ For he told them, "The son can do nothing of himself. He can only do that which he sees the father doing. And all things which the father does, so the son shall do as well."

³⁹ And when the master of the banquet had tasted the water, he found it had been transformed into wine. ⁴⁰ He therefore took aside the bridegroom, which is to say Jesus, and complimented him, saying, "Most would serve the best wine first, holding the lesser stock in reserve so it would go unnoticed when the guests are drunk. Yet you have saved the best for now!"

⁴¹ This he said to fulfill the command of Solomon:

⁴² Go and eat your food with gladness
    And drink your wine with joy
⁴³ For this is the time that God will favor all you do
    Ever clothed in white, your head anointed with oil
    Enjoy life with your wife, whom you love

⁴⁴ So they were married in this way on the third day, and in the course of time, she bore him a child. And their

daughter was named Sarah, which means Princess. Some say she was born in Egypt – for which reason she is called "the Egyptian" – and taken thence to the coast of Gaul with Mary and Joseph of Arimathea, a friend of Jesus who was among the Jewish leaders.

9

¹ After these things, Jesus took his disciples and journeyed to Galilee by way of Samaria. ² Now the people of this land were of diverse heritage, having within their veins the blood both of Israel and of foreigners. And for this cause were they looked down upon and ridiculed, so that many travelers avoided the place entirely, taking the long way around rather than passing through the heart of the countryside.

³ Jesus, however, did not aver from taking this journey. And it came about that as he traveled, he came upon a place called Jacob's well near the town of Sychar, which was the first capital of Israel. ⁴ Nearby this place was Mount Gerazim, which the Samaritans took for their holy place, believing it was here that Abraham had offered his son Isaac as a sacrifice to their god. (The Judeans, however, rejected this and worshiped in the temple at Jerusalem.) ⁵ Jesus, being weary, sat down by the well about the sixth hour of the day, and after a time, a Samaritan woman came there to draw out water.

⁶ "Will you give me a drink?" Jesus asked her.

⁷ She then marveled, for Jews by custom did not address Samaritans. And she answered him, saying, "You are a Jew, and I a Samaritan woman. How therefore do you ask me for a drink?"

⁸ "If you should have asked me," he said, "I would have given you living water."

⁹ But she thought he meant to draw water from the well and said to him, "Sir, you have nothing to draw with, and the well is deep. Our father Jacob dug this well and drank from it himself, as did his sons and all his flocks and herds. Are you therefore greater than he, that you can bring forth water from it without aid?"

¹⁰ Jesus therefore said to her, "Everyone who drinks of this water shall thirst again, but whosoever drinks of the water I give him shall never thirst. Indeed, this water will become in him a spring of water, welling up to life eternal."

¹¹ "Sir," she said, "then give me this water so that I may thirst no more, and henceforth will no longer need to come to this place and draw water."

¹² "Then go," he told her, "and call your husband, then return."

¹³ But she said, "I have no husband."

¹⁴ And Jesus said to her, "You have truly said that you have no husband, for you have had five husbands, and the man you have now is not your husband."

¹⁵ She was amazed and said to him, "Sir, I see well you are a prophet. Therefore tell me this: Our fathers worshiped here at this mountain, but you Jews say we must worship in Jerusalem."

[16] But he said to her, "Hearken unto me now, for a time is coming when you shall reverence the father neither on this mountain nor in Jerusalem. [17] Indeed, a time is coming and now is when those who do reverence truly shall approach the father in spirit and in truth, for such are the manner of men and women the father seeks. [18] God is spirit, and they that reverence him must do so in spirit and in truth."

[19] The woman therefore went from there and spread the news of it in the village, saying to the townsfolk, "This man told me everything I ever did." [20] Then did the Samaritans come out to him, and they urged him to stay with them. He then stayed with them two days. [21] But there were those who heard of these things and scorned him for accepting their hospitality, for these men bore no good will toward the Samaritans. [22] After these things, Jesus returned to his hometown, where he began to speak in the synagogue, and many marveled at his words.

[23] Some said, "Is this not a wise man!" Yet others began to grumble, asking, "Where did he get these ideas? Is this not the son of Mary, the brother of James and Joses and Judas and Simon? Are his sisters not also among us?"

[24] And they were offended.

[25] Jesus therefore said to them, "Only in his hometown, in his own house and among his kinfolk, is a prophet without honor."

[26] And he went from there to speak in the synagogues in one village and the next, drawing many people to hear his wisdom.

²⁷ During this time, he was addressing the multitudes when his mother and his brothers arrived, wishing to speak with him. But they were prevented from reaching him by the crowds. ²⁸ Therefore did someone came up to him and say, "Your mother and your brothers are here to see you." ²⁹ Yet he answered and said to them, "Who are my mother and my brothers? Behold! Whoever does the will of my father in heaven, these are my brothers and my sisters and my mother!"

³⁰ But when his enemies, heard this, they said that he was exalting himself, making himself equal to God – even though this is not what he had said. Rather, he had proclaimed that all who follow the ways of the father were the sons and daughters of heaven.

³¹ He also said plainly, "The father is greater than I."

³² Even so, they came forth to accuse him of blasphemy and picked up stones to use against him. ³³ Therefore he said to them: "Behold, is it not written in your own law, 'I have said that you are gods'? ³⁴ And if he called them gods to whom the divine word was revealed – and the scripture cannot be annulled – why do you accuse me of blasphemy for saying I am God's son? Do not believe me unless I do what the father does!"

³⁵ They had no answer for him, as they could not dispute with the wisdom of his words. And so, enraged, they sought to seize him, but he slipped away from their grasp. ³⁶ He did not strike at them, but exhorted his followers, saying, "Love your enemies and pray for those who persecute you, that you may be sons of your father in

heaven."

The Father and the Mother

[37] Philip therefore asked him, "Show us the father!"
[38] And he wondered at this, saying, "How can you ask me to show you the father? Do you not realize that I am in the father and the father is in me? [39] I love the father and do his work in every detail. As the father has loved me, so I also have loved you. [40] Whoever does not love his father and mother as I do can never be my disciple. For my mother gave me flesh, but my true mother gave me life."
[41] But he warned them, saying, "He who knows the father and the mother shall be called the son of a harlot." [42] Some who heard him were vexed, saying to themselves, "Who is the mother?" and "Who is the harlot?" [43] But they dared not question him about these things, which they failed to understand. They knew not that the mother he spoke of was the great Sophia, whose name is wisdom, the same harlot who cries out in the streets for anyone who might come into her. [44] Some among them therefore scoffed, saying his earthly mother must have been a harlot, and so this rumor began to spread and persists until this day. [45] Others began saying that Mary, his consort, was a whore as well.
[46] So he taught them concerning the nature of the one spirit, saying, "Heaven stands firm with neither post nor column, yet it stands not on its own but through the power of the one spirit.

[47] "When an archer shoots an arrow, the arrow is seen, but not the archer. Yet the archer is there. In this way do we know the power of the one spirit to sustain the heavens and the earth, which neither crumble nor fall down. We do not see this power, yet we know it is there. [48] And once the arrow's force is spent, it falls to the ground. So it is also with heaven and earth, which would pass away were it not for the power of the one spirit.

[49] "The one spirit cannot be seen in heaven or on earth, just as the one soul cannot be seen within the body. As the soul is present throughout the body, so also the one spirit resides in all creation.

[50] "The spirit is never in only one place, nor is it bound to a single place, but resides in a realm that is beyond this world. In this realm, the spirit is in two places, the first of which is the second in time. [51] There time is an illusion, and it is always in the present moment. This realm is neither created nor made, just as the one spirit is neither created nor made.

[52] And he saw that they wished to question him, but he said, "Do not ask whether all things that exist lie within the realm of which I speak. Neither ask how a thing can be without place and beyond time. [53] Not by such questions will you know the one spirit. Such wisdom is beyond the realm of questions.

[54] "Truly, the one spirit resides within all things, abiding without end.

[55] "Among all things that reside under the heaven, some may be seen and others may not. But who has seen

God? For the face of God is like the wind, which no one sees. Ever abiding, God never ceases to move throughout the earth.

⁵⁶ "The children of men can only live by dwelling in the living breath of God. From sunrise to sunset they abide there; each sight and every thought resides within the divine breath. ⁵⁷ No one knows how the wind blows; they hear it, yet see not its form. It has no color, neither blue nor yellow nor white, and no one knows whence it comes.

⁵⁸ "Whosoever is born shall also die. This is the way of things for every living creature. We are born of the wind, and as we die, the wind passes from our bodies. ⁵⁹ Do our hearts and our minds belong to us? No! But they endure because the wind allows it, and when the wind departs, their lives are at an end.

⁶⁰ "No one can see when the wind will depart, and because the children of men cannot see it, they ask, 'Where is the heavenly father?' And they wonder that they cannot see him. ⁶¹ But how can earthly eyes see your father in heaven, who is not as a man that mortal eyes may perceive him? For no one can fully know the heavenly father."

The Disciples' Vision

⁶¹ One day, his disciples came to him and said, "We have seen a great house with a large altar inside it, and twelve men who appear as priests, receiving offerings."

⁶² Jesus asked them, "What are these priests like?"

And the disciples, answering, said, "They appear in this

place every two weeks. Some sacrifice their own children, others their wives, to the praise one of the other. Some commit murder, and other practice a multitude of lawless deeds. ⁶³ The men who stand at the altar invoke your name, and complete their sacrifice in the midst of their own want." Then they fell silent, for they were troubled.

⁶³ At length, Jesus answered them, saying, "For generations shall men plant trees without fruit, shamefully invoking my name." ⁶⁴And he offered them this interpretation: "The god of this altar is the god you serve, and you are the twelve men you have seen. The cattle you have brought to sacrifice are the many you lead astray."

And they questioned him no more.

10

¹ It came to pass that five thousand men gathered to hear Jesus on the far shore of Lake Tiberius, which is called the Sea of Galilee.

² Then their eyes became fixed all the more keenly on him, and many among them were murmuring, "Here is a prophet!" ³And they sought to take him away by force to make him their king. Yet he would not allow it, for he wanted no part of earthly kingdoms, so he withdrew by himself to a mountain.

⁴ The Pharisees, however, were vexed, thinking he purposed to start a rebellion. ⁵ They therefore followed after him, and when they had found him, inquired as to how he came to be there. ⁶ He answered and said to them:

"Even did my mother, the divine spirit, take me by a single hair on my head and bring me to the great mountain called Tabor."

⁷ They knew not what he meant, that he was under the protection of his divine mother, whose name is Isis. For this teaching would he give to his disciples: "The very hairs on your head are numbered! ⁸ Therefore I say to you, do not fear those who can kill the body but nothing more. Are not five sparrows sold for two pennies? Yet not one of them is forgotten by God! ⁹ Truly I say to you, anyone who speaks a word against this son of man will be forgiven, but anyone who curses the divine spirit scorns the hand stretched forth in forgiveness."

The Way of Forgiveness

¹⁰ He therefore taught them, "Forgive your fellows, that you may be forgiven in turn. And neglect not to forgive yourself! For just as you forgive others, so shall the One Spirit forgive you."

¹¹ Simon Peter asked him, "How often shall we forgive one who offends us? Seven times?"

¹² But Jesus said, "I say not seven only, but seventy times seven!"

¹³ It therefore began to be said among some men that, through forgiveness, he was inviting further transgression. ¹⁴ Yet did he not also say, "Do not cast your pearls before the swine"? And did he not also upbraid the Pharisees for their continual abuse?

¹⁵ He therefore spoke to them more fully of forgiveness, asking them, "Suppose one of you has a hundred sheep and loses one. Does he not therefore leave behind the ninety-nine in the open country and search for the sheep that was lost until he finds it? ¹⁶ And when he does, he puts it on his shoulders and returns home with it, calling his friends and neighbors to him and saying, 'Rejoice with me, for I have found my lost sheep.' ¹⁷ Truly I say to you, there is more joy in heaven over one who seeks forgiveness than over ninety-nine who say that they are righteous.

¹⁸ "Or suppose also that a woman has ten silver coins, yet loses one of them. Does she not light a lamp and sweep the house, searching carefully until she finds it? And when she does, she tells her friends and neighbors to come and rejoice with her that she has found the coin she had lost.

¹⁹ "Now a certain man had two sons. And the younger went to his father, saying, 'Give to me my share of the estate.' So the man divided his property between the two of them.

²⁰ "Not long afterward, the younger son gathered up all his belongings and set off on a journey to a distant land, and once there he squandered all his wealth on lavish, carefree living. ²¹ Then a severe famine came upon the land, and he began to be in need. So he went forth and hired himself out to a citizen of that country, who sent him into the fields to feed his pigs. ²² He longed to fill his stomach with the pods he gave over to the pigs to eat, but he received nothing from anyone.

²³ "In due course, then, he remembered his father's house, saying to himself, 'How many of my father's servants have food to spare, while here I sit starving? Therefore shall I set forth and return to my father and humble myself before him, for I have transgressed against him and against heaven. ²⁴ I shall tell him I am no longer worthy to wear his name, and I shall ask of him that he hire me as his servant.' " ²⁵ Therefore did he arise and return to the land of his father.

²⁶ "But while he was still a long ways off, his father caught sight of him on the road and was filled with compassion. Running to him, he threw his arms around his son and kissed him.

²⁷ "And his son said to him, as he had determined, 'Father, I have transgressed against heaven and against you. I am no longer fit to be called your son.'

²⁸ "But the father sent word to his servants, commanding them to be quick and bring the best robe to adorn his son who had returned. ²⁹ 'Put a ring on his finger and sandals on his feet!' he declared. 'Bring the fatted calf and kill it for a feast that we might celebrate. For this son of mine who was dead lives again, and he who was lost is now found!'

³⁰ "And they began to celebrate. ³¹ But soon it happened that the man's elder son, who was out in the field, returned to the house. And when he came near, he heard the sound of music and dancing. ³² He therefore called one of the servants to ask what had happened, and the man told him, 'Your brother has come, and your father

has slain the fatted calf to celebrate his safe return.'

[33] "But the elder brother was indignant and refused to go any further, so his father came forth and besought him to come in.

[34] Then he answered, saying to his father, 'All these years have I slaved for you, never once refusing your commands. Yet never have you given me so much as a young goat to celebrate with my friends. Yet this son of yours has squandered your wealth with harlots and now returns home, that you may kill the fatted calf in his honor.'

[35] "His father therefore said to him, My son, you were ever with me, and all I have is yours. But it was only right to celebrate and be joyful, for this brother of yours was dead and is now alive again. He was lost and has been found!"

The Sign of Jonah

[36] But the Pharisees heeded not his words and knew not their meaning. They looked only on the outside of the dish, neglecting to search inside. [37] Loving the law, they shunned the spirit. Holding to the way of judgment, they knew not the way of love. [38] Caring not for his message, they sought only to see him work miracles. Therefore did they challenge him, saying: "What wonder will you perform for us that we may see it and believe in you? Our fathers ate manna in the desert, as it is written: 'He gave them bread from heaven to eat.'"

[39] But he chastened them, saying, "This wicked unfaithful generation asks for a sign, but none will be given

except the sign of the prophet Jonah!"

⁴⁰ Then they were speechless, for they knew not the sign of which he spoke, which is the sign of renewal from the depths of despair. For they sought not renewal but an excuse to pass judgment upon him.

⁴¹ He therefore performed no wonder for them to see.

⁴² After these things, his disciples came to him and started to ask him about the kingdom of heaven, so he began speaking to them in stories and parables.

⁴³ They asked him, "Why do you speak to us in this way?"

⁴⁴ And he said, "To you have the secrets of the kingdom been imparted, but not to these others. For though seeing, they see not, and though hearing, the do not listen or understand. ⁴⁵ In them is fulfilled the word of Isaiah:

> ⁴⁶ You shall be ever hearing, but never knowing
>   You shall be ever seeing, yet not perceiving
> ⁴⁷ For this people's hearts have become calloused
>   ⁴⁸ They scarcely hear with their ears
>   And have closed their eyes
> ⁴⁹ Otherwise, they might see with their eyes,
>   And hear with their ears
>   And understand in their hearts
>   And turn, and I would heal them.

⁵⁰ "Yet blessed are your eyes because they see, and your ears because they hear." ⁵¹ (These were the teachings

of the Therapeutae, who brought forth the ways of their ancestors by way of allegory and parable, believing that words were but symbols that concealed deeper secrets.)

The Realm of Heaven

⁵² And Jesus told them many things about the realm of God, saying, "It is like a mustard seed, which a man took and planted in his field. ⁵³ Although it is the smallest of all seeds, when it grows it becomes the largest of garden plants, as large as a tree, so that the birds of the air come and perch among its branches."

⁵⁴ And he said also, "The realm of heaven is like yeast, which a woman took and mixed into a large amount of flour until it worked all through the dough."

⁵⁵ And again, "The realm of heaven is like a woman carrying a jar full of meal. And while she traveled a distant road, the handle of the jar broke and meal began to spill out behind her on the road. ⁵⁶ Yet she was unaware, not knowing her misfortune, until she returned to her own home and opened the jar to find it empty."

⁵⁷ And he told them still another parable: "The realm of the father is like a woman who took a little leaven and hid it within the dough and, working it through, made from it large loaves."

⁵⁸ Then he said to them, "The realm of heaven is like a treasure buried in a field. ⁵⁹ Now a certain man discovered it, and he hid it once more, then in his joy went and sold all he had to buy that field. ⁶⁰ And it is like a merchant who

went looking for fine pearls: When he found one of great value, he went and sold everything he had to purchase it.

[61] "To you I give the keys to this realm. And whatsoever you bind on earth will be bound in heaven; and whatsoever you loose on earth will be loosed in heaven. For this realm is fashioned after a realm imperishable."

[62] These things too were the teachings of the Eygptian magi, who had a saying, "As above, so below."

11

[1] Jesus' disciples therefore asked him, "What existed before heaven and earth came into being?"

[2] And he told them, "There was darkness and water, and spirit upon the water. And truly I say to you, what you seek and ask after, behold, it is within you."

[3] They marveled at his words, that something within them should have existed before earth and even heaven.

[4] And they saw a baby nursing at his mother's breast nearby.

[5] And Jesus said, "Truly I say to you, unless you change and become like little children, you will never enter the kingdom. [6] Therefore, whoever humbles himself like this child is the greatest in the kingdom of heaven."

[7] They asked him, therefore, "Are we to enter the kingdom as infants?"

[8] And he said to them, "When you make the two become one, and the inner like the outer, and the outer like

the inner, you will you enter. ⁹ When you make the upper like the lower, and the male and female into a single one, so that they are neither male nor female, then shall you enter.

¹⁰ "All nature, and everything there is, and every earthly creature – all these exist in and with one another. For the nature of earthly things is to dissolve into the root of their own being. He who has ears to hear, let him hear."

¹¹ They wondered at these things, not understanding that he spoke of the cycle of birth, death and renewal that was manifest each day all about them. As the wise king Solomon has said:

¹² Generations rise and fall
    But the earth endures forever
¹³ The sun rises up and sets again
    Then hurries back to where it rises
¹⁴ The wind blows to the south
    Then turns to the north
¹⁵ Round and round it goes,
    Ever returning to its course

¹⁶ All streams flow to the sea
    Yet the seas are never full
¹⁷ For the place streams come from,
    To this place do they ever return
¹⁸ The eye will never have its fill of seeing
    Nor the ear its fill of hearing
¹⁹ All that has been done will be done once again
    For there is nothing new under the sun

²⁰ Then they asked him, "When shall we rest, and when will the kingdom come?"

²¹ And he said, "What you look forward to is here already, yet you do not see it."

²² So then they asked him, "How will our end be?"

²³ But he admonished them, saying, "Have you already discovered the beginning, that you seek now for the end? Where the beginning is, there the end shall be! Blessed is he who takes his place in the beginning, for such a one shall know the end and will not face death."

²⁴ When he saw they did not comprehend his words, Jesus therefore spoke to them in plain terms.

Who Do You Say I Am?

²⁵ And he asked them, "Who do people say that I am?"

²⁶ They replied, "Some say you are Elijah. Others that you are John, the baptizer. Still others say that you are Jeremiah or one of the prophets." ²⁷ (Now by this they testified to the hope of taking on new flesh once their body was committed to the grave, for Jesus himself had said to them that John was Elijah in new flesh.)

²⁷ Jesus then told them, "The names that are given to worldly things are the cause of great deception. For they turn men's hearts from what is true to an illusion. The names which are heard belong to this world."

²⁸ And he told them a parable: "Some rulers wanted to deceive a man, for they saw that he was virtuous. So he

took the name 'good' and ascribed it to that which would not profit him. ²⁹ In doing so, they sought to deceive him by binding a name to that which was not good. ³⁰ And then, as though doing him a favor, they invited him to forsake that which was good by calling it 'not good.' For they wished to take the free man and make him their slave forever."

³¹ He therefore admonished them, saying, "You have heard that it was said in days of old, 'Do not break an oath.' But I tell you to make no oath at all, either by heaven which is the throne of God or by earth which is his footstool. ³² And do not swear by your head, for you cannot make one hair of it white or black. But simply let your yes be yes and your no be no."

³³ He spoke these things so that they might understand the power of the word to tear down, as well as to build up. For he said, "Truth did not enter the world naked, but came adorned in forms and images. Otherwise, the world could not perceive it."

³⁴ Having said these things, he asked them again, "Now, who do you say I am?"

³⁵ And one among them said to him, "Truly, you are the messiah, the son of the living God."

³⁶ But he urged them not to speak thus.

The Way of Humility

³⁷ And yet his brothers pressed him, saying, "No one who wants to become a public figure acts in secret.

Therefore, show yourself to the world!"

⁳⁸ He therefore spoke to them of the Pharisees and teachers of the law. ³⁹ "All they do is done for men to see! They make their phylacteries wide and adorn their robes with long tassels. They pride themselves in taking the place of honor at a banquet or the most important seats in the synagogue, and they love to be greeted as 'Rabbi' in the town market.

⁴⁰ "But I say to you, do not be called 'Rabbi,' for you have only one teacher, who is your father in heaven, and all of you are brothers. ⁴¹ I tell you plainly: Whoever exalts himself will be humbled, but the one who humbles himself is raised up.

⁴² "The greatest among you should be as the youngest, and the one who rules like the one who serves. ⁴³ I ask you, who is greater? Is it the one seated at the table or the one who serves him? Is it not the one at the table? But I am among you as one who serves." ⁴⁴ (In so saying, he exalted the tradition of the Therapeutae, who are called servants).

⁴⁵ And he instructed them, "Take heed that you do not perform acts of virtue to be seen by men, for if you do, you will have no reward from your heavenly father. ⁴⁶ Therefore when you give to the needy, do not announce it with great fanfare to be praised by men, as the hypocrites do in the streets and the synagogues. ⁴⁷ But instead, do not let your left hand know what your right hand is doing, that your giving may be done in secret. Then your father, who sees the secret things, will reward you."

⁴⁸ When men would praise him, therefore, he would

withdraw from them. And when they sought to exalt him, he practiced humility. ⁴⁹ It therefore came about that some of his followers sought to take him by force and make him their king. But he, knowing their hearts, removed himself from their presence and went away by himself to a mountain.

⁵⁰ He would go off early in the morning, seeking out lonely places in which to pray, telling his disciples: "When you pray, to not be like the hypocrites who love to stand and pray in the synagogues and on street corners to be seen by men. Truly I say, they have received their entire reward. ⁵¹ But when you pray, go to your room and close the door, and there pray to your father, who is unseen. Then he who sees what is done in secret shall reward you."

⁵² Likewise, when he healed men of their afflictions, he would instruct them to tell no one.

⁵³ On a certain day, a man afflicted with leprosy came to him and pleaded with him for help, saying, "Master, if you are willing, you can make me clean."

⁵⁴ Jesus therefore reached out and touched the man, saying, "I am willing. Be clean," whereupon the leprosy departed from him.

⁵⁵ In so doing, he announced an end to the ancient laws of uncleanness, which have in every age divided the sons of men. And he proclaimed a new age, wherein the walls of division would be torn down and the veils obscuring truth would be rent asunder.

12

¹ Now the Sabbath, which is the day of rest, had arrived. And Jesus was passing through some grain fields on that day. ² His disciples had grown hungry and began to pick some heads of grain to eat them. ³ When some Pharisees who were nearby witnessed this, they became alarmed and accused him, saying, "Behold! Your disciples do that which is unlawful in profaning the Sabbath!"

⁴ But Jesus said to them, "Have you not read what David did when he and his fellows were hungry? He entered the House of God, and they partook of the bread that had been consecrated, which was not intended for them but only for the priests. ⁵ Or have you not read in the law that the temple priests are innocent, though they desecrate the Sabbath? ⁶ Had you known the meaning of these words, 'I desire mercy, not sacrifice,' you would not have condemned the innocent. A son of man is lord of the Sabbath."

⁷ Then they asked him also, "Why do your disciples despise the traditions of the elders, for they do not wash their hands before eating?"

⁸ Yet Jesus replied in kind: "And why do you violate God's command for the sake of your tradition? ⁹ For God said 'Honor your father and mother' and 'Anyone who curses his father or mother must be put to death.' ¹⁰ But you counsel a man to withhold blessings from his mother and father, telling them, 'Whatever help you might

otherwise have received from me is a gift devoted to God!' In so doing you nullify the word of God for the sake of your tradition. ¹¹ You hypocrites! Isaiah spoke truly when he prophesied about you:

> These people honor me with their lips
> > But their hearts are far from me
> ¹² They worship me in vain
> > Their teachings are nothing more
> > than rules devised by men

¹³ Now a crowd had gathered, and Jesus spoke to them, saying, "Hear and understand. What enters a man's mouth does not make him unclean, but that which proceeds from his mouth defiles him."

¹⁴ Afterward his disciples came to him and said, "Do you know that the Pharisees were offended by your words?"

¹⁵ But he said, "Leave them. They are blind guides. If a blind man leads a blind man, they shall both fall into a pit."

¹⁶ Jesus then went from that place to a synagogue and beheld a man whose hand was shriveled. And his enemies, looking for cause to impeach him, went to ask him: "Is it lawful to heal on the Sabbath?"

¹⁷ So he asked them, "If any of you has a sheep that falls into a pit on the Sabbath, will you not lay hold of it and raise it up? And what value has a sheep and what value has a man? Therefore I say to you that it is lawful to do good on the Sabbath!"

Teachings of Jesus

[18] These are the teachings of Jesus.

[19] "Do not judge, lest you yourselves incur judgment. For as you judge others, so shall you be judged in like manner, and the measure you use shall be used to measure you.

[20] "Why do you look at the speck of sawdust in your brother's eye, yet heed not the log in your own? How can you say to your brother, 'Come, let me remove the speck from your eye,' when all the time is a log in your own? [21] You hypocrite! First remove the log from your own eye. Only then can you see clearly to take the speck from the eye of your brother. [22] Know what is before your face, and that which is hidden will be disclosed to you, for nothing is hidden that will not be revealed, and nothing is buried that will not be raised."

[23] Now without judgment, there is no vengeance. He therefore counseled them also against vengeance, saying, "You have heard it was said, 'Eye for eye and tooth for tooth.' But I tell you, resist not the evil one. [24] If someone strikes you on the right cheek, turn to him the left as well. And if someone wants to sue and take your tunic, offer him also your cloak. [25] If someone forces you to go a mile with him, accompany him for two. [26] Give to the one who asks of you, and turn not away from the one who seeks to borrow.

[27] "To whoever has, more shall be given. From the one

who has not, even what he thinks he has shall be removed.

²⁸ "You have heard it said, 'Love your neighbor and hate your enemy.' But I tell you: Love your enemies and pray for those who persecute you, that you may be sons of your father in heaven.' (In so saying, he reminded them that a son of God is not a man born of a miracle, but one who is born again from his own humility). ²⁹ For God, he told them, "causes the sun to rise on the evil as well as the good, and he sends forth rain upon men of honor and dishonor. ³⁰ If, therefore, you love those who love you, what honor do you deserve? Even tax collectors do as much."

³¹ For this reason, he warned them against abiding in anger, saying, "The one who curses, becomes angry or finds weakness in himself, yet does not remove it, remains far from perfection." ³² And he taught them, "Behold, you have heard it said from ages past, 'Do not murder, for a murderer brings judgment upon himself.' But I say to you that anyone who is angry with his brother incurs judgment."

³³ These things he said knowing that the thoughts of a man are made manifest in action.

³⁴ They wanted to know from him the essence of all things, so he shared with them four principles.

³⁵ The first is this: Begin by freeing yourself from all desire, for if the heart is set on something, it gives rise to every sort falsehood. And false thinking gives rise to false action.

³⁶ The second is this: Be still. Wear no mask and make

no pretense to being what you are not.

[37] The third is this: Do not trumpet your good deeds for people to hear. Do what is right and hold to the truth, but not to make a name for yourself. Practice the way of light to bring life to the truth; then you will know peace and joy.

[38] The fourth is this: Seek not to control your life. Do not take sides in disputes concerning good and evil, but accept all people equally and live from day to day. A clear glass reflects all things, in every color and down to the smallest detail. Be as a glass and reflect without judgment.

[39] Someone asked him, "What is the greatest commandment?"

[40] And he answered, "Love the lord your God with all your heart, soul and mind. This is the first and foremost commandment. And the second is like it: Love your neighbor as yourself. All the law and the prophets are based upon these two commandments." [41] He charged them: "Be not content, save when you regard your brother with love. [42] This is my command, that you love one another. Love your brother like your soul, guard him like the pupil of your eye. In everything do to others as you would have them do to you."

[43] This had also been the teaching of Ma'at in Egypt, and the great rabbi Hillel had counseled his disciples, "That which is hateful to you, do not do to your fellow. That is the whole of the Torah. The rest is explanation. Go and learn."

[44] Jesus therefore told them, "With respect to all living

creatures, always act in kindness and refrain from cruel thoughts. The one who does this shall find less cause for regret. The children of men should always do what is right toward all living things.

45 "Faith receives and love gives. No one can receive without faith, so also no one can give without love. And if anyone gives without love, he has no benefit from what he has given."

46 And some were perplexed, murmuring, "What then of the law?"

47 But he said, "Do not presume that I have come to abolish the law or the prophets; I have come not to abolish, but to perfect them! 48 I tell you truly, until heaven and earth pass away, not the smallest letter or the least stroke of a pen will disappear from the law until all things are accomplished! 49 Anyone who breaks the least commandments and teaches others to do the same will be called least in the realm of heaven, yet whosoever practices and teaches these commands will be called great in the realm of heaven!

50 "Truly I say to you, unless your virtue exceeds that of the scribes and Pharisees, you will surely not enter the realm of heaven."

Women Exalted

51 He therefore taught them: "You have heard it said, 'Do not lie with another man's wife.' But I tell you that anyone who looks at a woman with desire has already lain

with her in his heart. ⁵² And it has also been said, 'The man who divorces his wife must give her a certificate of divorce. But I tell you that any man who divorces his wife, except if she be unfaithful, causes her to commit adultery. And the man who marries a divorced woman commits adultery in like manner.'

⁵³ He said these things because it had become the habit of men to send their wives away upon a whim, each that he might marry another. ⁵⁴ In so doing, it was said, they brought shame upon the ones rejected. Yet in truth, through their folly, they brought shame upon themselves.

⁵⁵ Some among his companions found these sayings hard to accept. These spoke out against the women who were among them, rebuking Jesus for the sake of his consort, Mary. ⁵⁶ One day, Simon Peter rebuked him, "Let Mary leave us, for women are not worthy of this life." But Jesus resisted him. ⁵⁷ So Simon took the others aside, saying, "Has he really spoken privately with a woman and not openly with us? Did he prefer her over us, and are we to therefore hearken to her?"

⁵⁸ Mary therefore wept when she heard this.

⁵⁹ And another among them disputed with Simon, saying, "You have always been quick to anger, and now you are contending against this woman as though she were an adversary. ⁶⁰ But if the master made her worthy, who are you to reject her? Surely he knows her well, and this is why he has loved her more than us."

⁶¹ For this reason, she was called an apostle.

⁶² And in this same way did Jesus give honor to all

women.

Teachings of the Disciples

[63] As Jesus shared wisdom with his followers, they in turn shared what was received of him.

[64] These, therefore, are their teachings:

[65] They spoke of wisdom: "If any of you should lack wisdom, let him ask of God, who gives to all generously and without reproach. And it shall be given to him."

[66] And then, that all things are connected: "For the body has not one part, but many. And if the foot should protest, 'I am not a hand, therefore I am not of the body,' this would in no way make it so. And if the ear should say, 'Since I am not an eye, I am not of the body,' it would not for this reason belong to the body any less. [67] If all the body were an eye, where would hearing be? And if all the body were an ear, how could there be smell?

[68] "So there are many parts, but one body. The eye cannot dismiss the hand, saying it is not needed. Neither can the head declare that it does not need the feet. [69] On the contrary, those parts which seem weaker are indispensable, and the parts that seem to us less honorable are treated with great honor. [70] If one part suffers, all others suffer with it, and if one is honored, all the others likewise rejoice."

[71] And again, on the excellence of love: "Love one another, for love is of God. They that love are born of God and know God. They that do not love know not God, for

God is love."

⁷² "If I speak in the tongues of men and angels, yet have not love, I am a naught but a resounding gong or a clanging cymbal. ⁷³ If I prophesy and understand all mysteries and knowledge, and I have faith that moves a mountain, yet I have not love, I am nothing. ⁷⁴ If I give all my goods to help the poor and surrender my body to flames, but have not love, it profits me not at all.

⁷⁵ "Love is patient. Love is kind. It is not given to envy and does not boast. It is not prideful, rude or self-seeking. It is slow to anger and keeps no account of wrongs suffered. ⁷⁶ Love delights not in cruelty but rejoices in truth. It ever protects, ever trusts, ever hopes and perseveres always.

⁷⁷ "Love never fails."

13

¹ In those days, it came to pass that Jesus received word from Bethany that Simon the Pharisee, the brother of Mary and Martha, was sick. ² This was the rich man who had been afflicted with leprosy, at whose home Jesus had stayed. And Mary had gone home to minster to him.

³ Messengers therefore came to him on the road with this news, but Jesus plainly told them, "This illness will not end in death," and he tarried two more days before he arrived, making ready for the task that lay ahead of him. ⁴ This was the great mystery of the heavenly father Osiris,

whose name was Al Asar or Eleazar, which in the Greek is Lazarus.

⁵ From days of old, the Egyptian priests had raised up and purified the fallen king from among the sleeping in the great necropolis at Heliopolis, declaring, "I have come for you that I might clean you, cleanse you and revive you. Rise up and live!"

⁶ So now Jesus set about to raise and purify Simon from his afflictions. Therefore was he set in a tomb for four days and given the name Lazarus after the manner of the heavenly father who had risen up before him, that he might partake in his mystery. ⁷ As it was written, "Horus dispels the evil that was upon you for four days."

⁸ At the end of these four days, Jesus went forth to him in the manner of Horus.

⁹ When she heard Jesus was coming, Mary stayed behind, but Martha came out to meet him on the road, reproaching him for the delay. But he told her, "Your brother will rise again."

¹⁰ At length he came to the place where they were, in Bethany, where a great crowd had gathered, for Simon was both rich and influential. ¹¹ The Pharisees had gathered there as well, for Simon himself was a Pharisee, but a great many of those who had come out to him were enemies of Jesus who had come to spy on him and report to the ruling council, called the Sanhedrin.

¹² When she saw Jesus coming, Mary came out weeping and lamenting over her brother, so that Jesus was deeply moved in spirit and troubled. He therefore asked her,

"Where have you laid him?"

[13] She said, "Come. Behold."

[14] Jesus wept.

The Raising of Lazarus

[15] Simon had been laid within a cave and wrapped in burial cloths, as was the custom through all the ages, and a rock have been placed across the entryway. [16] These things were done in homage to the earth, who takes the fallen again to her bosom and brings forth new life from the darkness of her womb. As Jesus had said, "You must be born anew." [17] Now was Simon's time to be born anew and be cleansed of the leprosy with which he was afflicted.

[18] Then did those standing by remove the stone from the mouth of the cave, releasing the stench of his sickness.

[19] And Jesus proclaimed, "Lazarus, come forth!"

[20] In this moment, Simon came out to them, still wrapped in the burial garments they had placed on him, a cloth set over his face and his hands bound in strips of linen. [21] And Jesus said, "Remove these garments and let him go!"

[22] Now the Pharisees who had come to spy on Jesus went back to those who had sent them and reported everything they had seen. And their reports reached the ears of the chief priests, whereupon they called a meeting of the Sanhedrin to discuss these matters.

[23] "What are we accomplishing?" they asked. "Here this man is performing deeds of wonder. If we allow him to

continue, all the people will flock to him and the Romans will come to take away our both our temple and our nation."

²⁴ They said this because Caesar had entrusted them with keeping the peace, and they feared losing their positions of influence on the council. But they were loath to lay their hands on him because they feared the crowds he commanded.

²⁵ Yet one named Caiaphas, who was the high priest at that time, silenced them, saying, "You know nothing at all! Do you not understand that it is better for you that one man die for the people than that the entire nation perish?"

²⁶ So they resolved then and there to kill him.

14

¹ After these things, Jesus decided to travel to Jerusalem for the Passover feast, so he began making his way toward the city.

² And he came to Jericho, that ancient city near the west bank of the Jordan, and there found a wealthy tax collector named Zacchaeus who had climbed a sycamore tree in order to see him above the crowds. ³ Catching sight of this man, Jesus said, "Come down at once, for I must stay at your home this night."

⁴ Zacchaeus therefore came down from where he had been watching and welcomed him. But some who were nearby were grumbling, because Jesus was to stay at the home of a tax gatherer.

⁵ But Zacchaeus stood up and declared to all within hearing, "This very day I give half my possessions to the poor. And to any man who I have cheated, I shall repay that one four times!"

⁶ Jesus replied, "Vindication has come to this house today!"

⁷ After these things, he sent two of his disciples ahead of him to a village near the Mount of Olives, which is just outside the city, and told them, "Go into that village, and there you shall find a colt tied up by the entrance to the place. Untie it and bring it to me. ⁸ And if anyone asks you what you are about, tell them that I need it and will return it shortly."

⁹ And they followed his instructions, finding everything as he had said. ¹⁰ Seeing a donkey's colt outside in the street, secured to a doorway, they went to untie it. Some people nearby asked them what they were doing, but when they told them Jesus had need of it, they let them continue about their business.

¹¹ They therefore returned the colt to Jesus and tossed their cloaks over its back so he could ride it, for the donkey was an animal of Set. ¹² In this way, he set an example for humility by following in the way of the seer and sorcerer Balaam, who in the same manner rode on the back of a donkey to bless the nation of Israel. ¹³ If anyone can accept this, Balaam was a forerunner of Jesus. He had said before him, "I cannot do anything of my own accord, for good or ill, that goes beyond the command of the Lord. And I must say only what the Lord says." ¹⁴ In like manner had Jesus

declared, "The words I speak to you are not my own, but they are the words of the father who speaks from within me."

¹⁵ But Balaam, when he set forth on his journey, had been waylaid by a messenger from the god of Israel, who stood in the midst of the road so that his ass could go no further. ¹⁶ And in his anger, he beat the animal that had been faithful to him many years, so that she cried out to him, protesting this treatment.

¹⁷ Yet the ass Jesus rode neither strayed from its course nor cried out, continuing onward toward Jerusalem.

¹⁸ Him who has ears to hear, let him hear.

The Humble Entry

¹⁹ And men came forth and laid their cloaks before him on the road and spread branches they had cut in the fields, for they wished to proclaim him their king, shouting, "Hosanna! Blessed is he who comes in the name of the lord! Blessed be the coming kingdom of our father David! Hosanna in the highest!"

²⁰ But again they had not understood him. For he had said: "He who has become rich, let that one be a king. But let he who has power renounce it! He who knows everything but fails to know himself misses everything!"

²¹ Yet not perceiving his humility as an example to be followed, they instead sought to lift him up. ²² He therefore tarried not long inside the city, but departed from that place and returned with his companions to Bethany. ²³ And his

anger burned within him, for no man had understood his message. The blessing he might have brought into the city instead became a curse.

²⁴ When, therefore, he went forth again the next morning and saw a barren fig tree standing by the road (for it was not the season for figs), he laid his curse upon it, saying, "May you never again bear fruit!"

²⁵ For just as his teachings had failed to bear fruit among the people, so had the fig tree failed to bear its fruit.

²⁶ But his disciples saw him do this, and it brought to mind a parable he had shared with them:

²⁷ A farmer went out to sow some seed. ²⁸ Some of it fell along the byways, and the birds of the air descended to eat it. ²⁹ Some also fell upon the rocky soil, and it sprang up at once but withered just as quickly for it had no place to take root. ³⁰ Other seed still fell among the thorns, which choked out the newly planted crops, preventing them from yielding any grain. ³¹ Only a portion of the seed fell on fertile soil, whence it sprang up and produced a crop a hundred times greater than what the man had planted.

³² So now had this seed fallen among the thorns of men who had no ears to hear and whose minds were closed to wisdom.

15

¹ The Passover feast was near at hand, and Jesus looked down upon the city and wept, saying, "Jerusalem,

Jerusalem! If only you had known this day what would bring you peace ... yet now, it is hidden from your eyes!"

² When he came again into the city, he went straightway to the temple and began to confront the men who had corrupted it. ³ In this place were merchants selling sheep and doves and cattle to be sacrificed, and also money changers who made their living exchanging Greek and Roman coins for Jewish money, which alone was accepted in the temple courts.

⁴ So making a whip of cords, Jesus began to flail it about, driving out the merchants and overturning the tables of the money changers, railing against them. ⁵ "It is written," he declared, "that my father's house will be a house of prayer. Yet you have transformed it into a den of thieves!"

⁶ Jesus watched as the wealthy came and put their gifts into the temple treasury, and presently he saw also a poor widow approach carrying two small copper coins called lepta. ⁷And he told those standing by there, "Truly I say to you, this poor widow has given more than all the others. Everyone else gave gifts out of their abundance, but she in her want gave all she had to live on."

⁸ And he visited a dye works owned by a man named Levi, where he took seventy-two cloths of varied colors and put them in the vat. But when he removed them, all were white as snow. And he said, "Even so is this son of man come as a dyer."

⁹ Now there were seventy-two members of the Sanhedrin in Jerusalem, and these men were tainted by

corruption of every sort.

¹⁰ The high men on the council were afraid at his actions in purifying the seventy-two cloths, because they thought he meant to remove them and install his disciples in their place. ¹¹ For he had appointed seventy-two of his own followers and sent them out ahead of them in pairs to seek out those who would receive his message. ¹² He had told them, "I am sending you out like sheep amongst the wolves. Take no bag or sandals, and greet no one on the road. ¹³ When you enter a house, say, 'Peace be upon this house.' And if a man of peace is there, he will receive your blessing. Stay in this house and partake of all that is set before you, but do not move from house to house."

¹⁴ He said this because he knew the dangers of sending them forth, for the authorities even then had been convinced that they planned to start a rebellion.

¹⁵ After this, he began to teach the people of the city about the realm of God.

A Blind Man Healed

¹⁶ Now near the Sheep Gate of the city lay a pool called Bethesda, around which there were five porches. And upon these were gathered the blind and the lame and the infirm, for it was said that at certain times a divine messenger went down into the pool and stirred up the waters. ¹⁷ And they believed that whoever was the first to step into the waters would be made whole of whatever afflicted him.

¹⁸ A certain man lay there who had been sick for thirty-

eight years. And when Jesus saw him there, he asked him, "Do you wish to be whole?"

[19] The man answered him, "There is no one to put me into the pool when the waters are stirred, so while I approach, someone always arrives before me."

[20] Jesus told him, "Arise, take up your mat and walk."

[21] And the man did so.

[22] But his enemies were moved to anger, for he had done this on the Sabbath. Yet he told them, "My father is still working, therefore I also work."

[23] As he passed along there, he came upon a certain man who had been blind from birth. His disciples therefore asked him, "Rabbi, who has sinned, this man or his parents, that he should have been born blind?"

[24] Jesus said to them, "Neither has this man nor his parents sinned." [25] In this way did he rebuke them for their error, for where they might have shown mercy, they sought instead to cast blame. For blame is the handmaiden of judgment, and these together beget conceit.

[26] So it is that conceited men have perverted the truth, calling forth judgment on all men for the evils they themselves have inflicted. Such men say that all are vile and wretched creatures, incapable of virtue because of Adam's error. [27] Yet they know not what they say. Have they not read where it is written, "Men shall not be slain for the crimes of their fathers, nor fathers for the crimes of their sons. Nay, each man shall answer for his own crimes"? [28] And do they not know that man was created in the image of God? So therefore if man is called evil, what may be said

of God?

²⁹ Jesus therefore told his disciples, "We have come here that the work of God may be displayed in this man's life."

³⁰ Then he spat on the earth, making some mud out of the spittle. And this he put into the blind man's eyes, saying, "Go now, wash in the Pool of Siloam." ³¹ Therefore did the man go forth as Jesus bade him, and when he went home again, his sight was restored.

³² Some of his neighbors, seeing this, began saying to themselves, "Isn't this the same man who used to beg by the side of the road?" Yet others said no, that he only resembled him.

³³ But the man himself insisted, saying, "I am he!"

³⁴ "How then have your eyes been opened?" they asked him. So he told them what Jesus had done.

³⁵ Therefore did these men take him before the Pharisees, who asked him the same questions. And he told them, "The man Jesus put mud on my eyes, and I washed, so now I see!"

³⁶ But some of the Pharisees said to him, "This man is not from God, for he does not keep the Sabbath. Tell us, what do you have to say about him?"

³⁷ The man replied, "He is a prophet."

³⁸ They took the man then to his parents and asked them about it. But they said, "This is our son, and he was born without sight. Yet as to how he now sees, we do not know. He is of age and can speak for himself." ²⁵ They said this because the leaders of the synagogue had said that any

follower of Jesus would be removed from the fellowship.

39 So the Pharisees told the man, "Give glory to God. As for this man, we know he is a sinner."

40 "Whether he is a sinner or not, I do not know," said the man. "I do know that I was blind, yet now I see."

41 They pressed him, saying again to him, "What did he do to you? How did he open up your eyes?"

42 But the man answered, "I have told you this already, and do you now want to hear it again? Do you wish also to become his disciple?"

43 So they heaped scorn upon him, saying, "It is you who are his disciple. We are disciples of Moses! We know that God spoke to Moses, but as to this one, we do not even know whence he came."

44 The man said, "This is a wonder of wonders! You know not whence he came, yet he opened my eyes. We know God does not hearken to sinners, but he listens to the godly man who does his will. 45 The eyes of a man born blind have been opened, a thing that has never been heard of before in Israel. If this man were not from God, he could do nothing."

46 "You were steeped in sin at birth!" they said, casting judgment against him for his infirmity. "How dare you lecture us!"

47 And they cast him out.

16

1 After this, they found Jesus and confronted him about

the man. Jesus therefore said to them, "For this have I come into the world, that the blind may see and those who see may become blind."

² The Pharisees said, "What then? Are we blind, also?"

³ But Jesus told them, "If you were blind, you would be free of guilt. Yet because you claim to see, your guilt remains."

⁴ During these days, it is said that an old woman approached the group to hear him more fully, but she was pushed aside by one who was there to spy upon him. This one sought to block her from hearing his words, placing himself before her. ⁵ But Jesus told him, "It is not fitting that a man should set aside his mother and take her place. Whoever respects not his mother, who is the most sacred being after his God, is unworthy to be called a son.

⁶ "Listen, therefore, to what I tell you: Respect woman, for she is the mother of the universe, and all the truth of divine creation lies within her. ⁷ She is the foundation of all that is good and beautiful, and she is the germ of life and death. On her depends man's entire existence, for she supports him both by her nature and her honor.

⁸ "Woman gives birth to a man in the midst of suffering and rears him by the sweat of her brow, enduring from him the greatest anxiety, even to her death.
⁹ Therefore do bless and exalt her, for she is your friend and supporter in this life. Respect her and honor her; in so acting, you will win her love and her heart. And you will find favor in the sight of God, with much forgiveness.

¹⁰ "In this way also, love and respect your own wives,

for they will be mothers tomorrow. Offer them your forgiveness, for their love ennobles a man and softens his hardened heart, taming the brute in him so he becomes like a lamb. ¹¹ Your wife and your mother are priceless treasures bestowed by God. They are the fairest things in all existence, and of them shall be born the inhabitants of this world."

¹² They marveled at these words, for it seemed that he was exalting woman to make her the equal of man. ¹³ To this some men objected. Was it not Lilith who defied God and parted from Adam? And was it not Eve who tempted Adam in the garden? ¹⁴ Yet they forgot that it was Adam who sought lordship over Lilith, who had been created as his equal, and it was Adam who sought to blame Eve for his own transgression.

¹⁵ And they chafed at how he had rebuked them, seeking therefore a way to entrap him using guile.

Cast the First Stone

¹⁶ One day, they brought him a woman who had been caught in lying with a man who was not her husband. They made her stand before the group that had gathered to hear Jesus, and they said, "Rabbi, this woman was found in the act of adultery. The law of Moses commands us to stone such a woman. What then do you say?"

¹⁷ Jesus did not answer them directly, but instead bent down and began to write on the ground with his finger. (Now when a wise man seeks to invoke God's power or

protection, he will draw a circle on the earth, as the righteous Honi had done when he brought rain to end a great drought that was upon the land.)

[18] The men who were seeking to trap Jesus, however, continued to question him, so that he stood up and challenged them: "If any of you is without sin, let him be the first to cast a stone at her!" And he returned to writing on the ground.

[19] At this, those who had heard him began to depart that place one at a time, the older ones first, until only Jesus was left with her. [20] He therefore stood up again and asked her, "Woman, where are they? Has no one condemned you."

[21] "No one, sir," she said.

[22] "Then neither do I condemn you. Go your way and turn from your transgressions."

[23] Now a rumor arose that Jesus had stayed behind with her in arrogance, thinking he had not sinned. Yet he, too, refused to condemn the woman. This rumor was spread by his enemies in order to mock him and by his own followers who sought to exalt him, but Jesus himself remained silent and took no part in it.

Sons of Abraham

[24] Having failed in their purpose, his enemies sought to entrap him once again. And they came to him demanding to know on whose authority he was teaching.

[25] But he responded by asking them, "Was John's

baptism from heaven or from men?"

²⁶ They therefore took counsel among themselves, but they could not agree upon an answer. ²⁷ "If we say it was from heaven, he will ask us why we did not believe his words. But if we say it came from men, the people will stone us because they all thought John was a prophet." So they finally told him, "We do not know."

²⁸ Jesus therefore said to them, "Then neither will I tell you by what authority I am doing these things!"

²⁹ And he told them: "If you understood my teaching, you would know the truth, and the truth would set you free."

³⁰ "We are the sons of Abraham," they said. "We have never been slaves to anyone. How then can you say we will be set free?" ³¹ (In saying this, they betrayed their ignorance of the scripture, wherein the sons of Abraham enslaved to both the Egyptians and the Babylonians.)

³² Jesus replied: "I know you are sons of Abraham, yet you are ready to kill me because you have no place for my words. ³³ If you were Abraham's children, you would do the works of Abraham. As it is, you are determined to kill me for telling you the truth I heard from God. Abraham did no such thing."

³⁴ Being offended, his enemies grew angry with him and began to accuse him: "Are we not right in saying that you are a Samaritan and possessed by demons?" For they knew he had been doing wonders, healing those who were afflicted and curing those who were said to be possessed by demons. ³⁵ So they said to him, "You cast out demons by

Beelzebul, who is the prince of demons!"

³⁶ Jesus therefore said to them, "A kingdom divided against itself will be ruined, and a house divided is sure to fall. If Satan is divided against himself, how can his kingdom prevail? ³⁷ If, therefore, I drive out demons by Beelzebul, by whom do your followers drive them out? But if I drive out demons by the finger of God, then the realm of God has come to you!"

³⁸ His adversaries failed to understand that all power comes from God, and that it falls upon the sons of men to use it wisely.

The Riddle of the Coin

³⁹ And they became all the more eager to entrap him, for his words were drawing even greater crowds to hear him. ⁴⁰ So they came to him with false praise and said to him, "Teacher, we know that your teachings are correct, and that you show no partiality but teach the way of God in truth. Tell us, therefore, is it right for us to pay taxes to Caesar or not?"

⁴¹ They asked him this knowing that many of his followers sought to make him a king (though he did not seek this for himself) so they might be free of Roman taxes. ⁴² If, therefore, he were to say "It is right," these men would declare him false and leave him. ⁴³ If, to the contrary, he were to say, "It is not right," his inquisitors would have grounds to arrest him for treason against the emperor.

⁴⁴ Jesus, however, knew their intentions.

⁴⁵ He therefore asked them, "Show me a denarius. Whose image does it bear?"

⁴⁶ And they produced the coin for his inspection. "The image of Caesar," they replied.

⁴⁷ So he said to them, "Then render to Caesar what is Caesar's and to God what belongs to God."

⁴⁸ They were astonished at his words, knowing that the coin indeed bore the image of Caesar but that all things belonged to God. And being unable to entrap him, they fell silent and went their way.

⁴⁹ Such men were those who accused him of fellowship with harlots and sinners, saying he had therefore become unclean. ⁵⁰ "John's disciples come fasting and praying," they said to him, "as do also the disciples of the Pharisees, yet yours come eating and drinking."

Parable of the Wineskins

⁵¹ But he answered them plainly, saying, "Would you compel the guests of the bridegroom to fast while he is among them? Yet the time will come when the bridegroom shall be removed from their presence, and in those days will they fast.

⁵² "No one tears a patch from a new garment and sews it onto an old one! If he does, the new garment will be ruined, and the patch he has taken from it will not match the old. ⁵³ In the same way, no one pours new wine into old wineskins. If he does, the new wine will pour forth from the skins, and they also will be ruined. ⁵⁴ No, new wine

must be poured into new wineskins. And no one who has partaken of the old wine wants the new, for he says, 'The old is better.' "

⁵⁵ This he said to them because he knew their hearts, that the teachers of the law would consult the scriptures and counsel men, saying "do this" or "do that" because it was written in the law and the prophets. ⁵⁶ They were like physicians who always prescribed the same treatment, neglecting to examine a single one who came to them infirm.

⁵⁷ They were drunk on old wine that had become like vinegar, while the new wine of each man's spirit was poured out as a sacrifice before them. ⁵⁸ And many toiled in vain seeking after a righteousness that was but falsehood, because the skins these so-called teachers had provided were poorly suited to their contents.

⁵⁹ "To what shall I compare this generation?" he said to them. "They are like children who sit in the marketplaces and call out to others: 'We played a flute for you, and you did not dance. We sang a dirge for you, yet you did not mourn.'

⁶⁰ "For John came neither eating nor drinking, and they say, 'He has a demon.' This son of man comes eating and drinking, and they say, 'He is a glutton and a drunkard, a friend of tax gatherers and sinners!' ⁶¹ Yet wisdom is vindicated by her actions."

⁶² These men had no wisdom. They scorned her presence, resisted her entreaties, turned their back when she cried out to them, shunned the tears she cried for them.

⁶³ Therefore did Jesus condemn them.

Woes Against the Pharisees

⁶⁴ "You Pharisees clean the outside of a dish, but inside you are full of greed and strife. Fools! Did not the same one who made the outside of the dish make the inside also? But give what is inside the dish to the poor, and everything will be clean for you!

⁶⁵ "Woe to you scribes and Pharisees, hypocrites! You give God a tenth of your mint, rue and other garden herbs, yet neglect justice and the love of God! You blind guides! You strain out a gnat and swallow a camel!

⁶⁶ "Woe to you Pharisees, for you love the seats of honor in the synagogues and cherish the greetings you receive in the marketplace. Woe to you! You are like unmarked graves, which men tread upon unaware.

⁶⁷ "Woe to you scribes and Pharisees, hypocrites! You cross land and sea to make a single convert, and when this is accomplished, you make him twice as much of a son of hell as you are!"

⁶⁸ "Woe to you scribes and Pharisees, hypocrites! You are like whitewashed tombs that look beautiful on the outside but on the inside are filled with dead men's bones and all things unclean. You appear on the outside as blameless and good, but inside you are full of hypocrisy and bitterness.

⁶⁹ "And you experts in the law, woe to you! You load people down with burdens they can hardly bear, while you

lift not one finger to aid them!

[70] "Woe to you who have no hope, who rely on things that will never come to pass!

[71] "Woe to you caught in the fire that burns you, for it cannot be quenched. The wheel turns within your minds, yet you are hostage to the burning that is in you, which will devour your bodies openly and secretly consume your souls!"

[72] "Woe to you who build tombs for the prophets, when it was your forefathers who killed them! You testify that you approve of what your forefathers did, yet they killed the prophets and you build their tombs! [73] For this reason the wise God has said, 'I will send them prophets and messengers, whom they will kill and persecute.' [74] Therefore this generation will be responsible for the blood of every prophet shed since the beginning of this age!

[75] "Woe to you experts in the law, for you have hidden the key to knowledge. You yourselves have not entered, and you have hindered those who sought to enter!"

[76] And when he had spoken thus, he left that place and returned again to Bethany.

17

[1] When the time came to reveal what was to come, Jesus took his disciples aside and told them plainly that he would be handed over to the authorities in Jerusalem and

be killed, and that in three days he would rise again after the manner of his father, Osiris.

² His disciples were therefore grieved, wondering at what lay ahead once he had left them.

³ But he comforted them, saying, "Where two or more of you have gathered together, I am there in the midst of you. Behold, I am in all. Cleave the wood, and I am there. Lift a stone, and there you will find me."

⁴ And he told them this parable of a king and his servants, that the king would say to those who had been faithful: "Come you who are blessed of the father, inherit the kingdom that was prepared for you from the foundation of the world. For I hungered and you nourished me, I thirsted and you gave me drink, I was a stranger and you invited me in, I was naked and you clothed me, I was sick and you cared for me, I was imprisoned and you came to visit me."

⁵ For, he said, "whenever you do these things to the least of my brothers, you do them also for me. And whatever you do not do for the least of these, you likewise withhold from me."

⁶ "Be not troubled. Trust in God and also in me. In my father's house are many chambers. If it were not so, I would not have told you. ⁷ I go to prepare a place for you, and I will return to take you with me that you may join me there. You know the way to this place I speak of.

⁸ "If you love me, you will be glad that I go to the father, for the father is greater than I. ⁹ Believe me when I tell you that I am in the father and the father is in me. Truly

I say to you that anyone who has faith will do what I have done and even greater things! ¹⁰ If you have faith as small as a mustard seed, you can say to a mulberry tree or even a mountain, 'Be uprooted and planted in the sea!' and it will obey you.

¹¹ These things he said to encourage them, but upon hearing them, Simon Peter took him aside to admonish him.

¹² Jesus therefore rebuked him, saying, "Are you my adversary? Get behind me! You do not consider the things of God, but only the concerns of men."

¹³ He said these things because they knew not his intentions, which had been spoken of by the priesthood of the phoenix in Heliopolis. For he sought to present an example to them, that they should yield up everything and become servants of all.

¹⁴ Therefore, he admonished them to humble themselves, saying, "The greatest among you will be your servant, for whosoever exalts himself will be humbled, but the one who acts in humility will be raised up."

Sacrifice You Did Not Desire

¹⁵ Behold, he told them, "It is more blessed to give than to receive."

¹⁶ Yet still they did not comprehend his words. And there arose a pernicious teaching that he meant to offer himself up as a sacrifice, and that this sacrifice would annul the sin of Adam. ¹⁷ These men spread this teaching to many

ears, not remembering the words of David: "Sacrifice and offering you did not desire. Neither did you desire burnt offerings or offerings for sin." [18] Yet these false messengers, regarding themselves as wise teachers, polluted the message of Jesus by saying that he came to be a sin offering – a thing which God did not desire!

[19] For it is not through burnt offerings and sacrifices that sins are atoned for, but this comes alone through love and faithfulness. As it is written:

> [20] To what purpose do you offer me these multitudes of sacrifice?
> [21] I have had enough of your burnt offerings of rams
> And the bloated fat of your cattle
> [22] I delight not in the blood of bulls or lambs or goats
> [23] He who kills a bull is as if he slays a man
> And he who sacrifices a lamb
> as if he breaks the neck of a dog

[24] Let the reader therefore heed the words of the prophet who said, "I desire mercy, not a sacrifice," and listen not to these men who flout the scripture. [25] For mercy is not paid for with a sacrifice, but rather is freely given. [26] Does a judge show mercy if he is paid to render a verdict? Or is such a one corrupt and without justice? [27] Does a ruler show mercy if he is bribed to provide favors? Or is such a one far from the light? [28] As it is written: "The wicked man accepts a bribe in secret and so perverts the course of justice" And again: "Woe to those

who acquit the guilty for a bribe, yet deny justice to the innocent."

²⁹ Yet Jesus said, "Blessed are the merciful, for these shall be shown mercy."

³⁰ He therefore told this parable: "A man was traveling from Jerusalem to Jericho, when he fell into the hands of robbers. These men stripped him of his clothes, beat him and went on their way, leaving him half-dead. ³¹ A priest who was traveling this same road saw the man, but passed by on the far side. In the same way, a Levite came upon the man but also passed by on the far side.

³² "Yet a Samaritan, when he came to where the man lay, took pity on him. He went to him and bandaged his wounds, pouring oil and wine on them. He put the man on his own donkey, took him to the inn and cared for him. ³³ The following day, he gave two silver coins to the innkeeper, saying, "Look after him, and when I return, I will pay you for any extra expenses you may have."

³⁴ And Jesus asked an expert in the law which of the three men showed the victim mercy.

³⁵ And the man answered and said to him, "The one who showed him mercy."

³⁶ Jesus therefore told him, "Go therefore and do likewise."

18

¹ Now Jesus knew that the Sanhedrin was seeking to arrest him and had been prevented from doing so only by

the crowds. So he spoke to some of his followers inside the city, who sought out a place where he might partake of the Passover meal in peace. ² When this was concluded, he knew, he would no longer be able to forestall what lay before him. ³ He therefore called his brother Judas and instructed him to prepare for his arrest, discussing these things with him in secret, knowing that others would seek to prevent it.

⁴ He told his disciples, "When you enter the city, a man bearing a jar of water will come to meet you. Follow this one and enter that house which he enters. ⁵ Say to the owner of the house, 'The rabbi asks: Where is the guest room, that I may eat the Passover with my disciples?' ⁶ He will show you to a large upper room, which is furnished. Prepare yourselves there."

⁷ They found everything as he had arranged it.

⁸ When the meal was served, he rose from the table and removed his outer clothing, wrapping his waist in a towel and pouring some water into a basin. He then began to wash his disciples' feet, using the towel to dry them.

⁹ But his brother Simon protested, saying, "Surely you will not wash my feet!"

¹⁰ Jesus answered and said to him, "You know not what I am doing, but you will come to understand. Unless I wash you, you will have no part of me."

¹¹ Simon then adjured him to wash his entire body.

¹² But Jesus said, "The one who has bathed need only wash his feet; then shall his entire body be clean. ¹³ Now that I have washed your feet, you also should wash one

another's. I have set this as an example for you, and you will be blessed if you follow it."

¹⁴ Then he took bread and broke it, saying, "Behold, my body shall be broken for you. Whenever you break bread, remember me." ¹⁵ And he took the cup and blessed it, saying, "Behold, this cup shall be as a covenant of my blood, which I will pour out for you. I tell you truly, I will not again drink of the fruit of the vine until I drink it anew with you in the kingdom of my father."

¹⁶ Then James said to him that he would therefore not break bread again until Jesus should complete that which must be done.

¹⁷ And Jesus said, "Even now the hand of he who will betray me is at the table. This son of man shall go as has been decreed, but woe to the one who shall betray him."

¹⁸ And they all began to murmur among themselves, questioning who among them he might mean.

¹⁹ Simon spoke up, saying, "I am willing to endure prison or even die for you!"

²⁰ But Jesus said, "Truly I tell you, before the rooster crows this day you will deny me three times over!"

²¹ Then, when the meal was nearly finished, Jesus handed Judas a piece of bread, which was a signal, saying, "What you must do, do quickly."

²² Judas departed.

²³ And the story arose among them that it was Judas who would betray him, though Judas acted according to Jesus' own instruction.

²⁴ It was to Simon, however, that he spoke this warning:

"Simon, our adversary has asked to sift you like wheat. I pray for you, my brother, that your faith does not fail you and, when you have returned to your senses, that you strengthen your brothers." [25] For Simon was a Zealot whose wish was to conquer by the sword, having not understood when Jesus admonished him to turn the other cheek. [26] And it was Simon, not Judas, who would deny him.

Gethsemane

[27] So it was that they left that place and went forth to the Mount of Olives. But Judas went to the chief priests and officers of the temple guard and, drawing them aside, proposed to deliver Jesus into their hands. [28] This assistance they accepted gladly, having sought a way for some time to arrest Jesus in solitude, away from the multitudes who followed him. [29] Jesus, though, knew well their intentions, though they knew not that he had commissioned Judas to speak with them.

[30] For Judas alone among his brothers had understood when he said, "Resist not your enemy." [31] Simon had proclaimed him messiah, the savior sent to deliver Israel from the bonds of the Roman occupation. He and many others had sought to crown him king of an earthly realm.

[32] Yet time and again he had refused them, and now he would refuse them yet again. [33] These were a hard-hearted people, but perhaps they might learn through the power of example. For he told them, "Greater love has no man than

this, that he should lay his life down for his friends."

³⁴ Some therefore thought he meant to die, yet he sought only the death of desire that begins in meekness and blossoms into servanthood. For service is the fruit of humility, and such is the way of the Therapeutae.

³⁵ Jesus knew the authorities were determined to arrest him, and he lacked any means to prevent it. ³⁶ He would therefore yield himself up of his own accord, so that all things might be fulfilled and that he might be delivered. As it is written: "He crowns me with deliverance."

³⁷ And again: "Pride walks boldly to its own destruction, and a spirit of arrogance leads to a fall. Far better it is to be oppressed and be humble in spirit than to share the plunder with men of conceit."

³⁸ And as he himself had taught them, "Whoever exalts himself will be humbled, but the one who humbles himself is raised up."

³⁹ For he knew this must be fulfilled: that he be raised up on the cross of the phoenix and be reborn, just as the great father Osiris was reborn from days of old. ⁴⁰ Now, as he had raised Simon the Pharisee as Osiris from the tomb in Bethany, so he too would be raised from the tomb to a new life. ⁴¹ There were men on the council, he knew, who could assist him in this purpose: one Joseph, a wealthy man from Arimathea who counted himself among Jesus' disciples; and a friend named Nicodemus.

⁴² It was Nicodemus whom he had counseled that truly, "no man can behold the realm of God unless he is born anew."

⁴³ "How can a man be born when he is old?" Nicodemus had objected. "Surely he cannot enter a second time into his mother's womb!"

⁴⁴ But Jesus had said, "Behold, I tell you truly that no one can enter the realm of God unless he is born of water and the spirit. Flesh gives birth to flesh, but the spirit gives birth to spirit. ⁴⁵ You should not marvel that I say, 'You must be born anew.' For the wind blows wherever it pleases. You hear the sound, but you cannot say whence it comes or where it flies. So it is with everyone born of the spirit."

⁴⁶ He had spoken of his mother, the spirit of wisdom. And Nicodemus had understood. Jesus therefore told him, "Just as Moses lifted up the serpent in the desert, so must this son of man be lifted up."

⁴⁷ For it is written that serpents came against the children of Israel in the desert, and Moses fashioned an image of bronze after their likeness and raised it up upon his staff. ⁴⁸ And it is said that whosoever had been bitten by one of the serpents could look upon the image Moses created and live.

⁴⁹ The serpent was an image of wisdom, and like the phoenix was a sign of the second birth, for it shed it skin to appear renewed.

⁵⁰ Now Jesus would likewise be renewed, setting an example for all who were to follow: "If anyone wishes to come after me, he must deny himself and take up his cross. For whoever wants to save his life will lose it, but whoever loses his life because of me and my words shall find it.

⁵¹ Indeed, what does it profit a man if he gains the whole world yet forfeits his soul? What can a man give in exchange for his soul? ⁵² If any man be ashamed of me and my words, this son of man will likewise be ashamed of him before the father."

⁵³ These words he spoke also to foretell the fate of Simon Peter, whose bold declarations of faithfulness would soon give way to shame.

Jesus Arrested

⁵⁴ Now, however, did Peter and the others go out with him to the Mount of Olives on the eastern side of the city, and to the garden that was called Gethsemane at the base of it. ⁵⁵ Here, he knew, Judas would find him and bring his enemies to arrest him if all went according to plan. So he took Simon Peter and two others with him to stand watch as he made ready to pray, telling them, "My soul is grieved to the point of death. Remain here and keep watch with me."

⁵⁶ He went on farther and prayed, but returning, found them asleep.

⁵⁷ "Can you not even keep watch with me one hour?" he asked them. "The spirit is willing, but how the flesh is weak!"

⁵⁸ And shortly afterward there was a commotion, and a large crowd of men armed with swords and clubs appeared, led by the men on the council and Judas alongside them.

⁵⁹ Jesus therefore greeted him, saying, "My friend, do

what you have come for."

⁶⁰ Judas stepped forward and kissed him in greeting, whereupon the others laid hands upon him to arrest him. ⁶¹ But Simon Peter, drawing a sword, lashed out in force at the high priest's servant so that his ear was cut off. Even now he failed to comprehend, seeking to establish a kingdom by force of arms. ⁶² Yet Jesus rebuked him. "Lay down your sword!" he said. "For all who draw the sword will likewise perish by the sword."

⁶³ Then he turned to the mass of people assembled there and said to them, "Am I leading a rebellion, that you come forth with swords and clubs to capture me? Each day I sat in the temple courts teaching, yet still you did not arrest me."

⁶⁴ But they held him fast.

⁶⁵ Now a young man wearing nothing but a linen garment had been following Jesus. ⁶⁶ Catching sight of him, some in the crowd sought now to seize him, yet he escaped them and fled, leaving the garment behind in his haste. And so did the rest of his disciples do likewise, though Simon Peter followed at a distance behind him.

19

¹ They brought Jesus to the house of the high priest, though it was late in the evening and the council met formally only in daylight. ² Still, they were determined to question him and find evidence against him that was worthy of death. So they assembled in that place, all the

chief priests and elders and members of the council with them, along with the high priest, whose name was Caiaphas. ³ These brought any number of witnesses to speak against him, but they could come to no decision, for their statements did not agree.

⁴ At last two men came forward and said, "We heard this man say he was able to destroy the temple of God and rebuild it again in three days."

⁵ The high priest demanded that Jesus answer the charge, but he remained silent.

⁶ Now while these things were happening, a crowd of people had gathered outside, and when some among them lit a fire in the courtyard, Simon Peter came to sit amongst them. ⁷ But a servant girl caught sight of him and began to look closely at him. Then she said, "This man was with them."

⁸ Yet he denied it, saying, "Woman, I know him not."

⁹ Shortly afterward, another among their number spied him and accused him: "You are one of them."

¹⁰ But he denied it again, saying, "Man, I am not!" And he moved away from them to stand in the entryway.

¹¹ An hour had passed when yet another spoke up and said, "Certainly this man here was with him, for he is a Galilean."

¹² Simon therefore began to curse and denied it: "Man, I know not what you are about!" ¹³ But at that moment, a cock crowed, and Jesus turned to look at Simon where he stood watching in the doorway so that he remembered the words spoken to him only hours before: "Before the

rooster crows this day, you will deny me three times."

¹⁴ And Peter moved away, going from that place.

¹⁵ Yet inside ,they persisted in their questioning, asking Jesus directly: "Are you the messiah, son of the blessed one?"

¹⁶ But he told them only, "Those are your words."

¹⁷ Yet they deemed the testimony sufficient to condemn him, and they ordered him bound and taken to Pontius Pilate, the Roman prefect in Jerusalem, that he might pass judgment.

Before Pilate

¹⁸ Now Pilate was known among the people for his cruelty and inflexible disposition. Not long before, he had earned the enmity of the people by bringing images of Caesar into the holy city, where it is unlawful to set up any graven image. ¹⁹ He set them up in the city under cover of darkness, so as not to inflame the people, yet when they saw them, there arose a clamor and the men of that city came before Pilate to petition for their removal.

²⁰ But Pilate, not wishing to grant their request for fear of offending Caesar, instructed his soldiers to surround them and call death down upon them should they resist him. ²¹ Yet instead, they bared their necks to him and cast themselves upon the earth, saying they would willingly suffer death rather than see the laws of their fathers so transgressed. ²² And Pilate, being vexed, removed the images from their presence and returned them to Caesarea,

whence they had come.

²³ No sooner had this crisis passed than another arose to take its place. For Pilate, seeking to build an aqueduct to bring water into Jerusalem, made use of money from the temple fund to do so. ²⁴ The people therefore, being offended, gathered together in a crowd and began to hurl abuses at him for this act, insisting that he should set aside his program.

²⁵ But he, growing weary with them, set among the crowd his own men armed with daggers beneath their vestments. And at a signal, they withdrew their weapons and set themselves against the crowd in vengeance, sparing neither the unarmed nor the innocent.

²⁶ A great number of men were slain that day, and the rest were put to rout, in which manner Pilate brought an end to their sedition.

²⁷ Pilate's disposition in these matters bode auspiciously for Jesus' accusers that he might act in the same manner now against their prisoner.

²⁸ Bringing him therefore before the prefect, Jesus' enemies told Pilate, "This man subverts our nation by opposing Caesar's taxes and claiming to be the messiah, a king. He was born of fornication and deceives the people by means of sorcery. Were he not a criminal, we would not have brought him here to you."

²⁹ "Take him, then, and judge him by your own laws," Pilate told them, but they objected, saying "It is not permitted for us to put a man to death."

³⁰ So Pilate withdrew to the palace and summoned

Jesus to him, asking, "Are you the king of the Jews?"

[31] Jesus said: "Is that your idea, or did others say this of me?"

[32] "Am I a Jew?" Pilate scoffed. "It is your own countrymen who have delivered you up to me. Tell me, therefore, what it is that you have done."

[33] But Jesus said, "My kingdom is not of this world. Were it so, those who follow me would have fought to prevent my arrest. Yet my kingdom is from another place. I was born and came into this world to testify of truth, for which reason everyone on the side of truth marks my words.

[34] "What is truth?" Pilate asked him.

[35] And he went back out to the people and told them, "I find no grounds to charge this man." [36] But they persisted, saying, "This man stirs up people all across Judea with his teaching. He came out of Galilee and now has come down here!"

Jesus Acquitted

[37] Now upon hearing that Jesus was from Galilee, Pilate sought to be rid of the matter by transferring it to Antipas, the tetrarch of that region and who had come to Jerusalem for the Passover.

[38] Antipas for his part was greatly pleased at the sight of Jesus, for he had wanted to speak with him for some time and hoped to see him perform a great wonder. He asked him many things, but Jesus remained silent and answered

not, so his soldiers, mocking, dressed him in a grand robe and sent him back to Pilate.

⁹³⁹ The prefect therefore summoned the members of the council before him and told them, "You brought me this man accused of fomenting a rebellion, yet I have examined him before you and found no basis for your charges against him. Likewise has Antipas sent him back here, finding also that he has done nothing deserving death. I will therefore scourge him and release him."

⁴⁰ But a crowd had gathered, and there arose a great commotion. Some among them cried, "Away with him!" Yet others said, "Release to us Barabbas!" (which means "son of the father," a name Jesus had used for himself – for many among them were pleading that he might be released).

⁴¹ And other voices still arose, shouting, "Crucify him!" ⁴² And the rabble would not be stilled, even though Pilate urged them to silence. ⁴³ But while Pilate was seated there, a courier arrived with a message from his wife, saying, "Have nothing to do with this innocent man, for in a dream today I was sorely afflicted because of him."

⁴⁴ So Pilate stood and took a basin of water, dipped his hands in and washed them in front of the entire crowd. "I am innocent of this man's blood!" he declared. "Do with him what you will." ⁴⁵ And he ordered him flogged, then surrendering him to their will.

20

¹ Joseph of Arimathea was a member of the council who esteemed the teachings of Jesus. ² He therefore went to Pilate and asked him to take custody of the Galilean. And he took him forth from that place as the crowd followed after. ³ Among these were some women who lamented him, and he said to them, "Daughters of Jerusalem, weep not for me, but for yourselves and for your children. Behold, the day is coming when it shall be said, 'Blessed are the wombs that never bore and the breasts that never nursed.' ⁴ Then shall the sons of men cry out to the mountains, saying, 'Fall on us!' and beseech the hills, saying, 'Cover us!' For if they do these things when the tree is green, what more will they do when it has withered?"

⁵ At length they came to a parcel of land belonging to Joseph called Golgotha, which means "place of the skull" and had, in days of old, been home to Aphrodite's temple. ⁶ So it was that he returned now to the place of his mother in spirit, the great goddess known also as Isis, to take up the mantle of the phoenix, which is the cross.

⁷ As it is written, "I am naught but dust and ashes." Yet it was from these ashes that the phoenix would arise anew.

⁸ All this was to be done according to his own plan. As it was written by the prophet Job, whose life was taken from him but returned in greater measure:

⁹ O, for the days of my prime
>   When God was a friend who blessed my house
>   When the Almighty was yet with me
>   And my children did surround me
¹⁰ When my path was bathed in cream
>   And the rocks poured forth olive oil in streams
>   When I went to gate of the city
>   And took my seat in the public square
¹¹ I rescued the poor who cried out helpless
>   And the orphan with none to assist him
>   The dying man blessed me
>   And the widow's heart sang
¹² I clothed myself in virtue
>   With justice my robe and headpiece
>   I was eyes to the blind and feet to the lame
>   A father to the needy and an advocate for the stranger
¹³ I broke the fangs of the wicked
>   Snatching victims from their teeth
>   I said to myself, "I will die in my own nest
>   And my days shall be as the days of the phoenix"

¹⁴ Now some men say that the Romans crucified Jesus, but they know not what they say. For Pilate, finding no guilt in him, released him. ¹⁵ And others began to murmur against the Jews, saying his blood was on their children. But these, too, are in error. For did not the leaders of the council say, "It is not lawful for us to put a man to death"? Nor would they have crucified a man, but would have

stoned him, as commanded in the law.

¹⁶ It was therefore his own followers who believed in him that took him forth to the place of death and renewal, where he would be raised up as the phoenix, a symbol of life eternal.

The Phoenix Raised Up

¹⁷ So they put him on a cross and raised it up there. It was the third hour of the day.

¹⁸ Some came to offer him wine mixed with myrrh, but he refused it. And there stood at the foot of the cross Mary Magdalene, with his mother and his mother's sister, the wife of Clopas, and also Salome.

¹⁹ And it came to pass that, at the sixth hour, the sky was darkened and the sun removed from their sight until the ninth hour, just as the skies are darkened in the depths of winter, when the sun descends to its nether point on the horizon and dwells there three days before ascending.

²⁰ Jesus therefore cried out, "Eloi! Eloi! Lama sabachthani!" which translated means, "My god! My god! Why have you forsaken me?"

²¹ Someone ran to get him drink and offered it to him at the end of a hyssop branch. Now some say it this was wine vinegar, yet surely it was not, for he had pledged to his disciples, "I will not drink again from the fruit of the vine again until the day I drink it anew with you in the realm of my father." ²² Yet when he drank it, he declared, "It is finished!"

²³ And they pierced him with a spear, as it is written in the Book of Going Forth By Day. For the gatekeeper of the fifth portal in death is "the one who spears the disaffected." ²⁴ When they did this, blood and water poured forth from his wound, for he yet lived, even as he journeyed through the gates of the underworld. This was a marvel of marvels.

²⁵ So they took him down from there and salved his wounds with spices, and they wrapped him in linen cloths. ²⁶ And Joseph took him to the tomb hewn from out of rock which was to be his own, and laid him there in a garden, at the place he had been crucified.

²⁷ And Mary Magdalene was there in that place also, with Mary who was his mother. At length these two departed to prepare spices and ointments, that they might minister to him.

The Empty Tomb

²⁸ And they rested on the Sabbath, but on the third day, before it was light, they returned to the place where he had been laid and found the tomb disturbed, and Jesus was no longer there. ²⁹ At this they were vexed. But they spied a young man in white, sitting beside the tomb, one of his disciples who had been appointed to stand watch. ³⁰And he said to them, "Do not be dismayed. You seek Jesus, who was crucified. But he has arisen."

³¹ Mary Magdalene went forth from that place and found his brothers John and Simon Peter, declaring to

them, "They have taken away my lord, and I know not where they have laid him." ³² She said this in a mystery, for she had known of his intentions. For just as Isis had searched for her slain consort Osiris in days of old, she now would take up the mantle of the goddess and search for her fallen husband who was taken from her.

³³ But the men were disbelieving, for Jesus had not told them of his plans lest they prevent him. Therefore did they make haste to Joseph's garden and, finding the tomb, found it all as she had said, with only the linen cloths left lying there. ³⁴ So they went away to their own homes, leaving Mary there alone beside the tomb, weeping, for she was afraid.

³⁵ And a voice from behind came to her, saying, "Woman, why do you weep?"

³⁶ She therefore turned to see Jesus, who appeared to her as the gardener, which is the title of Osiris. At first, she did not recognize him, but then he spoke her name to her.

"Mary."

³⁷ And at once she knew him and ran forth to hold him, crying, "My teacher!"

³⁸ Now Jesus went forth to James, who had sworn that he should not eat bread again until he should see Jesus risen from among those who sleep. ³⁹ So therefore Jesus came to him, saying, "Bring a table and some bread!"
⁴⁰ And he took the bread and broke it, and gave it to James, saying, "My brother, partake of your bread, for this son of man has risen from among those who sleep!"

⁴¹ During this time, Mary also went her way, and she

ran to tell his followers that Jesus was alive, but they did not believe her. (For they did not know that Joseph was a friend to Jesus, and they believed he had acted as a member of the council in taking him away, that he might be killed). [42] Now two other men also came to them, reporting that they, too, had seen him. [43] Jesus had come also after them, and in that moment he arrived to stand among them. [44] But the disciples were terrified, for they believed that they were seeing a ghost.

[45] He therefore said to them, "Why are you troubled? Why do doubts arise within your hearts? Look now upon my hands, and on my feet, and see that it is truly I. Touch me and see, for a ghost has neither flesh nor bone as I have."

[46] And he asked them, "Have you anything to eat?"

[47] They brought him a broiled fish and some honeycomb, whereupon he ate them in their presence.

[48] So it was for him as it had been for Osiris, who proclaimed:

> I am yesterday, the dawn and tomorrow
> I oversee the rebirth of souls, of all nature
> And her mysteries

[49] I am the Creator of the gods
> Who nourish the hosts of heaven,
> They that inhabit the Western sky

[50] I am the master of the East, I have two faces
> I arrange the rising of the sun,
> Whose rays rise up into the sky
> And which descends at dawn

THE PHOENIX CHRONICLES

To transform the dwellings of the dead

⁵¹ Abundance is my name: I am generous,
   Yet my true self is hidden
   I am the ray of light which appears at your door
   And goes where it will

⁵² I supply every need of the blest,
   Sending forth blessing in vessels beyond number

⁵³ I am in charge of this wealth,
   Bestowed according to its time
   On the day when we shall see
   The companions of Orion,
   Of whom there number twelve

⁵⁴ I came to Heliopolis
   To tell the phoenix about what passes in heaven

⁵⁵ Let me rise up and see the light of the sun
   Let me travel in peace
   And walk upon the celestial waters

⁵⁶ Let me fly toward the splendor of the blest,
   Toward Ra who gives life
   Anew each day to everyone

⁵⁷ I am Osiris, whose name is owner
   Of lands beyond measure
   I embraced the sycamore and she did protect me
   The doors of heaven opened for me

⁵⁸ I went to see Ra at his setting
   I was one with the wind when he returned
   My hands were purified in adoring him,
   Yet I can do all that the living do

⁵⁹ I was resurrected,

I flew up to the sky and I rested on earth
My eyes saw what I wished to see
⁶⁰ I am the one who brought into the world
The One who knows the plan for life on earth
And in the kingdom of the dead

Doubting Thomas

⁶¹ Now Judas Thomas, who had delivered him at Gethsemane, was not there with them when he came to them, for he dared not risk coming close to him again for fear of the authorities. ⁶² When, therefore, the others told him that Jesus had returned, he would not credit them, for he had been filled with doubt that Jesus would succeed in his intentions. ⁶³ And he said to them, "Unless I see the scars upon his hands and touch his side where the spear did pierce him, I will not believe."

⁶⁴ So it was that eight days later, Jesus returned to meet with them again. ⁶² Now the doors had been locked, so only those with the proper key could enter. But Jesus, arriving in their midst, greeted them, saying, "Peace be upon you." ⁶⁵ And he said to Thomas, "Stretch forth your fingers and see my hands. Reach out your hand and touch my side. Now do you believe?"

⁶⁶ Judas, seeing that he was alive, cried out to heaven, "My lord and my God!"

⁶⁷ And Jesus said to him, "Because you have seen me, you have believed. Blessed are those who believe without seeing."

⁶⁸ So it was that Jesus fulfilled all things that are given a son of heaven to fulfill, and he did so in a mystery, a baptism and anointing. ⁶⁹ The mystery was the mystery of birth and everlasting. The baptism was the wonder of new birth. The anointing was the work of Magdalene. ⁷⁰ So also did he fulfill all things in a feast, which is the bridegroom's, and in a sacrifice, which is the death of self, and in the bridal chamber, which is the holy of holies.

⁷¹ These things have been written that you may believe in the realm of God which is unseen. ⁷² It is not found in books or temples or laws laid down by men. For will God really make his dwelling on the earth, when even the highest heaven cannot contain him? Will he really dwell in a temple made by human hands, or in words on a printed page? ⁷³ But the words of God are written on your hearts, for the realm of God resides within you and in every fiber of creation. ⁷⁴ This realm is one, just as God is One. And just as Jesus became a child of heaven, so you may also be.

⁷⁵ Blessed is the one who adds to what has been written here with the fruit of his own life.

Selah.

Stephen H. Provost

The author writes about American highways, mutant superheroes, mythic archetypes and pretty much anything he wants. A journalist, historian, philosopher and novelist, he lives on the Central Coast of California. And he loves cats. Read his blogs and keep up with his latest activities at stephenhprovost.com.

www.ingramcontent.com/pod-product-compliance
Lightning Source LLC
Chambersburg PA
CBHW070733170426
43200CB00007B/509